FACING THE HOLOCAUST

Edited by
GILA RAMRAS-RAUCH *and*
JOSEPH MICHMAN-MELKMAN

Introduction by
GILA RAMRAS-RAUCH

Afterword by
GERSHON SHAKED

THE JEWISH PUBLICATION SOCIETY
Philadelphia · New York · Jerusalem
5746 · 1985

FACING THE HOLOCAUST
SELECTED ISRAELI FICTION

Library of Congress Cataloging in Publication Data
Main entry under title:

Facing the Holocaust.

  Bibliography: p.
  Contents: The name / Aharon Megged—The lead soldiers / Uri Orlev—Enemy
territory / Hanoch Bartov—[etc.]
  1. Short stories, Israel—Translation into English. Short stories, English—Translations
from Hebrew. 3. Holocaust, Jewish (1939–1945)—Fiction. 4. Holocaust
survivors—Fiction. I. Ramraz-Ra'ukh, Gilah. II. Michman, Jozeph.
PJ5059.E8F33   1985   892.4′301′0895694   85–12570
ISBN 0–8276–0253–7

Designed by ADRIANNE ONDERDONK DUDDEN

ACKNOWLEDGMENTS
"The Name" by Aharon Megged. From Blocker, Joel, ed. *Israeli Stories.* Schocken
  Books, New York, 1962.
"The Lead Soldiers" by Uri Orlev. A chapter from the novel *The Lead Soldiers.* Peter
  Owen Publishing House, London, 1979.
"Enemy Territory" by Hanoch Bartov. A chapter from the novel *The Brigade,* published
  in Hebrew by Am Oved Publishers, Tel Aviv, 1965. Also published in English with
  translation by David S. Segal, Holt, Rinehart and Winston, New York, 1968.
"The Phosphorus Line" by Itamar Yaoz-Kest. The second part of a novella, *The
  Phosphorus Line,* published in Hebrew by Ekked, Tel Aviv, 1972.
"Mrs. Eckhardt's Story" by David Schütz. A chapter from the novel *The Grass and the
  Sand,* published in Hebrew by Sifriat Poalim, Tel Aviv, 1970.
"Lands of Peach, Apricot, and Bread" by Ben-Zion Tomer. A chapter from the novel
  The Way of Salt, published in Hebrew by Tarmil, Tel Aviv, 1978.
"Bertha" by Aharon Appelfeld. From Penueli, S.Y., and Ukhmani, A., eds. *Hebrew Short
  Stories.* The Institute for the Translation of Hebrew Literature Ltd. and Meggido
  Publishing House, Tel Aviv, 1965.
"Twilight" by Shulamith Hareven. From *Modern Hebrew Literature,* vol. 6, nos. 3–4,
  Winter 1981. Orginally published in Hebrew in her collection of short stories, *Solitude,*
  Am Oved, Tel Aviv, 1980.
"Weger" by Yossel Birstein. A revised version of the story that appeared in *Ariel: A
  Quarterly Review of Arts and Letters in Israel,* no. 37, 1974.
"Klein" by Yitzhak Ben-Mordechai. From the collection of short stories *Hunting Iguanas,*
  published in Hebrew by Hakibbutz Hameuchad, Ramat-Gan, 1979.
"La Promenade," part of a triptych by Michal Govrin. From the collection of short stories
  Hold On to the Sun, published in Hebrew by Siman Kriah Books, Tel Aviv, 1984.
"The Times My Father Died" by Yehuda Amichai. From the collection of short stories
  The World Is a Room. The Jewish Publication Society of America, Philadelphia, 1984.

CONTENTS

FACING THE
HOLOCAUST

INTRODUCTION

1

It would seem that a "Holocaust literature" is an impossibility—that, indeed, the phrase itself is a contradiction in terms. The reasons are at least threefold: first, there is no way to link a life-affirming enterprise such as literature with a death-bound phenomenon of such magnitude; second, no gift for literary description, no matter how blessed that gift, could possibly encompass the horror of the Holocaust experience itself; third, since any writing involves some degree of distance, such "detachment" would violate the sanctity of the actual suffering and death undergone by the victims. The grounds for the contradiction could be multiplied, undoubtedly. Yet the three we have mentioned ought to be sufficient to make us question the warrantability of this—or any other—anthology of Holocaust literature.

Art is never entirely remote from death—as we soon realize, for example, in our first acquaintance with the music of Gustav Mahler. Yet inasmuch as the Mahler songs and symphonies achieve a transcendence of death, we may well ask whether the Holocaust could possibly admit the hope of a similar transcendence by way of art. This "limitation" (if it is that) has been perceived in the very theme of the Holocaust itself. Thus, one recent scholar has spoken of recurrent motifs "that illustrate the aesthetic problem of reconciling normalcy with horror: the displacement of consciousness of life by the imminence and pervasiveness of death; the violation of the coherence of childhood; the assault on physical reality; the disintegration of the rational intelligence; and the disruption of chronological time."*

We may easily speak of certain ontological categories associated with ordinary life—categories such as life's finality and irreversibility—that are part of its being comprehensible. Yet in relation to the Holocaust, these take on an altogether different ontological dimension: Indeed, the finality and irreversibility of the Holocaust only add to its incomprehensibility, and they are carved into language as wounds that will not heal. Thus, the Holocaust is located in the nether side of human existence, a materialization of the darkest reaches of human imagination. Counterpoised to this, there is human language as an affirmative vehicle of thought—and as such it can do no more than resort to metaphor, simile, metonymy, or synechdoche in approaching the Holocaust in its full scope.

And yet, the seeming contradiction in the term "Holocaust literature" is belied by the fact that that literature does exist. The question we are thrown back upon, therefore, is how that literature can at all come into being. Obviously, there are some fallacious assumptions about its impossibility. The view that a "literature" of the Holocaust would demean its sanctity makes certain assumptions about literature in its descriptive and explanatory functioning—and we may wish to question those assumptions in order to allow for

*Lawrence L. Langer, *The Holocaust and the Literary Imagination,* New Haven, 1975, p. xii.

the open-endedness of Holocaust literature. It was Aristotle who advanced the idea that literature, rather than history, could provide the means for comprehending human existence *in extremis*. Certainly, language rests upon shared human experience; yet it is in literature that language can attempt to make the impossible possible and believable—but only if we first divest language of its explanatory role.

To see this, we might want to go back to the literature of suffering in the broad tradition of Hebrew writing. In this light, Holocaust literature—written in Hebrew, in Israel, after the war—is clearly tied to a long line of writing of catastrophe. From a literature of divine wrath and human lamentation, from prophecies of destruction onward to records of forced conversions, *autos-da-fé,* and pogroms, the Hebrew language is saturated with the deposits of these experiences. Thus the reality of the Holocaust, in time and place, is connected to these dire memories. But as yet it is devoid of an analogue; it is an experience that is *sui generis,* lacking any other to equal it. The Holocaust is in the process of becoming an archetype—perhaps to expand, eventually, beyond the specifically Jewish concern to become a part of the literary memory of Western civilization.

The tradition of Hebrew literature abounds in thematic material that can and does find its way into Holocaust literature. For example, there are the themes of exposure and nakedness—and the interrelation between revealment and concealment runs through the religious as well as the secular heritage. The elements of "covering" and clothing refer to the tie between God and His people—as in the symbols of head-covering, the bridal canopy, the prayer shawl and *tallith katan* worn by Orthodox males. In view of the prevalence of these thematic elements in the living tradition, they may be expected to manifest themselves in Holocaust literature—touching as it does the religious and secular dimensions. Indeed, in the modern writer's exertions to find *some* symbolic analogue to the Holocaust experience, he or she will inevitably come to this traditional material, since it is this material that allows itself to be used as symbol, metaphor, or simile of what would be otherwise inexpressible.

Although Biblical themes abound in Holocaust literature, they are often given an inverted meaning. The Fall, for example, is traditionally seen as a fall *into* humanness (concomitant with moral awareness). In Holocaust literature, it is often used to symbolize a falling *away* from humanness and human awareness. Analogously, the Holocaust experience is seen to deprive man of his "covering," his *raison d'être,* so that his fall reduces him to an elemental nakedness devoid of meaning. Thus, the Fall is not a transition from innocence to experience, as the result of man's assertion of selfhood, but rather a change outside all context, and leaving him with no "lesson," no moral residuum. As another example, there is the theme of *akeda,* the binding of Isaac, taken as the ultimate test of faith and the meeting-point for divine will and unquestioning human submission. In Holocaust literature, the theme of *akeda* is used to emphasize the absence of divine intervention to save those about to be sacrificed. This evokes yet another theme in the literature of Jewish suffering: that of God averting His face, turning His back on Israel—with the feeling of utter abandonment on the part of those sacrificed.

Beginning with the Book of Genesis, the Hebraic tradition bases the tie between the nation of Israel and its history on four elements: promise, dialogue, trial, and exile (with redemption encompassed in the promise). These elements constitute the thinking of the Biblical writers as much as the consciousness of the nation. In the literature of the Holocaust, these elements have their meaning violated or denied altogether. For example, the theme of dialogue (between God and man) made for comprehension of one's fate and for coming to terms with the sufferings of the nation. From Abraham to Job to the Ba'al Shem Tov to the Rabbi of Berdichev, the Jew felt that he could call upon God to plead for an explanation or even to argue with Him. But with God averting His face, the Jew in the literature of the Holocaust is represented as suffering an *irreversible* abandonment, in a world devoid of God's providence.

As a result, we see an attempt to come to terms with the Holocaust as meta-personal—even if it is translated into personal terms as loss of one's own image as human. The personal experience is that of total desertion; of being torn from time and space; of existing in a world of eternal winter, eternal flight, outside the natural cycle of existence.

On the other hand, we see an attempt (especially in poetry) to find images that might approximate one's personal state of being in the complexity of Holocaust experience. A recurring theme is that of the inversion of world order, with a consequent inversion of human expectations. This inversion is applied to some of the traditional themes already mentioned. Thus, in Amir Gilboa's poem "Isaac" it is the father who is the sacrificed: "It is I who am slaughtered, my son,/And my blood is already on the leaves." It is the father, as model of the son's future, who is being killed—the father to whom a promise was made by God, the father who might have served as guide.

Above all, with the loss of any meta-personal meaning, survival itself becomes meaningless. The theme of survival is constant in Genesis (where the pattern of self-perception is set for the entire people). Abraham is a survivor (leaving for Egypt when famine comes; passing off his wife as his sister to avoid attack), as are Isaac (who has a parallel incident with Rebecca) and Jacob (who wrestles with the angel, and prevails). The theme of survival is sanctified in the Covenant, guaranteeing return for exile, rebuilding for destruction. This traditional framework has led to two possible ways of relating to the Holocaust: either as part of a long history of destruction *(ḥurban, shoa)* or as something altogether beyond historic precedent. On the personal level, nothing in past experience could mitigate the present—which is why, for many of the characters in Holocaust literature, the entire sequence of events marks the end of an era when all was comprehensible and the beginning of a consciousness that is autistic and incommunicable.

2

The two major events affecting Jewish existence in our century are the Holocaust and the subsequent establishment of the State of Israel.

Hebrew literature is still wrestling with those two events and their repercussions. What we must bear in mind, as readers, is the complexity of emotions felt by the young Israeli writer regarding those events during the 1940s and '50s. On one hand, there was the love and compassion, the opening of hearts and gates to the victims of the Holocaust as they entered the land of Israel. On the other hand, those same young writers could feel a deep sense of shame, even estrangement, regarding the many millions who went to their deaths with little or no resistance, whereas the War of Independence, in which the fledgling state repelled the combined onslaught of five Arab nations, was a scene of heroism.

In the eyes of Israeli writers at that time, this difference served only to emphasize the gulf, once more, between Israel and the Diaspora. The individual Israeli, engaged as he was in the battle for national survival, felt what he regarded as the passivity of European Jews during the Holocaust to be incomprehensible. Thus, the "Israeli nature" was once again pitted against the "Jewish nature." This became polarized in a difference of affiliations—the Israeli, as writer and citizen, felt that *his* basic loyalty was to the land and its future, while he felt that what characterized the European Jew was his domination by a past that included a recurring cycle of persecution, exile, and extermination.

In the 1980s, after five wars and the unending threat of annihilation, the Israeli feeling has softened with regard to the European Jew: Along with the heightened awareness of national extinction as an ever-imminent possibility, there has come a consciousness of a common destiny, shared by Israel and the Jewish people everywhere.

We may distinguish two groups among Israeli writers concerned with the Holocaust. The first consists of those who lived through the Holocaust, most of them as youngsters, who came to Israel after the war through Youth Aliyah. The prominent writers in this group are Aharon Appelfeld, Uri Orlev, Shamai Golan, and Itamar Yaoz-Kest. Within this group of foreign-born writers, there is a subgroup consisting of those born outside Israel, who left Europe before the catastrophe. (The poet Yehuda Amichai was born in Germany and came to Palestine with his family before the war.) The second main group of writers are those who were born in Palestine and lived there as children during the war. In a way, they too are survivors, at least by dint of the fear of imminent destruction. We must remember that the extermination of the Jewish population in Palestine was part of the overall German plan. In May 1941 General Rommel's armed force reached as far as El Alamein, a mere one hundred kilometers west of Alexandria, and it was not until October 1942 (eighteen months after) that he was defeated at El Alamein, thus breaking the German front in North Africa. Therefore, from the outbreak of war until that time the Jewish population in Palestine lived in danger of destruction, and it has given voice to its "survivorship" in its writing.

Apart from this distinction regarding the writers there is another division to be made, concerning two major trends in the Hebrew literature of the Holocaust: the realistic trend as against the symbolic/fantastic trend. This loose division reflects two very different orientations—and yet the line of demarcation is an ambiguous one, since elements of both trends are often found in the same work. Indeed, we might perhaps see it to be a result of the enormity of the Holocaust experience, that the reality of it goes over into the fantastic.

In general, the writing of the realistic trend is concerned with portrayal, in fiction, of direct experiences, and especially of the effect of the Holocaust experience on children. We may therefore expect to find depictions of places and occurrences, as pervasive elements. The mimetic approach here involves a combination of autobiographical and fictional structures, varying from direct description of the horror to stories of imprisonment, escape, or rescue. In many of these stories, the third-person technique gives the author the position of omniscience that was not to be had amidst the experience itself. The selective power of fiction allows for the recreation of experience in a new guise.

We can venture the general observation that whereas writers of the realistic trend are attracted to the heart of the experience itself, writers of the symbolic/fantastic trend try to transcend the experience in its spatial and temporal dimensions. They do this by making the human psyche the center of the event, and the psyche will possibly have undergone a disorientation, even a disintegration. An author such as Aharon Appelfeld goes even further in detaching experience from its temporal setting and plants it in a primordial cycle of time.

A fascination with the past, a reassessment of the past so that one places oneself at some *point* in a temporal sequence (perhaps thereby to give a "place" to a displaced psyche)—all this may culminate in a return to one's "hometown." The primary aim here is to remember and comprehend—but it may also be more basic than that: to reassure oneself that the experience actually occurred, as though we must go to a place so that we might be sure that something "took place."

Thus, we encounter in this literature the constant theme of "return." The return to the landscape of one's childhood and to the place of one's ever-possible death—this theme appears again and again, as though reflecting some dark fascination with places connected to a multitude of inexpressible fears.

The "return" is in a way prompted by the succession of tears in the fabric of childhood. These include not only the Holocaust experience but also, in much smaller scope, the geographic transfer to a new soil and new possibilities for life. But any such transition (major or minor) may bring the natural process of individuation to a halt. A new process of individuation began for many of the survivors arriving in Palestine. This involved not only the release from the previous setting and entrance into a new society dedicated to the preservation of one's life (as the prior one was dedicated to one's death) but also, quite often, taking a new name, learning a new language—in every concrete sense being reborn and acquiring a new identity.

Beneficial as that surely was, the acquisition of a new identity may leave a person even more haunted by the old one. What we often find in this literature, therefore, is the protagonist as a mature individual, strangely attracted to the past and to his prior "homeland." That attraction leads to a return, and in Holocaust literature this is always of a very unsettling nature (as we might well expect). In Appelfeld's novel *The Age of Wonders* the protagonist's return stirs up emotions long buried; and those individuals he meets, loaded with suppressed memories, expect the protagonist to go back to Jerusalem and leave them with their memories suppressed.

In any event, the return is a catharsis one has to go through in order to be able to come to terms, it would seem, with one's new Israeli identity as a matter of choice and not of necessity. For many who came to Palestine as children, the coming there was not a result of a conscious decision; rather, the post-war reality landed thousands of parentless children on the shores of Palestine—resulting in an often traumatic experience that called for quick adjustment to change of name, to new language and experience. This transition, as I said, may lead to a realistic approach in the eventual writer; but as often it leads to fantastic, even surrealistic, fiction.

The theme of return to one's "hometown" features in the surrealistic story "Twilight" by Shulamith Hareven. The story opens with the words, "Last night I spent a year in the city where I was born." This cathartic story has the quality of a well-rehearsed *mise en scène*. Theatrically, the frozen city repeats its demise nightly in a ghostly scene at the opera house. Every night after the performance the audience is rounded up and shoved into trucks. Every successive night they are returned to the theater, somewhat less alive, yellowing like the pages of an album. The narrator is saved by a man who will be her husband, the father of her son who will be born, who will grow and speak within days, only to be lost, drawn to the singing and the opera house. She steps out of her dreams to find herself in her home in Jerusalem—in the domain of daylight, the sun, the voices of her husband and children. The opening line of the story, "Last night I spent a year in the city where I was born," corresponds to the words over the gates of Dante's Inferno: "Through me the way to the doleful city; through me the way to the lost people . . ."—except that, unlike Dante's, Hareven's hell has no God dispensing justice and mercy: Here, both values are absent. Her "return" is a final cutting of the connecting cord, a reaffirmation of life and sun.

In *The Phosphorus Line,* a novella by Itamar Yaoz-Kest, the protagonist's "return" is motivated by his mother, who believes that her husband's death in Israel was brought about by their acceptance of German reparations (as though she and her husband were somehow helping the Germans expiate their sins). She wishes to return to the camp where her parents perished, to ask for their forgiveness. The camp and its surroundings make up a phantasmagorical world, a sterilized inferno eroded by creeping fungi. The protagonist is tempted and detained by a child/woman who infests him with fear and desire. The camp, the desertion of his mother in the snow— everything suggests an inferno of desire, fear, and hesitation, a state of being into which he is thrown. In the mind of the non-Jewish caretaker of the camp, himself a form of inmate, Germany is a state of being, a condition but not a country. The mother seeks death in the infinite domain of the snow but is snatched up by the son taking her to the train that will lead them not to death but to the sunlight, the reality that defies memories and changes them.

In the David Schütz novel *The Grass and the Sand,* the protagonist returns to Germany with his brother for what is to be a family reunion. The mother, a German woman of Jewish origin but of no Jewish persuasion was in Germany throughout the war and remained there. While she wandered, her four children were cared for by a non-Jewish neighbor. The protagonist spends an entire night in a spiritual struggle with his mother but she remains unmoved, devoid of a sense of guilt or even of any desire to dwell on the past. The image we are left with is that of the old woman, biting into a sausage with her bright white teeth.

If the modern Jewish experience is to be seen as a continuation of the historical past, then it ought to be possible for Jews to find solace for their suffering in the ongoing tradition. If, on the other hand, the Jew's modern experience is altogether unique, then no guidelines derived from past experience can be of any help in answering the question, "Why?" For someone who is committed to the truth of the continuous heritage, the matter is settled. Yet for the secular Jewish individual—as for the secular Jewish state—the choice is there to be made, and it must be made day after day, in regard to innumerable problems that are presented.

Is Israel a continuation or a new genesis? Are we to reaffirm the established past, or are we to base ourselves on the here-and-now? These questions have beset Jewish thinkers since the nineteenth century, when thought began to be directed toward the idea of a Jewish national entity. The establishment of the State of Israel only intensified the questioning (rather than settling the issue, as some thinkers thought it would, with the inauguration of a Jewish state). After the Holocaust, that same questioning was refueled, not in regard to Jewish *national* identity but rather in regard to the cogency and vitality of Jewish *cultural* identity, following the Holocaust. Obviously, it was the Jewish cultural identity that marked millions for death. Is it therefore a badge of shame, to be rejected and overcome? Or is it, on the contrary, to be the source of strength for those who have survived?

The story "The Name" by Aharon Megged touches upon all these questions and more, and is as timely now as when it first appeared, in the early days of the State. Megged describes—quite movingly—a confrontation between a grandfather, living in Israel but raised in the Ukraine and steeped in memories, and his grandchildren, who are Israeli-born and entirely Israeli-oriented. Naming a newborn child for someone who has died is a traditional way of preserving the memory of the deceased. The old man wants their newborn son to be named for a grandson of his who perished in the Holocaust. The grandson's name was Mendele. To the ears of the young Israelis, this is a ghetto name, ugly and horrible; they would prefer to forget the past. For the time-haunted old man, however, "Ties are remembrance." To him, the name is the essence of meaning and memory. The young couple see themselves connected to the land rather than to memory. Despite this, the Holocaust has called modern Israel back to a self-definition that goes beyond the present.

Hanoch Bartov's novel *The Brigade* describes the firsthand encounter of Israeli-born Jews with a defeated Germany and survivors of the Holocaust. The Jewish Brigade was composed of Israelis who fought in the British army in World War II. The personal encounter with the survivors is the affirmation of hope and its denial. The first meeting with a Jew who came "from there" has almost a mystic quality: "This stranger, who had come to us from out of the darkness, awesome in his appearance, was actually one of us, speaking our language, coming to us straight from the forest, directing his feet to this spot on the border as though to a star." This revelation of brotherhood transcending boundaries is coupled with personal horror. Elisha Krook, the young protagonist, realizes that a relative of his has survived Auschwitz by working at the crematorium: "More than anything else, I was filled with revulsion at the thought of being connected with him." The encounters of Brigade members with individual Germans is complex as well, leading to new questions: How does one hate? What is the moral price of revenge? Can an individual wage a private war? Is the Brigade an army of liberation or an army of retribution? The abstract notion of the enemy must be translated into terms befitting the everyday encounter with individual Germans.

The young protagonist, thrown into a situation that is devoid of precedent, is left with a self-questioning that is ultimately doomed by a sense of impotence and ambiguity. The final mystery is the survival itself. In light of the horror, what price must any survivor pay? If survival is bought at the expense of one's humanness, must not the survivor embrace his own animalism as the ultimate value?

Another expectable reaction must be a retreat into autism. In milder form, this is translatable into solitude and withdrawal. And what has been especially ironic is that the survivors have as often withdrawn from the society that has welcomed them—simply because the welcomers cannot possibly understand what the survivors have undergone. There have been many stories about Holocaust children who reached the shores of Palestine in the 1940s. Thrown out of childhood by the horror, they were then "thrown" (in a milder way) into a new society. That society did not accept them readily. Their accents, their rolled socks, their round glasses, their pallor—all this accentuates their "strangeness."

Shulamith Hareven's sensitive story, "The Witness" (not included in this anthology), is a subtle and ironic incrimination of Israeli society of the '40s for its sense of smugness and self-satisfaction. The witness is a boy, Shlomek, who is an early arrival from the inferno. His personal story of the horror—the massacre of his parents and brothers—is rejected by Israelis as the fruit of an overdeveloped imagination and is not taken seriously. The boy's lonely refusal to acclimate himself and let the past be forgotten creates a gap between himself and the acrimonious kibbutz society—its pat remedies for all ills are counterpoised against the three-dimensionality of his pain.

In Holocaust literature, the fantastic emerges both as a thematic element and as a structural element. Generally, fantastic literature demands a suspension of disbelief on the part of the reader—and we are willing, usually, to overcome our disbelief for the sake of a partial fulfillment of our wishful thinking or the reaffirmation of social values. In the case of Holocaust literature, however, all this becomes far more problematic—and literary premises, hitherto unchallenged, are now challenged in new and forceful ways. Thus, we cannot suspend our belief in the actual events, but at the same time no suspension of disbelief can be demanded—because the real *is* so fantastic in character!

Despite all these inherent limitations, the element of the fantastic is prominent in the literature. The writer transcends historical reality and yet aims at a *mimesis* of reality. He creates a special universe, an airless existence within the psyche of the character that need not heed the laws of logic. The writer may create (as does Yaoz-Kest) a fantastic world made up of symbols and metaphors, a world that does not exist. Or he may build a world around a character whose inner life is a mystery—to the writer, to the reader, and to the other characters.

A master of modern anti-tales, Aharon Appelfeld relates to the Holocaust as to a metaphysical wound. His tales, like those of other writers in this collection relying on the fantastic (e.g., Yaoz-Kest, Hareven, Ben-Mordechai), create a subtle interplay between the inevitable factuality of the Holocaust and the poetic attempt to go beyond it.

Thus, through a partial *suspension* of the realistic element, the writer will try to find new ways to reach the subject and its reality. This creates a tension between narrative distance and proximity—or perhaps an impossible combination of the two, an oxymoron involving deterministic features that coexist with a psyche in chaotic freedom. Appelfeld often detaches experience from its historic mooring, so that the psyche is seen in its essential changes, but without the cause of those changes being visible to the reader. Many of his characters, like Bertha (in the short story of his that is included in this collection), are fragments of human beings, caught in the curve of time and never to emerge from it. Bertha lacks all sense of self, all individuation, all projection of a future. She has insulated herself against change, and she lives on almost a pre-cognitive level, without the play of possibilities. The outer world has betrayed her; none of it can make for her security, and therefore her safety lies within. (Notice, therefore, that in the Holocaust the characteristics of existence are precisely those befitting psychosis in the ordinary world.) Bertha enters oblivion upon arriving in Israel. "You couldn't make her disclose anything from the past, nor was she capable of absorbing anything new."

Often the Holocaust experience, since it cannot be explained by the rules of the familiar world, is transmuted into the symbolic or fantastic—as an attempt to make it comprehensible in *those* terms, lacking any other. Appelfeld's characters live beyond the organic cycle, in the absurd. Bertha's existence is totally insular, connected to no social world. To the outer world, she is a young retarded child, a victim of the Holocaust. To her protector, Max, she is a mysterious being, exercising a magic hold on him.

Do we not impose rationality on a story by telling it? By now, it would be platitudinous to say that the irrationality of the Holocaust initiated a literature that made the irrational itself a thematic and structural element. If so, is the irrational rationalized in the telling? It would seem, nevertheless, that there is a quantum of the irrational that remains—unresolved—and often we may detect its presence through its association with irony.

In "The Times My Father Died," Yehuda Amichai gives us a highly imaginative and poetic tale, unique in form and tone. On the realistic level it reiterates the idea of the countless deaths experienced individually by European Jews. The major image—that of the author's law-abiding father—is embedded ironically within that milieu. The father—a humanist, loyally devoted to the causes of pre-war Germany—is nevertheless exposed to a slow and remorseless degradation. Anti-Semitism forces him out of a Germany in which he had his roots as a German and as a devout Jew. The changing reality does not alter his convictions, but it does corrode his life and make it a chain of painful deaths. His one response to these deprivations is unquestioned humanism. During the First World War, when he fought in the German army, he gave some French prisoners all the water in his canteen. Decades later, in Jerusalem, on his deathbed, he tells his son: "There's the cat mewing on the neighbor's roof. Maybe it's shut in and wants to get out."

The irrational quality that has dominated human fate in modern life and fiction has forced its fictional characters into unrelieved contradiction. Hegel says that if one approaches the world rationally, the world will respond by presenting a rational image of itself. In the Holocaust, on the other hand, it is the world that has approached us with its irrationality, and we respond to it by recasting that world in irrational fiction. The twentieth century "celebrates" —shrilly and unabashedly—the decline of man as a paradigm of reason and nature. The attendant virtues of truth, justice, and mercy have therefore been shunted aside as inauthentic relics. Again and again in Holocaust literature, life appears as an unreal game in which the old rules no longer hold. And yet there is the fact of that literature itself to be accounted for: Amidst the ruination of reason and meaning, that literature has been the most profound attempt, in our time, to find a meaning for the otherwise absurd, to find reason in what is otherwise inexplicable.

GILA RAMRAS-RAUCH

THE
NAME

Aharon Megged

G randfather Zisskind lived in a little house in a southern suburb of the town. About once a month, on a Saturday afternoon, his granddaughter Raya and her young husband Yehuda would go and pay him a visit.

Raya would give three cautious knocks on the door (an agreed signal between her and her grandfather ever since her childhood, when he had lived in their house together with the whole family), and they would wait for the door to be opened. "Now he's getting up," Raya would whisper to Yehuda, her face glowing, when the sound of her grandfather's slippers was heard from within, shuffling across the room. Another moment, and the key would be turned and the door opened.

"Come in," he would say somewhat absently, still buttoning up his pants, with the rheum of sleep in his eyes. Although it was very hot he wore a yellow winter vest with long sleeves, from which his wrists stuck out—white, thin, delicate as a girl's, as was his bare neck with its taut skin.

After Raya and Yehuda had sat down at the table, which was covered with a white cloth showing signs of the meal he had eaten alone—crumbs from the Sabbath loaf, a plate with meat leavings, a glass containing some grape pips, a number of jars, and so on— he would smooth the crumpled pillows, spread a cover over the narrow bed, and tidy up. It was a small room, and its obvious disorder aroused pity for the old man's helplessness in running his home. In the corner was a shelf with two sooty kerosene burners, a kettle, and two or three saucepans, and next to it a basin containing plates, knives, and forks. In another corner was a stand holding books with thick leather bindings, leaning and lying on each other. Some of his clothes hung over the backs of the chairs. An ancient walnut cupboard with an empty buffet stood exactly opposite the door. On the wall hung a clock that had long since stopped.

"We ought to make Grandfather a present of a clock," Raya would say to Yehuda as she surveyed the room and her glance lighted on the clock; but every time the matter slipped her memory.

She loved her grandfather, with his pointed white silky beard, his tranquil face from which a kind of holy radiance emanated, his quiet, soft voice that seemed to have been made only for uttering words of sublime wisdom. She also respected him for his pride, which had led him to move out of her mother's house and live by himself, accepting the hardship and trouble and the affliction of loneliness in his old age. There had been a bitter quarrel between him and his daughter. After Raya's father had died, the house had lost its grandeur and shed the trappings of wealth. Some of the antique furniture that they had retained—along with some crystalware and jewels, the dim luster of memories from the days of plenty in their native city—had been sold, and Rachel, Raya's mother, had been compelled to support the home by working as a dentist's nurse. Grandfather Zisskind, who had been supported by the family ever since he came to the country, wished to hand over to his daughter his small capital, which was deposited in a bank. She was not willing to accept it. She was stubborn and proud like him. Then, after a prolonged quarrel and several weeks of not speaking to each other, he took some of the things in his room and the broken clock and went to live alone. That had been about four years ago. Now Rachel would come to him once or twice a week, bringing with her a bag full of provisions, to clean the room and cook some meals for him. He was no longer interested in expenses and did not even ask about them, as though they were of no more concern to him.

"And now . . . what can I offer you?" Grandfather Zisskind would ask when he considered the room ready to receive guests. "There's no need to offer us anything, Grandfather; we didn't come for that," Raya would answer crossly.

But protests were of no avail. Her grandfather would take out a jar of fermenting preserves and put it on the table, then grapes and plums, biscuits and two glasses of strong tea, forcing them to eat. Raya would taste a little of this and that just to please the old man, while Yehuda, for whom all these visits were unavoidable torment, the very sight of the dishes arousing his disgust, would secretly indicate to her by making a sour face that he just couldn't touch the preserves. She would smile at him placatingly, stroking his knee. But Grandfather insisted, so he would have to taste at least a teaspoonful of the sweet and nauseating stuff.

Afterwards Grandfather would ask about all kinds of things. Raya did her best to make the conversation pleasant, in order to relieve Yehuda's boredom. Finally would come what Yehuda dreaded most of all and on account of which he had resolved more than once to refrain from these visits. Grandfather Zisskind would rise, take his chair and place it next to the wall, get up on it carefully, holding on to the back so as not to fall, open the clock and take out a cloth bag with a black cord tied around it. Then he would shut the clock, get off the chair, put it back in its place, sit down on it, undo the cord, take out of the cloth wrapping a bundle of sheets of paper, lay them in front of Yehuda and say:

"I would like you to read this."

"Grandfather," Raya would rush to Yehuda's rescue, "but he's already read it at least ten times. . . ."

But Grandfather Zisskind would pretend not to hear and would not reply, so Yehuda was compelled each time to read there and then that same essay, spread over eight, long sheets in a large, somewhat shaky handwriting, which he almost knew by heart. It was a lament for Grandfather's native town in the Ukraine which had been destroyed by the Germans, and all its Jews slaughtered. When he had finished, Grandfather would take the sheets out of his hand, fold them, sigh and say:

"And nothing of all this is left. Dust and ashes. Not even a tombstone to bear witness. Imagine, of a community of twenty thousand Jews not even one survived to tell how it happened . . . Not a trace."

Then out of the same cloth bag, which contained various letters and envelopes, he would draw a photograph of his grandson Mendele, who had been twelve years old when he was killed; the only son of his son Ossip, chief engineer in a large chemical factory. He would show it to Yehuda and say:

"He was a genius. Just imagine, when he was only eleven he had already finished his studies at the Conservatory, won a scholarship from the government, and was considered an outstanding violinist. A genius! Look at that forehead. . . ." And after he had put the photograph back he would sigh and repeat, "Not a trace."

A strained silence of commiseration would descend on Raya and Yehuda, who had already heard these same things many times over and no longer felt anything when they were repeated. And as he wound the cord around the bag the old man would muse: "And Ossip was also a prodigy. As a boy he knew Hebrew well, and could recite Bialik's poems by heart. He studied by himself. He read endlessly, Gnessin, Frug, Bershadsky . . . You didn't know Bershadsky; he was a good writer . . . He had a warm heart, Ossip had. He didn't mix in politics, he wasn't even a Zionist, but even when they promoted him there he didn't forget that he was a Jew . . . He called his son Mendele, of all names, after his dead brother, even though it was surely not easy to have a name like that among the Russians . . . Yes, he had a warm Jewish heart . . ."

He would turn to Yehuda as he spoke, since in Raya he always saw the child who used to sit on his knee listening to his stories, and for him she had never grown up, while he regarded Yehuda as an educated man who could understand someone else, especially inasmuch as Yehuda held a government job.

Raya remembered how the change had come about in her grandfather. When the war was over he was still sustained by uncertainty and hoped for some news of his son, for it was known that very many had succeeded in escaping eastward. Wearily he would visit all those who had once lived in his town, but none of them had received any sign of life from relatives. Nevertheless he continued to hope, for Ossip's important position might have helped to save him. Then Raya came home one evening and saw him sitting on the floor with a rent in his jacket. In the house they spoke in whispers, and her mother's eyes were red with weeping. She, too, had wept at Grandfather's sorrow, at the sight of his stricken face, at the oppressive quiet in the rooms. For many weeks afterward it was as if he had imposed silence on himself. He would sit at his table from morning to night, reading and rereading old letters, studying family photographs by the hour as he brought them close to his shortsighted eyes, or leaning backward on his chair, motionless, his hand touching the edge of the table and his eyes staring through the window in front of him, into the distance, as if he had turned to stone. He was no longer the same talkative, wise, and humorous grandfather who interested himself in the house, asked what his granddaughter was doing, instructed her, tested her knowledge, proving boastfully like a child that he knew more than her teachers. Now he seemed to cut himself off from the world and entrench himself in his thoughts and his memories, which none of the household could penetrate. Later, a strange perversity had taken hold of him that was hard to tolerate. He would insist that his meals be served at his table, apart, that no one should enter his room without knocking at the door, or close the shutters of his window against the sun. When anyone disobeyed these prohibitions he would flare up and quarrel violently with his daughter. At times it seemed that he hated her.

When Raya's father died, Grandfather Zisskind did not show any signs of grief and did not even console his daughter. But when the days of mourning were past it was as if he had been restored to new life, and he emerged from his silence. Yet he did not speak of his son-in-law, nor of his son Ossip, but only of his grandson Mendele. Often during the day he would mention the boy by name as if he were alive and would speak of him familiarly, although he had seen him only in photographs—as though deliberating aloud and turning the matter over, he would talk of how Mendele ought to be brought up. It was hardest of all when he started criticizing his son and his son's wife for not having foreseen the impending disaster, for not having rushed the boy away to a safe place, not having hidden him with non-Jews, not having tried to get him to the Land of Israel in good time. There was no logic in what he said; this would so infuriate Rachel that she would burst out with, "Oh, do stop! Stop it! I'll go out of my mind with your foolish nonsense!" She would rise from her seat in anger, withdraw to her room, and afterward, when she had calmed down, would say to Raya, "Sclerosis, apparently. Loss of memory. He no longer knows what he's talking about."

One day—Raya would never forget this—she and her mother saw that Grandfather was wearing his best suit, the black one, and under it a gleaming white shirt; his shoes were polished, and he had a hat on. He had not worn these clothes for many months, and the family was dismayed to see him. They thought that he had lost his mind. "What holiday is it today?" her mother asked. "Really, don't you know?" asked her grandfather. "Today is Mendele's birthday!" Her mother burst out crying. She too began to cry and ran out of the house.

After that, Grandfather Zisskind went to live alone. His mind, apparently, had become settled, except that he would frequently forget things that had occurred a day or two before, though he clearly remembered, down to the smallest detail, things that had happened in his town and to his family more than thirty years ago. Raya would go and visit him, at first with her mother and, after her marriage, with Yehuda. What bothered them was that they were compelled to listen to his talk about Mendele his grandson, and to read that same lament for his native town that had been destroyed.

Whenever Rachel happened to come there during their visit, she would scold Grandfather rudely. "Stop bothering them with your masterpiece," she would say, and would herself remove the papers from the table and put them back in their bag. "If you want them to keep on visiting you, don't talk to them about the dead. Talk about the living. They're young people and they have no mind for such things." And as they left his room together she would say, turning to Yehuda in order to placate him, "Don't be surprised at him. Grandfather's already old. Over seventy. Loss of memory."

When Raya was seven months pregnant, Grandfather Zisskind had in his absent-mindedness not yet noticed it. But Rachel could no longer refrain from letting him share her joy and hope, and told him that a great-grandchild would soon be born to him. One evening the door of Raya and Yehuda's apartment opened, and

Grandfather himself stood on the threshold in his holiday clothes, just as on the day of Mendele's birthday. This was the first time he had visited them at home, and Raya was so surprised that she hugged and kissed him as she had not done since she was a child. His face shone, his eyes sparkled with the same intelligent and mischievous light they had in those far-off days before the calamity. When he entered he walked briskly through the rooms, giving his opinion on the furniture and its arrangement, and joking about everything around him. He was so pleasant that Raya and Yehuda could not stop laughing all the time he was speaking. He gave no indication that he knew what was about to take place, and for the first time in many months he did not mention Mendele.

"Ah, you naughty children," he said, "is this how you treat Grandfather? Why didn't you tell me you had such a nice place?"

"How many times have I invited you here, Grandfather?" asked Raya.

"Invited me? You ought to have *brought* me here, dragged me by force!"

"I wanted to do that too, but you refused."

"Well, I thought that you lived in some dark den, and I have a den of my own. Never mind, I forgive you."

And when he took leave of them he said:

"Don't bother to come to me. Now that I know where you're to be found and what a palace you have, I'll come to you . . . if you don't throw me out, that is."

Some days later, when Rachel came to their home and they told her about Grandfather's amazing visit, she was not surprised:

"Ah, you don't know what he's been contemplating during all these days, ever since I told him that you're about to have a child . . . He has one wish—that if it's a son, it should be named . . . after his grandson."

"Mendele?" exclaimed Raya, and involuntarily burst into laughter. Yehuda smiled as one smiles at the fond fancies of the old.

"Of course, I told him to put that out of his head," said Rachel, "but you know how obstinate he is. It's some obsession and he won't think of giving it up. Not only that, but he's sure that you'll willingly agree to it, and especially you, Yehuda."

Yehuda shrugged his shoulders. "Crazy. The child would be unhappy all his life."

"But he's not capable of understanding that," said Rachel, and a note of apprehension crept into her voice.

Raya's face grew solemn. "We have already decided on the name," she said. "If it's a girl she'll be called Osnath, and if it's a boy—Ehud."

Rachel did not like either.

The matter of the name became almost the sole topic of conversation between Rachel and the young couple when she visited them, and it infused gloom into the air of expectancy that filled the house.

Rachel, midway between the generations, was of two minds about the matter. When she spoke to her father she would scold and contradict him, flinging at him all the arguments she had heard from Raya and Yehuda as though they were her own, but when she spoke to the children she sought to induce them to meet his wishes, and would bring down their anger on herself. As time went on, the question of a name, to which in the beginning she had attached little importance, became a kind of mystery, concealing something preordained, fearful, and pregnant with life and death. The fate of the child itself seemed in doubt. In her innermost heart she prayed that Raya would give birth to a daughter.

"Actually, what's so bad about the name Mendele?" she asked her daughter. "It's a Jewish name like any other."

"What are you talking about, Mother"—Raya rebelled against the thought—"a ghetto name, ugly, horrible! I wouldn't even be capable of letting it cross my lips. Do you want me to hate my child?"

"Oh, you won't hate your child. At any rate, not because of the name . . ."

"I should hate him. It's as if you'd told me that my child would be born with a hump! And anyway—why should I? What for?"

"You have to do it for Grandfather's sake," Rachel said quietly, although she knew that she was not speaking the whole truth.

"You know, Mother, that I am ready to do anything for Grandfather," said Raya. "I love him, but I am not ready to sacrifice my child's happiness on account of some superstition of his. What sense is there in it?"

Rachel could not explain the "sense in it" rationally, but in her heart she rebelled against her daughter's logic, which had always been hers too and now seemed very superficial, a symptom of the frivolity afflicting the younger generation. Her old father now appeared to her like an ancient tree whose deep roots suck up the mysterious essence of existence, of which neither her daughter nor she herself knew anything. Had it not been for this argument about the name, she would certainly never have got to meditating on the transmigration of souls and the eternity of life. At night she would wake up covered in cold sweat. Hazily, she recalled frightful scenes of bodies of naked children, beaten and trampled under the jackboots of soldiers, and an awful sense of guilt oppressed her spirit.

Then Rachel came with a proposal for a compromise: that the child should be named Menahem. A Hebrew name, she said; an Israeli one, by all standards. Many children bore it, and it occurred to nobody to make fun of them. Even Grandfather had agreed to it after much urging.

Raya refused to listen.

"We have chosen a name, Mother," she said, "which we both like, and we won't change it for another. Menahem is a name that reeks of old age, a name that for me is connected with sad memories and people I don't like. Menahem you could call only a boy who is short, weak, and not good-looking. Let's not talk about it any more, Mother."

Rachel was silent. She almost despaired of convincing them. At last she said:

"And are you ready to take the responsibility of going against Grandfather's wishes?"

Raya's eyes opened wide, and fear was reflected in them:

"Why do you make such a fateful thing of it? You frighten me!" she said, and burst into tears. She began to fear for her offspring as one fears the evil eye.

"And perhaps there *is* something fateful in it . . ." whispered Rachel without raising her eyes. She flinched at her own words.

"What is it?" insisted Raya, with a frightened look at her mother.

"I don't know . . ." she said. "Perhaps all the same we are bound to retain the names of the dead . . . in order to leave a remembrance of them . . ." She was not sure herself whether there was any truth in what she said or whether it was merely a stupid belief, but her father's faith was before her, stronger than her own doubts and her daughter's simple and understandable opposition.

"But I don't always want to remember all those dreadful things, Mother. It's impossible that this memory should always hang about this house and that the poor child should bear it!"

Rachel understood. She, too, heard such a cry within her as she listened to her father talking, sunk in memories of the past. As if to herself, she said in a whisper:

"I don't know . . . at times it seems to me that it's not Grandfather who's suffering from loss of memory, but ourselves. All of us."

About two weeks before the birth was due, Grandfather Zisskind appeared in Raya and Yehuda's home for the second time. His face was yellow, angry, and the light had faded from his eyes. He greeted them, but did not favor Raya with so much as a glance, as if he had pronounced a ban upon the sinner. Turning to Yehuda he said, "I wish to speak to you."

They went into the inner room. Grandfather sat down on the chair and placed the palm of his hand on the edge of the table, as was his wont, and Yehuda sat, lower than he, on the bed.

"Rachel has told me that you don't want to call the child by my grandchild's name," he said.

"Yes . . ." said Yehuda diffidently.

"Perhaps you'll explain to me why?" he asked.

"We . . ." stammered Yehuda, who found it difficult to face the piercing gaze of the old man. "The name simply doesn't appeal to us."

Grandfather was silent. Then he said, "I understand that Mendele

doesn't appeal to you. Not a Hebrew name. Granted! But Menahem
—what's wrong with Menahem?" It was obvious that he was con-
trolling his feelings with difficulty.

"It's not . . ." Yehuda knew that there was no use explaining;
they were two generations apart in their ideas. "It's not an Israeli
name . . . it's from the *Golah* *"

"*Golah,*" repeated Grandfather. He shook with rage, but somehow he maintained his self-control. Quietly he added, "We all come
from the *Golah*. I, and Raya's father and mother. Your father and
mother. All of us."

"Yes . . ." said Yehuda. He resented the fact that he was being
dragged into an argument that was distasteful to him, particularly
with this old man whose mind was already not quite clear. Only
out of respect did he restrain himself from shouting: That's that, and
it's done with! . . . "Yes, but we were born in this country," he said
aloud; "that's different."

Grandfather Zisskind looked at him contemptuously. Before
him he saw a wretched boor, an empty vessel.

"You, that is to say, think that there's something new here," he
said, "that everything that was there is past and gone. Dead, without
sequel. That you are starting everything anew."

"I didn't say that. I only said that we were born in this
country. . . ."

"You were born here. Very nice . . ." said Grandfather Zisskind
with rising emotion. "So what of it? What's so remarkable about
that? In what way are you superior to those who were born *there*?
Are you cleverer than they? More cultured? Are you greater than
they in Torah or good deeds? Is your blood redder than theirs?"
Grandfather Zisskind looked as if he could wring Yehuda's neck.

"I didn't say that either. I said that *here* it's different. . . ."

Grandfather Zisskind's patience with idle words was exhausted.

"You good-for-nothing!" he burst out in his rage. "What do
you know about what was there? What do you know of the *people*

*The Diaspora; the whole body of Jews living dispersed among the Gentiles.

that were there? The communities? The cities? What do you know of the *life* they had there?"

"Yes," said Yehuda, his spirit crushed, "but we no longer have any ties with it."

"You have no ties with it?" Grandfather Zisskind bent toward him. His lips quivered in fury. "With what . . . with what *do* you have ties?"

"We have . . . with this country," said Yehuda and gave an involuntary smile.

"Fool!" Grandfather Zisskind shot at him. "Do you think that people come to a desert and make themselves a nation, eh? That you are the first of some new race? That you're not the son of your father? Not the grandson of your grandfather? Do you want to forget them? Are you ashamed of them for having had a hundred times more culture and education than you have? Why . . . why, everything here"—he included everything around him in the sweep of his arm—"is no more than a puddle of tap water against the big sea that was there! What have you here? A mixed multitude! Seventy languages! Seventy distinct groups! Customs? A way of life? Why, every home here is a nation in itself, with its own customs and its own names! And with this you have ties, you say . . ."

Yehuda lowered his eyes and was silent.

"I'll tell you what ties are," said Grandfather Zisskind calmly. "Ties are remembrance! Do you understand? The Russian is linked to his people because he remembers his ancestors. He is called Ivan, his father was called Ivan and his grandfather was called Ivan, back to the first generation. And no Russian has said: 'From today onward I shall not be called Ivan because my fathers and my fathers' fathers were called that; I am the first of a new Russian nation which has nothing at all to do with the Ivans.' Do you understand?"

"But what has that got to do with it?" Yehuda protested impatiently. Grandfather Zisskind shook his head at him.

"And you—you're ashamed to give your son the name Mendele lest it remind you that there were Jews who were called by that name. You believe that his name should be wiped off the face of the earth. That not a trace of it should remain . . ."

He paused, heaved a deep sigh and said:

"O children, children, you don't know what you're doing . . . You're finishing off the work which the enemies of Israel began. They took the bodies away from the world, and you—the name and the memory . . . No continuation, no evidence, no memorial and no name. Not a trace . . ."

And with that he rose, took his stick, and with long strides went toward the door and left.

The newborn child was a boy and he was named Ehud, and when he was about a month old, Raya and Yehuda took him in the carriage to Grandfather's house.

Raya gave three cautious knocks on the door, and when she heard a rustle inside she could also hear the beating of her anxious heart. Since the birth of the child Grandfather had not visited them even once. "I'm terribly excited," she whispered to Yehuda with tears in her eyes. Yehuda rocked the carriage and did not reply. He was now indifferent to what the old man might say or do.

The door opened, and on the threshold stood Grandfather Zisskind, his face weary and wrinkled. He seemed to have aged. His eyes were sticky with sleep, and for a moment it seemed as if he did not see the callers.

"Good Sabbath, Grandfather," said Raya with great feeling. It seemed to her now that she loved him more than ever.

Grandfather looked at them as if surprised, and then said absently, "Come in, come in."

"We've brought the baby with us!" said Raya, her face shining, and her glance traveled from Grandfather to the infant sleeping in the carriage.

"Come in, come in," repeated Grandfather Zisskind in a tired voice. "Sit down," he said as he removed his clothes from the chairs and turned to tidy the disordered bedclothes.

Yehuda stood the carriage by the wall and whispered to Raya, "It's stifling for him here." Raya opened the window wide.

"You haven't seen our baby yet, Grandfather!" she said with a sad smile.

"Sit down, sit down," said Grandfather, shuffling over to the shelf, from which he took the jar of preserves and the biscuit tin, putting them on the table.

"There's no need, Grandfather, really there's no need for it. We didn't come for that," said Raya.

"Only a little something. I have nothing to offer you today. . . ." said Grandfather in a dull, broken voice. He took the kettle off the kerosene burner and poured out two glasses of tea, which he placed before them. Then he too sat down, said, "Drink, drink," and softly tapped his fingers on the table.

"I haven't seen Mother for several days now," he said at last.

"She's busy . . ." said Raya in a low voice, without raising her eyes to him. "She helps me a lot with the baby. . . ."

Grandfather Zisskind looked at his pale, knotted and veined hands lying helplessly on the table; then he stretched out one of them and said to Raya, "Why don't you drink? The tea will get cold."

Raya drew up to the table and sipped the tea.

"And you—what are you doing now?" he asked Yehuda.

"Working as usual," said Yehuda, and added with a laugh, "I play with the baby when there's time."

Grandfather again looked down at his hands, the long thin fingers of which shook with the palsy of old age.

"Take some of the preserves," he said to Yehuda, indicating the jar with a shaking finger. "It's very good." Yehuda dipped the spoon in the jar and put it to his mouth.

There was a deep silence. It seemed to last a very long time. Grandfather Zisskind's fingers gave little quivers on the white table-cloth. It was hot in the room, and the buzzing of a fly could be heard.

Suddenly the baby burst out crying, and Raya started from her seat and hastened to quiet him. She rocked the carriage and crooned, "Quiet, child, quiet, quiet . . ." Even after he had quieted down she went on rocking the carriage back and forth.

Grandfather Zisskind raised his head and said to Yehuda in a whisper:

"You think it was impossible to save him . . . it was possible. They had many friends. Ossip himself wrote to me about it. The manager of the factory had a high opinion of him. The whole town knew them and loved them. . . . How is it they didn't think of it . . . ?" he said, touching his forehead with the palm of his hand. "After all, they knew that the Germans were approaching . . . It was still possible to do something . . ." He stopped a moment and then added, "Imagine that a boy of eleven had already finished his studies at the Conservatory—wild beasts!" He suddenly opened eyes filled with terror. "Wild beasts! To take little children and put them into wagons and deport them . . ."

When Raya returned and sat down at the table, he stopped and became silent, and only a heavy sigh escaped from deep within him.

Again there was a prolonged silence, and as it grew heavier Raya felt the oppressive weight on her bosom increasing till it could no longer be contained. Grandfather sat at the table tapping his thin fingers, and alongside the wall the infant lay in his carriage; it was as if a chasm gaped between a world that was passing and a world that was born. It was no longer a single line to the fourth generation. The aged father did not recognize the great-grandchild whose life would be no memorial.

Grandfather Zisskind got up, took his chair and pulled it up to the clock. He climbed on to it to take out his documents.

Raya could no longer stand the oppressive atmosphere.

"Let's go," she said to Yehuda in a choked voice.

"Yes, we must go," said Yehuda, and rose from his seat. "We have to go," he said loudly as he turned to the old man.

Grandfather Zisskind held the key of the clock for a moment more, then he let his hand fall, grasped the back of the chair and got down.

"You have to go. . . ." he said with a tortured grimace. He spread his arms out helplessly and accompanied them to the doorway.

When the door had closed behind them the tears flowed from Raya's eyes. She bent over the carriage and pressed her lips to the baby's chest. At that moment it seemed to her that he was in need of pity and of great love, as though he were alone, an orphan in the world.

Translated by MINNA GIVTON

THE LEAD
SOLDIERS

Uri Orlev

Formations of soldiers faced each other across the floor, taking cover in domino houses and bunkers of colored blocks. Yurik and Kazik lay by their soldiers. Yurik took a coin and flicked it at his brother's troops. It fell among their ranks, leaving dead and wounded in its path.

"I killed Robin Hood!" Yurik exulted, jumping to his feet.

"That wasn't him."

"You rotten liar, you said that the one without a bayonet was Robin Hood."

"No, I didn't," Kazik maintained.

Yurik threw down the soldier in his hand. "I'm not playing with you any more," he said, getting up again. "You keep changing him from one to another to keep him alive. It's against the rules."

"Don't play, then! I didn't change him."

"All right, but remember." Yurik returned to the game. "It's my turn again. Watch. I'm firing at your capital." He paused and rose on his elbows to listen to the footsteps coming up the stairs. "Who's that coming?"

Kazik listened for a moment.

"Those are the quick footsteps that live across from us," he said.

"She's back already," said Yurik, surprised. "All right, here goes," he added in a lower voice.

"Pan Petrushka," said the whiny voice of a woman from the staircase. "Pan Petrushka, what's new in town?"

"Nothing's new," the man's voice answered. "Did you hear that Marishka's going with Yanek?"

"That's as old as the hills, Pan Petrushka, and with a beard on it."

"And did you hear that they found some Jews over at Kowalska's place?"

"What are you telling me?!" The woman was astonished. "A good Catholic like her hiding Christ-killers? How's your daughter, Pan Petrushka?"

"Better, Pani, better. The doctor said she can get out of bed in a few days' time. Could you perhaps let me have the loan of a kilo of potatoes? My wife's coming back from the village tomorrow and we'll return them with interest."

"She's talking to the shuffling steps down below," said Yurik. "I'm advancing. Take a good look so that you don't say I cheated."

Captain Nemo had led Yurik's troops to the very wall of Kazik's capital. Thaddeus Kosciusko in person, mounted on a white horse, now charged from the flank at the head of a regiment of saber-wielding cavalry that Yurik had drawn and cut out of cardboard. Tadek Swierczewski, his old friend from Zoliboz, joined the fray with a long column of reserves, horsemen and infantry, who advanced from position to position toward the front. General Boehm trotted on his horse before his batteries of cannon. Artillery, fire!

Victory was at hand. The walls of the capital crumbled before a barrage of heavy coins fired at close range. The last of Kazik's soldiers broke and ran for an isolated fortress at the far end of the floor. Yurik took the city and bombarded the fleeing defenders with their own guns. Three times he raked them with fire; three times they retreated the maximum distance, the width of Kazik's outspread hand. Only one of Kazik's soldiers was still alive, at a distance of one more hand from the fort. Yurik aimed and fired. The coin struck the soldier, who somersaulted in the air and landed again on his feet.

"He's still standing!" Kazik shouted.

"Let me have him, but remember where he was. Don't move him." Yurik turned the hero over and looked at his base. "He already has two decorations," he said. He took a pencil and drew a third cross next to them. "He gets a name."

"He's mine," Kazik boasted. "I'll call him . . . Ironhand."

"I've already reserved that," Yurik protested. "I read the book first."

"No, you didn't."

"All right," he conceded. "But it's your turn."

"Ironhand gallops off on his horse," Kazik said.

"He doesn't have a horse," declared Yurik.

"Yes he does. Don't interrupt me."

Yurik fired.

"Missed!"

Ironhand reached the gates of the fort and vanished inside. Yurik staged a massive assault. Cavalry, foot soldiers, and horse-drawn artillery poured forth from every direction. Colorful regiments formed a broad arc in front of the fortress walls. The heroes of novels, famous generals, and the bearers of titles Yurik had invented led his forces against the enemy's last stronghold. Ironhand faithfully deployed his three cannons and shelled his attackers with each in turn, but still they drew nearer. Lead and paper soldiers, pistol bullets and rifle cartridges, queens, bishops and chess pawns, stood at the foot of the fort.

"Surrender!"

"Ironhand never surrenders!"

"Let me have him, I'm taking him prisoner."

"You'll have to find him. He's hiding."

"Liar, you've got him in your pocket!" Yurik fell on his brother, struggling to get the soldier. Kazik fought as hard as he could. Yurik twisted his hand and discovered the fugitive in his clenched fist.

Kazik was close to tears. "Give him back!"

"No, he's my prisoner. My men are marching him back to me. On your knees, coward! Beg for your life from the Commander of the Universe, Jan Grenadier Tarzan. Ironhand is thrown to the floor and I personally slap him in the face." Yurik cut the air forcefully with his hand. "Off to the dungeon!" he commanded.

Kazik's eyes filled with tears at the injustice done to his hero. He threw himself in despair at his brother, trying to get Ironhand back. "Let me have him," he sobbed.

Yurik fought free and ran laughing around the table. Kazik ran after him, crying unrestrainedly. "Let me have him, you pig!"

"Idiot, don't cry so loud. The neighbors'll hear us."

Kazik restrained his sobs. Yurik began to feel sorry for Ironhand. "All right," he said. "Do you agree to my executing him with full honors and then we'll fight another war?"

"Yes," Kazik agreed.

Yurik leaned the prisoner against his fort and stood a squad of marksmen opposite him under the command of General Gordon of Khartoum.

"I'm tying his hands and eyes."

"You don't have to blindfold him," said Kazik bravely.

"What's your last wish?"

"To have this letter delivered to my wife."

The soldiers shouldered their rifles.

"Wait, drums," Kazik reminded him.

The drummers beat out a roll on their drums.

"Long live Poland the free and invincible!" cried Ironhand.

"Fire!" ordered General Gordon.

The rifles rang out. Ironhand still leaned against the wall, his head fallen on his breast.

"Do you want to give him a funeral?"

But Kazik had stopped playing and was listening to the stairs. "Christina's coming." He knew her steps. "She's bringing lunch."

A blonde, trim girl of about eighteen entered the room carrying a laundry basket and a bouquet of lilacs.

"See what I brought you? It's spring outside. The lilac's in bloom." She put the flowers in a vase and filled it with water from the pitcher. "I'm in an awful rush, because my mother has lots of laundry today. Hurry up and eat," she requested. She removed the washing from the basket and handed them the plates of food that were underneath it.

"Kazik's been crying," she said, studying his face.

"We were just playing a game," explained Yurik. "Can you exchange books for us?"

"Have you already finished the ones I brought you? I'll bring you new ones tomorrow," she promised. "I've got you some colored paper, and some cardboard and glue. I'll bring it all up tonight. I had nowhere to put it now."

The boys finished eating and Christina returned the plates to the basket.

"Don't forget to change the water in the vase every day. It's a shame to let them wilt right away." She took the basket and left.

"Ready for more?" asked Yurik.

"Let's have some peacetime first."

"And then we'll play war again?"

"Yes, but later."

Christina went down to the laundry.

QUICK AND CLEAN said the sign on the window at the front of the house. Christina, her mother, and two hired girls did the wash inside amid vaporous clouds of steam. Pani Sadomska, whose husband had been killed fighting in the defense of Warsaw, had agreed to take in the two Jewish boys in return for a handsome fee. Her own two-room apartment was attached to the laundry by a narrow corridor. She and her daughter lived in one of the rooms, and her sixteen-year-old son in the other. The room in which the two boys were hidden was seven flights up on the roof.

"There won't be any bill collectors here," Pani Sadomska had warned them when they arrived. "Don't open the door for anyone. Whenever we come we'll give three knocks three times. And try to be quiet. It's our luck that no one's living underneath you."

The thick wooden beam supporting the ceiling made the room look like a peasant cottage. The furniture was simple and very old. There were two broad wooden beds, a two-legged easy chair that rested against the wall with its springs sticking out, and a wobbly table that must have dated from Napoleon's time. A curtain serving as a partition between the room and the washing area, in which stood a sink, a pitcher of water, and a bucket, completed the scene. Two pictures adorned the walls, one of Jesus bearing his cross through the streets of Jerusalem, and the other of Saint Peter. By them hung a drawing, clipped apparently from an advertisement, of a sailboat on a lake.

"It's getting too dark to see anything," said Kazik.

"Let's put everything away." They threw all the toys in a chest and pushed it under a bed. They lay down next to each other and waited for their supper.

"Tadek's coming with her," announced Kazik.

Yurik went to open the door. Christina lit the kerosene lamp and started preparing the table. Tadek sat on a bed and followed a fly buzzing on the window pane with his watery expressionless eyes. He suddenly leaped up, crushed it against the glass, and returned to the bed again.

Christina liked talking with Yurik. She had never gone beyond the fourth grade and was amazed by how much he knew and thought. Her brother, who had been brain-damaged in infancy by a fall from his crib, had never even finished first grade.

If what Yurik said was true, Christina mused, the stars were really very strange. But what kept them burning all the time? He had told her something else too . . . oh, yes: about the Greeks who had died defending a narrow pass in the mountains. She remembered that they had written something on the stone walls of the pass. It was a nice story. She had tried telling it to Zbishek, but such things didn't interest him. "Let's dance," he had said.

"Will you marry him?" asked Yurik.

"I don't know. Maybe."

"Christina," whispered Yurik. "Look what's happened to Tadek."

Tadek, who had been sitting quietly on the corner of the bed, suddenly waved his hands spastically and keeled over with his eyes wide open. Christina rushed over, grabbed him by the arms, and began to drag him around the room. "Tadek," she cried, "wake up! Tadek!"

Tadek woke up and stood on his feet. "What happened?" he asked.

Christina calmed down. "It happens to him sometimes," she explained to the boys. "Afterwards he never remembers a thing. It's because the blood goes to the wrong place in his brain."

Tadek helped her collect the plates and pack the basket.

"It's already late," said Christina. "Good night."

Yurik lowered the wick of the lamp and lay down in bed. The

silence around them was broken at intervals by the sound of hoof-beats or the horn of a passing car.

"Kazik, do you want to play submarines?"

Yurik got out of bed and put the kerosene lamp under the table.

"Hang up your blanket too," he said to Kazik as he draped his own from the table top. The two of them crawled under it and sat there on pillows. Yurik turned up the lamp.

"Captain Nemo! Full speed ahead! We're heading for Treasure Island."

Afterwards they sat on the table and looked out over the dim rooftops at the stars. "The moon was on that side of the chimney before," Yurik showed his brother, "and now it's on the other side. Do you see? That means that the earth is really turning around."

The full moon rose over the pitch of the roof and looked into their room.

"It has a face," said Yurik. "Look carefully."

"It's a little cross-eyed," said Kazik.

Yurik awoke in the middle of the night. The lamp had nearly gone out. Someone tall and dark was standing in the corner of the room. Yurik strained to hear. A floorboard creaked by the door. Someone had come in through the shut door. The board creaked again. Someone was approaching his bed, coming nearer and nearer without touching it.

"Kazik."

"I'm not asleep."

"I'll give you ten free commands if you get up now and turn up the lamp."

"I can't," replied Kazik.

"I'll give you General Gordon too," said Yurik.

"I can't."

"If I turn it up myself will you come and sleep with me?"

"Yes," Kazik agreed.

Yurik quickly threw back the blanket from over his head and reached the lamp with a single bound. The shadows vanished. Kazik crossed over to his bed.

"But no kicking, and no pulling the blanket."

"It's always you who pulls."

The lamp went out by itself. Yurik and Kazik fell asleep, huddled together in the moonlight.

Strange footsteps mounted the stairs and stopped outside their door. The two of them listened tensely. The knocker knocked three times and three times again. It stopped.

"Should I open it?" asked Yurik in a whisper.

The knocker knocked three more times.

"That's nine. I'm going to open it."

A large stranger wearing a stiff, round hat entered the room. He looked at them and then looked for a place to hang his hat. In the end he put it by his briefcase on the table and sat down in the easy chair.

"Good morning, boys," he said. He smiled at Kazik and raised his chin. "What's your name, young man?"

Kazik didn't answer.

"His name is Kazimierz Stefan Kosopolski," Yurik answered for him.

"Be quiet!" the stranger said angrily. "I wasn't aware that anyone had asked you." He smiled again at Kazik. "Where did you live before coming here, young man?"

Kazik sat there bewildered. He couldn't for the life of him remember the complicated story he had been instructed to tell under such circumstances.

"We're from Lvov," Yurik said.

Sergeant Zuk wheeled around and slapped him in the face. "I asked you not to answer for him," he warned. "Are you Jewish?" he asked Kazik.

Kazik's bewilderment grew, but he shook his head.

"He isn't," said Yurik.

The sergeant spun around again. "Wise guy! I told you to shut up. Do you hear me?"

"He . . . he doesn't talk so well," Yurik apologized. "He's still little."

"Are you Jewish?" This time the question was finally directed at Yurik.

"No."

"What's your name?"

"Jerzy Henryk Kosopolski. We're Pani Sadomska's nephews. We came here from Lvov because the Russians were there. They killed our father and mother, and we were sent here by our uncles."

"You took the train to Warsaw?"

"Yes."

"And then?"

"We took a carriage."

"Did the driver have a moustache?"

"It was a long time ago," said Yurik.

"How do you like Warsaw, better than Lvov?"

Yurik forgot himself. "Oh, yes," he said. "Warsaw's much nicer. Especially Zoliboz."

"The train went through Zoliboz?"

"Yes," Yurik replied, giving himself away.

"Oh," said the sergeant.

Christina came with their afternoon snack and paused pale-faced in the doorway. The sergeant gave them a last look. "Oh well," he said. He took his briefcase and his hat. "Goodbye, boys," he said.

The two boys waited wordlessly for him to leave. Christina followed him out. He locked the door from outside and removed the key.

"He took it," whispered Yurik. They waited for the footsteps to disappear from the yard and lay down on one of the beds.

"What's going to happen?"

Yurik shrugged.

"Nothing's going to happen," Kazik suddenly said.

"How do you know?"

"I had a dream."

"What did you dream?"

"Brown Suit and Gray Suit came to the door and threatened us with pistols. Not real pistols, ones like ours. They were even made out of cardboard, and were flat."

"So?"

"We ran down some streets with Aunt Ella until we got here. Then the ceiling opened up and a naked man came out with lots of hair. There was a lot of light and he had a cross. I think it must have been Jesus."

"When did you dream it?"

"The night before last."

"You're not making it up? Swear to me."

"I swear," Kazik promised.

"Swear by Papa."

"I swear by Papa."

"Then what happened?"

"They got smaller and disappeared into the floor. You know," Kazik remembered, "Pani Sadomska said that when we become Catholics after the war Christina will be our godmother."

"Should we pray?" asked Yurik.

Kazik nodded.

"Hail Mary, full of grace," Yurik began.

"Full of grace," Kazik repeated after him.

"Pray for us now and at the hour of our death, Amen."

Sergeant Zuk of the secret police informed his superiors that his investigation had confirmed that two children were staying with Pani Sadomska, as a certain tenant in the house had reported, but that the boys were undoubtedly the lady's Catholic nephews who had come from Lvov.

Ella obtained his address and went to thank him. She offered him money but he refused. In token of her appreciation she sent him a present of considerable value together with a large bouquet of white lilies.

A bomb fell. Yurik and Kazik sat in the darkness on the table in their room. "Give us this day our daily bread," they prayed. The walls of the room shook and a window pane shattered from the explosion. "Forgive us our trespasses as we forgive those who trespass against us."

"I'm scared," whispered Kazik.

"It's the Russians," Yurik reassured him. "Look, you can see the anti-aircraft fire."

"Let's lie down and pray some more," Kazik suggested.

Yurik lay down next to him and Kazik wrapped his arms around him. There was another explosion.

"Do you know the Credo by heart?"

"No, but I'll say it after you."

"I believe," Yurik began, "in God the omnipotent Father, Creator of heaven and earth."

A majestic pageant of aerial warfare filled the night sky.

Translated by HILLEL HALKIN

ENEMY
TERRITORY

Hanoch Bartov

The appearance presented by our convoy the day we crossed the German border may easily be imagined. We had stretched ropes and webbing belts across the hoods of the trucks and hung our clothes out to dry, and we ourselves were wearing whatever had escaped the water. We looked like a band of gypsies on the move.

But only on the surface. We didn't wander from place to place like gypsies, we had certain very specific places in mind. And at the end of the four days, when we left by the other border, across the Rhine, we were not as carefree as before.

We traveled through the Tyrol, keeping close to the border. The road twisting through the mountain passes climbed from hill to hill and crossed the Italian border again, on the way to the Brenner pass, and after that we had left Italy behind us for good and we were already deep in the heart of the Tyrol. When we set out on this second journey there were no more cheers of conquest and victory among us—the six weeks they had kept us on the border, and then our expulsion, with the frank intention of closing the single gateway that necessity and will had opened—all this had choked the cries of victory in our throats. I don't know what was happening in all the other hundreds of trucks as they crossed the mountain passes, but I know what was happening in ours.

Why in ours? In me. I had spent my entire childhood within a radius of twenty kilometers—the citrus groves, the seashore, the gentle slopes of the hills of Ephraim. The first time I went up to Jerusalem by train, I felt as if I were climbing to the roof of the world; when I drove down the road from Bethshaan to the Jordan valley for the first time, sitting in the back of a truck, I felt as if I were plunging into a nether paradise. Who had ever seen such a river before, who had ever seen such a sea! And now we were crossing lofty peaks, driving through dense, endless forests, over bottomless chasms. And all around us were the mountains, plunging to the feet of lakes in whose clear waters the green forest mingled with the shining sky. The fairytale land, the imps and elves, the yodeling, the leather pants, the feathered hats . . . God Almighty, here they were, in the flesh—the old men leaning in the doorways of their cabins, smoking their long-stemmed pipes, and at the doors of the beer halls, men as square and sturdy as tree stumps, and Hansel and Gretel. Not even a single shell had scarred the shining walls, not even a single bullet had shattered the polished windowpanes. Here, of all places, God had set Himself aside a nature reserve, and the war had not upset the seasons of the year.

Until we left Innsbruck behind us. Inside Germany, the wounds opened up all along the convoy. Uncommanded, unorganized, the crumpled flags were spread over the hoods of the trucks again, the slogans were chalked on the dark green tarpaulins:

Deutschland kaput!

Kein Reich, kein Volk, kein Führer!

Die Juden kommen!

It all looked like that first journey, from the front to the border, except that now there was no singing, no shouting. We sat in silence, our eyes narrowed, with the soundless voice saying hypnotically over and over again: "Hate them, hate them . . ."

How to hate the loftiness of the sky, the glory of the mountains, the smells of the forest, the singing brooks? What, what could our hate take hold of? The mountains fell away, valleys opened out, in forest clearings broad harvested fields appeared. Sheaves of corn stood in the fields, stacked like conical hats. We'd come a long way since morning, and despite the delay in setting out, our officers seemed determined to reach the appointed camping site. A soft day dying into a deep, rich twilight, dark forest belts, church spires piercing the sky like spears, smoke hanging delicately over distant villages like veils. Where, where had the iron claw of war extracted retribution here? Where were the boiling pools of blood? Not one cruel, ineradicable hour—of all the ruin and destruction we had seen, from Taranto north, this alone had been saved.

I was sitting next to Brodsky, and Sonnenshein was sitting opposite us, near the back of the truck. From the moment we had crossed into Germany, something had happened to him. His pipe never left his mouth; as soon as it went out he quickly filled it again.

He took short, nervous puffs and kept his eyes fixed on the landscape outside the tarpaulin flaps. The look of calm intelligence that had appealed to me so strongly had gone from his eyes, and even their color seemed different, almost black. From time to time his facial muscles tightened in a kind of tense expectation, waiting for the next familiar scene to be revealed. Unusually for him, he talked a lot, describing the places we were about to pass before we reached them. "I know Bavaria well," he said. "I spent a lot of time in these parts when I was young. I studied for a while in Freiburg—much further west, and afterwards I stayed in Munich. Look," he cried suddenly in open emotion, "we're coming to the junction. We'll be there in a minute. The right-hand road goes down to Munich."

We took the road to the left, and Sonnenshein made haste to announce that not far from here was Oberammergau. There was something astonishing about this liveliness, about his joy whenever he discovered that his memory had not failed him, that every spot and road was so deeply etched in his heart, although—so he said— sixteen or seventeen years had passed since then. It's not just the memory, I said to myself. I suppose he must have been a young man then, almost as young as I am today, and now he's reliving the passionate feelings of his youth. It's not just the memory—deep feelings are rising to the surface, and you can see on his face how he's experiencing now only what happened then, and not what happened in the meantime. He pronounced all the place names with a distinct German accent, for as he had told me, he had been educated in that language. Prague Jewry was an important center of German culture.

"What's Oberammergau?" I imitated his accent, spitting out the rs and dwelling on the long vowels.

In Sonnenshein's eyes I saw that he had noted the mockery in my voice, and also the reasons for it. The muscles of his face slackened and his expression grew more composed.

"It's a small town, or a large village, where for the past three hundred years or more the villagers have been performing a Passion Play, or religious mystery pageant. It's not theater, but mystery, and both the participants and the spectators identify with the sufferings of Jesus, the savior who was crucified by the Jews. I was there once. And I found the spectacle with the hundreds of ecstatic peasants profoundly moving." Sonnenshein went on looking at me, but he spoke to everyone. "Thousands of people, students like me, enthusiasts of folk art, ordinary people, sat and identified. The thing goes on for hours, and as I sat there watching I felt myself filling with shame. At my Jewishness. And fear. That someone would discover the mark of Cain printed on my brow and they would drag me off to Golgotha overlooking the beautiful scenery of Oberammergau . . . It was only years later that I understood what that terrible place preserves . . . People say that Nazism began in the beer halls of Munich. Maybe so. But the deep roots of the murder of the Jews can be seen here, on the border of the Tyrol and Bavaria, in Oberammergau . . ." and his finger hung in the air, pointing.

We drove on, almost without stopping. The sun began sinking over the trees, but the twilight here went on for ages, not like at home. Night refused to fall, and the convoy refused to stop. Sonnenshein had concentrated my thoughts and made them even more confused. Give me hate, dear God, stick it in my body like nails, make it so much a part of my flesh that I'll scream, that I'll never be able to get rid of it.

Suddenly we stopped.

"Concentration camp!" cried Ostreicher, and we all jumped up and crowded to see.

The green summer lapped the road, and in the distance the forests darkened. But right here, next to the road, there were high barbed-wire fences and watchtowers of black wood. On the other side of the fence were two-story houses, which looked in the twilight like blocks of smoldering coal. Maybe there were huts too, I don't know. The convoy didn't stop, but it didn't move forward either. The drivers in front of us seemed to have slowed down of their own accord, ignoring the officers' commands to drive on. The trucks crept forward, hundreds of trucks, as if they were driving against the wind. And on the roadside for a few dozen meters stood people, waving hands, hats, and scarves, and shouting in broken voices. The people appeared suddenly, and only when our truck drove past the camp gates did we see how many they were. The gate was open and from the inside of the camp more of them came running. I cannot reconstruct those few moments in the land of the black forest, because we fell into them so suddenly, at the end of such a crazy day. One cry galvanized both them and us. Perhaps they sang, perhaps they called out, but among the sounds of singing and shouting two words rang out, "Shalom" and "Eretz"—that is to say, not as if they were shouted again and again, but as one long, continuous cry, from the moment the first people were seen on the road until both voices and faces were lost in the distance.

Or perhaps it was different. Who can remember how and what really happened? Wellsprings of emotion gushed out of us and poured into a cataract at the gates of the camp. We shouted at them like madmen, and someone remembered the empty ration boxes. Piles of sweets we couldn't stomach any more had accumulated in the empty boxes. Now we all jostled and shoved to throw a handful of our own into the little troop of Jews we had suddenly discovered, who were already receding into the distance. For two days we had been traveling in enemy territory, with stony faces, and suddenly we could be glad, see welcoming faces, boys whose eyes went out to us, women weeping with joy. Take, children, take sweets. Take, people, take cigarettes from us. Hey, friend, catch a pack. You'll get one too, here, catch! Take whatever we manage to give you before this moment passes.

We didn't manage much. The convoy moved slowly, as if it were stuck to the fence, but our truck was already past the last boy waving with all his strength at the truck behind us. We hadn't even managed to throw all the sweets at them, and now we sank back onto our damp gear. We had been cut off from the sight as if by a sword, and a strange silence fell on the truck, as if the picture still had to fix itself inside us, without being disturbed.

We went on driving, and the darkness was almost total. We drove through the outskirts of a town and our instincts told us that this was where we were going to stop. The long halts and slow progress indicated that the head of the column was already spreading out in the parking area. Everything proceeded with the usual routine of an army on wheels, and there was no need to think. Our truck drove into an open field, and we groped for our gear and jumped down onto the damp grass. It had already rained once here today, and from the clouds at the edges of the sky it seemed that we were in for another downpour. Sergeant Major Isaacson stood in the dark and grunted, and Corporal Kuperberg led us to a bit of field and said, "We bivouac here. Get organized and then we can eat."

In other words: After emptying the trucks of our personal gear they began chucking the folded tents onto the ground, and every pair of us grabbed hold of a wet and muddy canvas bundle and went to look for a patch of grass. Not much fun. And what a sweet evening all around us. A strange end-of-July feeling, the smell of wet fields, on one side a forest and on the other, at the edge of the field, rows of two-story houses with pointed roofs. Little windows shining in the attics. Men on bicycles riding down the road, women standing in the doorways looking at the field, their arms folded across their chests. Have they all gone mad, digging pegs into the soft ground, preparing to sleep on it? In the distance we could see a big barn; maybe we could find a dry corner there.

"We're not sleeping here, I can tell you that," stated Brodsky. "They'll sleep in their houses and we'll get rheumatism sleeping on the ground—God damn it . . ."

A sense of expectancy stirred in me. I knew exactly what he had in mind, and I was with him. Yes, God damn it, this was our night, maybe the only one, in spitting distance of a German suburb, and there were no more excuses. Here we were, in the wet field, with everything so bloody pastoral around us, and the books Noga had sent me, the books I didn't have the heart to abandon to the mercies of the wet field, and Hershler's death and the things Pinek had said in Venice . . . when was I there? Only three days ago?

Corporal Kuperberg dashed about in the dark urging everyone to hurry up, pitch their tents, take their mess kits, and go to get a hot meal. Company parade in half an hour. No one leaves the camp.

"No one leaves the camp. Hah!" grumbled Brodsky. "In Russian there's a name for someone like him . . ." and he said something in Russian.

"Translate, Kirschenbaum!" The name came to my lips of its own accord, and with it the memory of standing under the cherry tree.

"You still remember?" he said, surprised. "Never mind what I said in Russian. Let's take our stuff and move."

We took our guns and knapsacks, shut the flap of the tent, and turned in the direction of the houses. All of a sudden Tamari loomed out of the darkness.

"Well!" He embraced both of us affectionately, his eyes darting between us. I didn't know if he had mistaken us for somebody else in the darkness, or if he was suspicious because of our guns and the direction in which we were walking. "Did you see the Jews?"

"Where?"

"At Landsberg. What a reception!"

"Yes, we saw them. Why not?" said Brodsky. "And we can see the Germans too."

Brodsky couldn't stand Tamari, and the latter sensed it, even though he slapped his shoulder and smiled pedagogically at him. "Everything's going to be all right, Brodsky, I'm telling you, everything's going to be great! . . . I heard over the radio that Labor came in with a big majority in England. That means there's hope for us . . . There's something to be happy about today, boys . . ."

"I'm a man of peace, Tamari, and when the *goyim* celebrate I get scared."

"They're workers, buddy, friends of ours."

"My mother used to say, 'When the *goy* is sad—keep away, and when the *goy* is happy—run for your life.'"

"Well, well." Tamari embraced us again, looked into our eyes, and was swallowed up in the gathering dark.

"Did you hear that?" laughed Brodsky as we marched toward

the houses, and he belched with a loud, explosive sound. "The workers have won in England!"

From now on we walked in silence, tense with the anticipation of what had to happen, although neither of us had put it into words. I knew Brodsky. When he said, "I'm a man of peace," it was a sure sign that memories of horrors were rising in him, and that he would soon tell a story I hadn't yet heard. We were on the border of the field. A road streched between two rows of houses. The street lamps shone dimly. The sky was covered with low clouds, and there was no knowing how late it was. At the end of the road, facing our camp, stood a civilian, leaning on his bicycle. When we approached him, he bowed to us two or three times, as if he wanted to greet us or to attract our attention. He was wearing a tattered German army jacket with ripped-off shoulder straps and a pair of baggy civvie pants. We walked past him with blank, expressionless faces, to let him know that our intentions weren't friendly. He hurried after us, pushing his bicycle.

"Excuse me, gentlemen, please. Just a moment, please."

We waited. Against my will, I was overcome by a feeling that I indignantly resisted. I understood the man's German; it was as familiar to me as if I were back home again. And not only the words, but also the man himself: somewhere in his fifties, sturdy, getting fat, heavy-jowled, looked like one of the German Jews who had suddenly overrun my hometown. Not just like one of them, but Hollander to a T, Hollander who had introduced us to great innovations, turned an irrigation pool in one of the citrus groves into a swimming school. Hollander exactly. The resemblance horrified me. He leaned toward us and whispered, his index finger, hidden by the front of his body, pointing at the third house on the right-hand side of the road.

"You see that house? It's an S.S. house." Brodsky and I looked at him and at each other in astonishment. "Yes, yes. Over there, in the third house, that's where they live, the damn sluts. The man disappeared. A high-level S.S. officer, the swine."

And the moment he finished talking he put on a leather cap,

mounted his bicycle, and rode off. His heavy mountain boots, the confidence with which he rode the bicycle with its thick tires, all these seemed familiar and unexpected in that hostile landscape. Why was he standing there, on the edge of the road? How was it that he had put into words that which neither of us had yet dared to say to each other? Did he know who we were? What did he expect us to do? The man turned his bicycle around a corner, and our questions went unanswered.

We left the road and started down the path leading to the house. Brodsky strode on ahead with me behind him, the gravel crunching under our boots. I felt as if it weren't really me walking behind Brodsky, but a detached observer watching some fantasy being enacted. The steady tramping of our boots was like something in a movie, in a book, like the boots of the Gestapo. Brodsky stopped outside the dark-green–painted door, took down his gun, held it back to front, and started battering the door with the butt. The hollow knocking sounded as if it could be heard for miles around. Brodsky went on hitting the door with the butt of his gun. To the right of the door there was a dark little window. There was no answer from inside the house. And the dazed sense of unreality—that all this couldn't really be, that we weren't in Germany, that the house wasn't an S.S. house, grew stronger. That guy had been making fools of us—there wasn't a living soul behind the door. I too took down my gun and began to batter the door. To hell with it—if nobody opened, we'd knock the door down. There was no turning back.

"Wait," said Brodsky, "somebody's coming."

Behind the door we heard footsteps. Someone was descending a wooden staircase. An electric light went on in the little window. My knees trembled with excitement, and God knows why, but all this time I couldn't stop thinking of Felicia, of that luscious body that had abandoned itself to me with a kind of simplicity, of Pinek keeping her in that house on the Lido, Pinek, the hero of my childhood. Now I knew for sure—the whole picture had come vividly into my mind while Sonnenshein was telling us about Oberammergau—now I knew what else Pinek had said to me when he picked me up off the floor and put me in his bed. "Everything's burnt," Pinek said to me, "the whole world's one black market, and Europe's lying on her back with her legs wide open. So why not me, why shouldn't I have a house on the Lido, why shouldn't there be a woman warming my bed, why shouldn't there be money in my pocket? Don't remind me of the stuff I used to pour into your ears, Elisha. I told you what they told me. Forget it. Forget it all, Elisha, forget it. . . ."

A key turned in the keyhole, and the door opened a crack. The head of a woman peeped out. In the dim light shed by the street lamp we saw a fair head, a white collar, a dark dress. Brodsky hit the door with his gun and pushed it wide open. The woman recoiled and remained standing in the hall, her fingers clutching the frilly apron covering her dress. She didn't open her mouth; her eyes were clouded with fear. What now, I said to myself, what are we going to do next?

Brodsky stepped inside and looked around him. A nice house, a well-waxed floor, an embroidered sampler on the wall of the kitchen to the right of the hall, a sloping wooden staircase leading to the attic, wallpaper with green and pink flowers on it. This fair, neat woman, this devoted housewife, was the wife of an S.S. officer, according to our anonymous informer. What were we going to do to the woman, what were we going to do to the house, why had we broken in? Oh, why hadn't I stayed in the field . . .

"A room," said Brodsky in Yiddish, not even trying to make it sound like German, "we want a room." The woman understood. She spread her hands out in front of her, the right hand pointing to the stairs, as if to say, The room in the attic, but go ahead and take your pick. Take what you please, I'm at your mercy.

"Okay," said Brodsky, and started up the stairs. His face shone with a strange fire and there was a fixed, faraway look in his eyes. His boots thundered on the stairs, as if they wanted to drown out every other sound. We were storm troopers in a strange house, and the woman was standing below, in the doorway to her kitchen, and she was strangely silent. But it wasn't her, she could go to hell. Who was talking about her? What was *I* doing, trampling in nailed boots, battering down doors, glaring and scowling? What terrible thing was I about to do? I climbed the stairs, floating outside myself, as if I were playing the role of someone who wasn't me.

Brodsky opened the attic door and the two of us stepped inside. The room was trapezoid, with the two long walls sloping inward at the same angle as the roof. In the vertical wall there was a round window covered by a colored curtain. Two beds with flower-print covers. Above them a photograph of snowy mountains, an embroidered sampler in a frame, writing in Gothic letters. The smell of fresh sheets, of a room lived in by young girls. I opened the window, and the darkness came in from outside, the smell of a light rain beginning to fall, the distant forest, the wet field. Voices reached us from the street. Voices of soldiers from the brigade, looking for rooms as we were.

"We should have brought our kit bags and spread out our clothes to dry," said Brodsky.

"Let's go. We haven't eaten either."

But Brodsky hesitated, and so did I. If we started running backwards and forwards carrying kit bags we'd attract others, and there were only two beds here.

"Maybe a bit later," said Brodsky.

We were tired and dirty, we hadn't shaved for two days, our boots and pants were covered with mud. I wanted to lie down on the bed, but I didn't have the heart to do it. Brodsky too sat on the edge of the second bed in silence. Downstairs the door slammed. We heard the voice of a young girl rise shrilly and then break down into a whisper.

"This is a girls' room," said Brodsky.

"Uhmm."

"And the woman's not old either. No more than forty."

"Uhmm."

And we fell silent again. It was still early, we couldn't go to sleep yet, we couldn't go out, and we couldn't just sit around talking, as if we weren't here in this country, in this house. The women downstairs were probably terrified of us—ha!—a girls' room! And the woman wasn't old either.

"Krook, did I ever tell you about how we once lived in a house made of ice?"

He had told me. That day in Bologna, when we were hitching a lift back to the camp. But I said, "No, what do you mean—a house made of ice?"

"It was during my winter with the partisans. I was almost a child, and I'd been on the run for two years already. We were in the forest. Not like what we saw here today—a bit of town, a bit of village, a bit of forest. There a forest's a forest. And winter. Everything covered with snow. And the ground like iron. And we got an order to ambush a German convoy. I won't go into the details of how we knew they were coming, how we lay in the snow on both sides of the road, and suddenly opened fire. No one came out alive. No one. You know what we did? We put them one on top of the other, in layers . . ." Suddenly he fell silent, looked at me, and burst out laughing. "Bastard, I've already told you."

"When did you tell me?" I asked innocently.

"In Bologna. When we were waiting for a ride. You remember very well. The kids were there."

"I remember," I said. "But I like hearing you tell it. I like hearing you say, 'I'm not a man of war.' "

"That's right, I'm a man of peace. I only wish I didn't remember the things that I remember."

The stairs creaked. Light feet were ascending them. While I was listening to the story of the corpses turning to walls of ice, I was thinking of telling Brodsky about my conversation with Hershler, the night before we went to the front. He didn't believe he'd come out alive. And he asked me to look after his things and send them to his relative in Beth Yisrael. But before I could open my mouth we heard the light footsteps on the stairs. A hesitant hand knocked at the door.

"Yes!" I called.

The door didn't open. "Who's there?" I raised my voice. Nothing. I got up, went to the door, and threw it open dramatically. A young girl stood on the threshold. She recoiled slightly, but she was still very close to me. Her face was like the pictures on the toffee boxes—apple-cheeked and cherry-lipped. A white, plump throat. A bit shorter than me, but sturdy. From her throat down, a woman. With breasts filling her blouse like grapefruit. A dirndl dress gathered over plump thighs. Her light eyes were full of mortal fear.

"What's the matter?" I said sharply. She was milky and virginal and my head was suddenly full of the smell of Felicia, the tips of my fingers felt her nakedness. Only three days. She's a damned German, a voice screamed inside me. A Nazi. The daughter of an S.S. officer. You hate her.

"What do you want here?"

"Tell her to bring her sister too," said Brodsky.

"What do you want?" I yelled into her face, in Hebrew, and I knew that I was acting a part.

"Mother wants to know if you want to wash, or something hot to drink . . ."

She spoke German, in a strangled whisper. Somehow the German didn't connect with everything else here. I understood every word. I could hear our neighbors at home. I could hear Hollander's daughter calling in the twilight, *"Mutti . . ."*

"No!" I shouted. "Go away! Quick march!"

The frightened girl retreated to the top of the stairs. She didn't have to know Hebrew to understand me. She ran down the stairs. Down below, in the kitchen doorway, her mother was standing with another girl, even younger. I went back into the room and slammed the door.

"That was true Jewish revenge," laughed Brodsky. "You won't rape her, not even if she begs for it. And you won't even have a cup of tea. . . ."

"Kiss my ass, man of peace."

"You can't stand hearing the truth, eh, Krook? After all the speeches about revenge . . ."

"And what about you, Brodsky? What are you sitting on the

edge of the bed for, afraid to move in case you dirty their room?"

Brodsky didn't answer. His narrow eyes looked at the open window in unutterable sadness, and I felt helpless weeping at the defeat of my sick soul welling up inside me. It wasn't for nothing that we had broken into this house, nailed boots and rifle butts—ever since morning, ever since Giladi had told us about Hershler's death, that day on the border had reopened like a wound inside me, the identification parade, Hershler and Bobby's failure, the feeble show we put on with those two women—it was for that we had come here now, Brodsky and I, to do it, to do what Bobby and Hershler had failed to do the moment they crossed the threshold. And now look at us, a couple of lousy men of peace. . . .

"Come on, let's go and get the kit bags." Brodsky rose and went to the door. His broken nose overshadowed his lips, and there was nothing left of the cheeky vagabond who had stolen my heart. I'd provoked him, and unthinkingly had unlocked some safety catch in his heart. "I'd tell you a thing or two, but what's the use . . ."

We went down the stairs. The kitchen door was half open, and out of the corner of my eye I saw a heavy table and women sitting around it. Not only the mother and her daughter. They were sitting as if they had been turned to stone, listening to our footsteps. I almost said to them, "We'll be back in a minute," the kind of thing you say to people when you go out. We went out and shut the door behind us.

In the camp everything was quiet; only where the trucks were parked, headlights were on and soldiers gathered. We found our tent, collected our gear, and slipped back stealthily to the house. No one took any notice of us or asked us where we were going. When we tried to open the door we found that it was locked. My hands were full of bundles; my gun was dangling from my shoulder. I kicked the door with the toe of my boot, and heard hasty footsteps. The mother opened the door and stepped back with a welcoming smile. Everything was so cozy, it made you sick.

We spread the wet blankets and clothes on the floor, on the table, on the two armchairs, on hooks on the wall. I examined the books again. The damp had rotted them, the covers were coming apart, the color had run. But I couldn't even leave the math books here, because of the Hebrew letters. A lot of good they can do us, our holy letters, with our damned boring symbols. I wanted to go to sleep, I wanted it to be three days from now, as if this night had never happened.

We took off our clothes and lay down in the two spotless beds. I don't know what Brodsky was thinking about, but I myself, if I hadn't been ashamed to, would have lain down on the floor between my own wet blankets. We're not damned Christians, for God's sake, I repeated to myself, but I couldn't fall asleep. I saw Nehemiah on that last summer leave, when we came from Egypt to say goodbye. We sat in his room, Noga and I, and he held forth as usual. He had suddenly discovered the Sermon on the Mount, and read it aloud to us, with pathos, standing up, in the dying light of the end of October. And I, with the awe of the New Testament in me, shouted at him, "Leave me alone with the Kingdom of Heaven and the other cheek. What do you think's so noble about that sermon anyway, as if you've discovered something new, something that hasn't been stuffed down our throats until we choked to death? What's this sudden 'holy Gentile' stuff, Nehemiah? On the contrary, just let's be given a chance, for once, to be unholy Jews, and we'll jump at it, with all our hearts and souls. We've got to. How long can we go on hearing about how we were screwed from one end of Europe to the other?"

" 'The Depths of the Mire.' 'The Sanctification of the Name.' 'Three Presents.' 'My Sister Ruhama.' 'The Nemirov Eulogy' . . .* Do I look as if I need the Sermon on the Mount? Ever since first grade, ever since kindergarten, this nectar of the downtrodden has been making me sick. Why shouldn't we, just for once, be what we are, in the Old Testament, and I say amen to that, Nehemiah. A bit of an eye for an eye for a change, amen. A bit of visiting the sins

*Names of stories about Jewish suffering and martyrdom in the Diaspora, studied in the schools of the Jewish *Yishuv* during Elisha Krook's schooldays.

of the fathers on the sons, amen. A bit of innocent blood under our fingernails, so that we'll also have something to be sorry for and feel guilty about for a change . . ."

That was how I yelled then, a stage brute. And now, in the dark attic, I lay still, listening to the frightened whispering of the women in the kitchen below. Nazis, never mind the cleanliness and coziness, a murderer's wife and his seed, bitches who know only too well what they deserve and what they could expect tonight from the soldiers sleeping here—and there's only one little secret they couldn't possibly guess: What the measure of our heroism was. For one whole day, in the barn, we had acted out the fantasies of our revenge. How we had ranted and raved, what fire-eating speeches we had made, like my speech to Pinek, my speech to Nehemiah and Noga, like the sermon Giladi had preached to us. Yes, Giladi, the biggest talker of us all—and the feeblest when it came to action. Why had he stood there debating with Tamari, when he could have gone out and done it . . . he just wasn't capable of it, exactly like the two of us here and now. For what was stopping us, Brodsky and me, but the fact that we were impotent, impotent . . .

. . . in a world I have never seen in my life before, I run, and it's all as real as if my life has always been enclosed inside it. Our house stands at the edge of the village, alone among the black huts and thatched roofs. And I too play alone in the muddy road among the puddles, and down below, at the bottom of a gentle slope, there's a kind of lake, or dam, with flocks of white geese marching around its banks. The road emerges from the village, circles the dam, and climbs toward the railway line. That's the direction I look in because that's where everything comes from. A train emerges slowly from the forest, and there's no one to stop it, open cattle cars bearing horses and their riders, like in a picture, blue coats, Cossack hats and long carbines. The train doesn't stop at all, but as one of the cars reaches the dirt road horses leap from it, galloping through the air in a shallow arc and making straight for us. The geese squawk hoarsely, their proud march turning to flight. I too run for our cabin, to warn my mother and father, but the door's locked. With all my strength I bang on the door, and nobody opens it. They've forgotten that I'm outside, or they're afraid to come to the door, or perhaps they've gone to work. The road is empty and very long, like the streets in the curfew. I run to the far end, to the big synagogue, but there the giant three-wheeled beetles are already crawling. I escape through a hole in the fence into one of the courtyards, but here too I won't be saved unless I hide at the top of a tree. That eucalyptus, if only I could climb its slippery white trunk they wouldn't catch me. But there's no time. The Cossacks gallop on the cobblestones; from inside the houses women scream for help. I cling to the wooden boards, try to find a crack in the concrete foundations. I know that voice. It's Hollander's daughter screaming. . . .

Until you've woken like this, shuddering with electric vibrations, as if your body's been stitched up by a cold sewing machine, paralyzed by a dead current, you'd never believe it possible to experience a place, voices, a fate you never suffered yourself so vividly in a dream. Still hunted, digging my fingernails into the wooden wall, unable to stir, the voices coming from the kitchen, the German women, the dull thuds, the creaking furniture, the hoarse whispers of men, were transformed gradually into a wild reality. I lay on the spotless girlish bed, emerging from my nightmare as from a deep dive, but the voices dragged me down again like the coils of an underwater jungle. I dug myself a tunnel in the water and kept my head down until I had no more breath left. Something terrible was happening down below.

I tore myself awake and sat up.

"Brodsky!" I cried.

"What do you want?"

Instantly my head cleared. Brodsky wasn't sleeping; he was listening silently to what was going on downstairs. The women were struggling with men who had broken into the house. Strangled voices and the hard thud of body against body. The despairing scream of the girl.

"Listen to what's going on down there!"

I jumped out of bed and found my pants draped on the chair in the dark. I got dressed quickly.

"Where are you running?" Even in the dark his voice had a steely glint, like an oiled dagger. The girl's voice broke into sobbing.

"Are you crazy, Brodsky, or what? Can't you hear what they're doing there?"

I buttoned up my pants. My fingers groped for the light. My gun was unloaded; I had to find the bullets.

"Go back to bed, Elisha, it's our guys down there."

The light filled the room. And my eyes closed. I shaded them with my hand, and opened them into narrow slits. Brodsky was sitting on the bed in his underpants, his back against the wall, his whole body concentrated on the struggle downstairs. A smile clamped his face shut, like an invisible muzzle holding his feelings in check. He was participating in the events downstairs, and in his glassy smile I saw myself reflected.

It's our guys down there.

The girl's sobbing crept up the stairs, straining for salvation, and the nailed boots crushed it. I couldn't go on standing there and by my silence be part of what was happening downstairs. I didn't want to think about anything else; nothing else existed in the world at that moment, only that defeated sobbing. I grabbed a supply of bullets, pulled back the bolt, loaded the gun, cocked it, and shut the safety on the bullet in the barrel.

"You *shmuck!*" Brodsky jumped off the bed and leaped at me. Both of us were barefoot; he was in his underpants and I had a gun.

"Leave me alone, Brodsky!" With my back to the door I pressed the handle down. The butt of my gun was pointing at Brodsky, ready to hit him.

"You sonofabitch, Krook! You want to put your first bullet of the war into one of your friends?"

I had no control over my thoughts. Only the helpless sobbing downstairs called me to it. I ran down the stairs. The door of the kitchen was wide open, and so was the front door to the house. The kitchen was brightly lit, and I took in the whole scene from the door

—one soldier was standing over the woman and the younger daughter with his bayonet fixed, pushing them into the corner between the heavy kitchen cabinet and the wall, and the daughter who had come up to our room was lying on the floor. Another soldier crouched over her, his knees pinning her outspread arms to the floor and his hands holding her shoulders down. Her dress was torn and her body was exposed from the waist down. She cried as if she were forcing herself to cry with her last remaining breath, her plump legs quivering like a slaughtered chicken thrown into the dust. Between her open legs a third soldier knelt, the only one whose face could be seen from the door. He was red with sweat and with the blood rising to his head. There was real blood on his cheeks, and his lips were parted as if he were gasping for air. I knew all three of them. I remember their faces vividly and their names too, but I'll let them remain anonymous even today.

"Leave the women alone and get out of here. I'm counting to three. Anyone who's still here will be shot, without further warning."

I heard my voice as if it belonged to someone else. It had never sounded so calm and firm. The three of them were frozen with horror. The one pushing the mother and daughter into the corner turned to face me, and as his body turned so did his gun.

"Krook!" he yelled, not believing his eyes. "You . . ."

"Drop your gun or I'll shoot."

"You'll shoot? You lousy medic!" And he took a step toward me, as if he were on a bayonet charge. I released the safety catch, pointed my gun at the ceiling, and pressed the trigger. Inside the house, in the silence of the night, the shot sounded like a grenade exploding. The gun was steady in my hand. The smoke and smell of gunpowder were real. The first soldier flung down his bayonet, and the other two jumped to their feet, leaving the naked girl on the floor. They all retreated to the wall.

"Krook, you're crazy. What are you shooting in the middle of the night for . . ." said the one who had pinned the girl to the floor with his knees. His voice shook.

"All we need now is for the M.P.s to show up," said the third.

"Get out of here, you bastards." The fog surrounding me was beginning to dissolve, and the whole scene seemed impossible. "Or I'll shoot you like dogs. Go on, move!"

The three of them moved along the wall toward the door, like in a movie, and the first bent down to pick up his gun. I lowered the barrel of my gun in his direction and he straightened up and leaned against the wall.

"Krook, you're crazy. They're Nazis. The old whore's husband's in the S.S. One of the Germans outside in the street told us. He came up to us himself and told us, Krook. There weren't any Germans to protect Jewish women with their guns . . ."

"Get out of here!" An evil spirit took hold of me. I yelled without knowing what I was saying, I yelled to drown out all the other voices clamoring inside me. "Take your guns and get out. All three of you. I'm counting: one, two. . . ."

They took their guns and slipped out of the open door. I went out after them and saw them running silently in the direction of the camp, afraid that the shot had attracted attention. There was absolute silence in the street. Even if they heard their neighbors being murdered or raped they wouldn't leave their houses at night. I turned on my heel and started up the stairs to the attic. The woman stood in my path and grabbed my hand with both of hers as if she wanted to kiss it. A sudden rage seized hold of me and I pushed her violently away. I saw the gratitude on her face turn to astonishment. I saw her slip, lose her balance, bump into the wall, and fall on the bottom stair. I didn't stop. I ran up the stairs with my gun in my hand, my bare feet absorbing the weight of my body. Brodsky was still sitting on his bed in the same position as when I had switched on the light. His eyes were as glassy as before, but the thin smile on his lips had disappeared. I went up to my bed, turned to face the wall and unloaded the four remaining bullets. I took the cleaning materials out of the pouch on my belt and sat down to clean the barrel with a well-oiled cloth. All my actions were measured and drilled. I tried not to raise my eyes from the gun. When I saw that it was more or less clean I oiled the barrel once more, wiped my hand on one of the blankets spread out on the floor to dry, and went over to the switch to put out the light.

All of a sudden, as if some spring had been released, Brodsky jumped off his bed and stood facing me, smaller than me, with his long, broken nose and the sharp lines at the corners of his mouth. He's going to hit me, I said to myself, and what am I going to do? I stood by the switch and waited. Suddenly he spat on the floor, between our bare feet.

"*Parshivi Zhid!*" he hissed in Polish between clenched teeth. Filthy Jew. And then he stood still, waiting for a reaction. I said nothing. His face twisted in contempt and he lowered his head, spat between our bare feet again, and went back to his bed, lay down, turned his face to the wall, and covered his head with the blanket.

I switched the light off quickly, so that the darkness would swallow me up before the tears welling up inside me gushed out. They burst out with the darkness. I ran to the bed and buried my head in the pillow. I breathed in the smell of the young girl's body and recoiled. I swallowed my tears, got up, and began gathering my things and packing them. Activity restored my composure. With automatic movements I collected the gear in a fixed order, without any need of light, and put it in the kit bag, the big pack, the knapsack, all to turn my heart away from what had happened, to blot out my failure. But my heart would never turn away from what had happened, and I knew it even then. At long last I had done something, of my own free will, and what had I done—rushed to save my own purity. In a moment all the hymns of hate had been wiped out and I was my father's son again. Rotten with purity. A *mensch*. A lousy human being. Now I knew: We were what we were, condemened to walk the face of the earth with the image of God printed on our foreheads like the mark of Cain. Incapable of seeing a little girl raped. Incapable—lily-white Jewish soul . . . and already I could hear the sound of the shell growing on my back like a hump, the armor that would protect our hearts like the shield of a medieval knight: How would we vanquish them if we became like them? . . . Yes, we must, we must wallow in the muck, like the soldier wallowing between the legs of the naked girl, we'd go mad if we carried on like this now too, without Tartars, without Huns, without the S.S., if we carried on like this forever, groaning beneath the cross of the vengeance we hadn't taken, with the crows cawing: *In thy blood shalt thou live.* Crow, Satan, crow. . . .

The soundless tears of a weak child streamed down my cheeks and the mucus dribbled from my nostrils. I filled the kit bag, rolled up the blankets, put on my puttees, shirt, battle dress, loaded my gear onto my back, took my gun, and left.

"Elisha!" Brodsky shouted after me, but I was already halfway down the stairs. He went on shouting from above: "Where do you think you're going in the middle of the night, you ass?"

I wanted to run away. If only I could have, I'd have gone right on walking, out of the whole business, back into the normal world. I swore to myself that the day we arrived at our permanent base I'd begin to work on getting a quick discharge. I'd do anything I could to get out of this continent where there was no way in which I could be myself, neither with our dead nor with their living.

Downstairs in the kitchen the light was on; the woman and her two daughters were moving around in it. My heavy footsteps and Brodsky's shout brought the woman to the door. Again she spoke to me in the so-familiar words, and out of the corner of my eye I saw one of the girls bending over the other. Again the woman held out her hands, but I averted my face and refused the touch of her accursed gratitude. I opened the door and hurried toward the bivouac and the rest of the dark night in this place.

Translated by DALYA BILU

THE
PHOSPHORUS
LINE

Itamar Yaoz-Kest

A tree, a house, a tree, and the hillside whitening in slow motion through the windowpane. The figure of a man carrying a sack on his shoulders trudges wearily up a snow-packed path. Sometimes the man overtakes the crawling train, and sometimes it is the train that overtakes the bowed, wintry figure of the man. The silver twilight sun is still visible, flying low behind the triangular roofs of a mountain village suspended between earth and sky.

The windowpane accumulates layer upon layer of opacity, sparkling with flower-like frost flakes and cutting the treetops off from the ground.

And soon there is nothing to be seen at the window but the reflection of the man standing there, swaying backward and forward, with only his own sensations to act as his compass.

The electric light goes on in the compartment, spilling from side to side with the swaying of the train.

I turn my collar up and station myself at the corridor door, waiting for the conductor to appear. I can't see a thing.

The doors rattle in their frames, either because of the jolting of the train or because of the draft racing through the corridor. Someone must have opened the bathroom door and let the gale inside.

A whistle. Were we waiting or taking off?

Had I really started out?

My mother lay prostrate on the broad seat, huddled in her combination of winter and summer clothes, with only her eyes peeping out.

And indeed, the sun had still been quite strong at the beginning of our journey, two or three weeks ago, after I had finally given in to my mother's insistent demands that I accompany her. Or, to be more precise—to her announcement that she was going, with me or without me. And if without me—it was only too probable that I would never see her alive again; for the whole business of the journey had originated in the affair of the reparations, which, according to my mother, was to blame for my father's death. And this being the case, she was obliged—so she claimed—to set out at once and keep on going until she came to the place where my grand-mother and grandfather were buried, in other words, the German camp where they had been murdered together with a group of other outcast Jews. She was obliged to go and lie down on their mass grave and beg their forgiveness, in order to put a stop to the evil and prevent it from demanding any more sacrifices from our family, or so she blindly believed.

As for me, although I considered the whole thing a lot of superstitious nonsense, I was concerned for my mother's sanity and so I joined her.

That, it seems, is how it all began.

And now—the engine huffed and puffed and the carriage shook, and the suitcase slipped slightly backward, as if it were shying away from the exit, and slid from the door to the window wall.

The train suddenly stopped in its tracks. I flattened my nose against the winter-padded window and through the strips I managed to clear, I saw only the shadow of a mountain, bare tree trunks in a row, and some kind of a wall dragging the weight of its body upward. Perhaps it was only a wall of mist. There seemed to be no sign anywhere with the name of the station on it, and the train stopped with such a jolt that my face banged into the window and my glasses fell off my nose. They rolled away from me, sliding down the corridor along the slippery linoleum. My face felt exposed and utterly abandoned without my glasses. I wanted to hang onto some-thing, and I thrust my hand into the air. I almost went down on all fours in my search for my means of vision.

"Why don't you get off the train, sir?" I heard the voice of the conductor, upon whom I had scarcely laid eyes since the beginning of the journey, and who was now gripping my shoulder in order to help me up and holding my glasses in his hand. Drops of melted snow fell onto me from the peak of his cap. I thought at first that he was smoking, because of the gray-blue puffs that clouded the air between us when he opened his mouth, but it was the cold outside seeping through the body of the blond railway man, and when he flung the door wide open I saw my mother already sitting next to the railway tracks gleaming in the evening frost, sitting on the heavy suitcase and waiting for me. I wondered how she had managed to drag the heavy case down the carriage steps, and I decided that it must have been the conductor who had chivalrously exerted himself to help her while I was busy looking for my fallen glasses. At any rate, I thought, I'm lucky the lenses aren't broken.

My mother sat on the suitcase by the side of the railroad tracks and rubbed her legs.

"Are you hurt?" I asked, feeling guilty about not having helped her down the ice-covered steps, since that was the reason I had come with her in the first place, in other words—to assist her in difficult situations, and not out of any particular interest in this hellhole.

But I could not hear her answer, for at that moment the engine let out a thunderous blast and with a mighty clatter of its wheels hurtled forward, moving up the mountainside in a series of jerks until it disappeared into the vacuum on the other side.

We were left alone—my mother pathetically rubbing her leg without deigning to tell me what had happened to her, and I scanning the terrain for a sign of some living soul who would direct us to the gate of the camp.

My mother groaned. She pressed her left arm heavily and her groans grew louder.

"Hello! Hello!" I raised my voice to a shout, but instead of a human voice or an answering echo, a ray of light cut across the edge of the sky, like a beam from a projector, and rested for a second on the huge stone wall that I thought I had imagined seeing through the snow-covered window of the train. And even after the glare faded, the light went on glowing in the stones of the wall, which loomed up on the mountain face like a column of men and women supporting each other to keep from collapsing. The light shone from the stones as if they had been soaked in some phosphorescent material.

"It hurts . . . it hurts . . . here . . ." muttered my mother fearfully, utterly lost in herself and abandoned to the darkness.

I heard a creaking sound, or rather a kind of ringing. I hoped that it might be a car approaching, or perhaps a horse-drawn sleigh arriving, a little on the late side, to meet the evening train. But it was only two iron bars hanging from the opening to a nearby wooden shelter that were banging together in the wind. And it was lucky for me that I had heard their clanging, for now I was able to make out a sign with an arrow on it pointing in the direction of the official railway station.

I grabbed hold of my mother with my right hand and the suitcase with my left and began dragging them both in the direction of the arrow.

"I can't . . ." wailed my mother, pulling me down with her into a snowdrift.

I dragged her as far as the shelter, which had apparently once been used as an unloading depot for freight.

I put the suitcase down on the frost-cracked floor and seated my mother on it.

"I'll go for help," I said. "I'll run to the station and fetch someone to help."

I tied my mother's scarf around her head, taking care to cover her ears, and buttoned up her dark leather coat. I kissed her, but all I could taste was the annihilating winter. She made no response. She may not have seen me at all, for her eyes were fixed on the huge, luminous wall stretching all the way up the mountainside, which was still glowing with a faint green radiance that seemed to be welling up out of the earth itself.

And I ran off, without looking back or wasting any time on trivialities.

With the sound of the iron bars spinning behind me in the snowstorm buffeting the shelter entrance, I quickened my pace as I ran toward the station which had not yet come into view—toward the wall looming in front of me, with the rays of the projector crisscrossing the no man's land between us.

It was a stone wall about twice the height of a man, with barbed wire on top of it forming a prickly grill, to which lumps of heavy snow clung like distorted human forms.

Now I could see too the watchtowers of the abandoned camp, but they seemed somehow detached from the snowy reality around them, as if they were floating in the air, held up by some power of the night. But this, of course, was only an illusion created by the lighting, made doubly powerful by the dazzling glitter of the snow. Despite the blinding light, however, the guards keeping watch over the "Lager"—now transformed into a site of "historical interest" from the days of the war—apparently sighted me. For after a few moments the light narrowed to a thin line that seemed to be coming from a hurricane lamp swaying in front of me. I followed its wavering line, still breathing heavily from my running, which I now slowed to a walk.

Yes, without a doubt, it was a hurricane lamp, held in the hand of one of the guards.

"Hello! Hello!" I called again with all my strength, my frozen breath falling to the ground and shattering with a sound like metal nails.

The distance between us narrowed. The guard stood waiting for me, resting the lamp on his head.

At the sound of my loud shout, a fox sprang out of the thick pale tunic on the watchman's shoulders and fled in alarm, bringing the human form to the ground, where it disintegrated into lumps of snow, while the stars went on shining on the rusty helmet lying among the remains of the snowman.

And the barbed snowy wall stretched into the distance, as far away from me as ever.

In any case, I realized that the presence of the snowman meant that there were people, including children, not far from where I now stood. At the same time I began to feel afraid of the apparent infinity of the deserted death camp, accompanying me into the void while my mother lay beside the railroad tracks in the open shelter, exposed to the wind and the frost.

Should I turn back and return to her?

But what good would it do her if I went back empty-handed?

I exerted all my strength and advanced along the huge, luminous wall, comparing my movements with those of a man revolving on the axis of himself. All my limbs were dragging me downward, to the earth, exposing its icy jaws, the wall electric with the bright moonlight, and I was terrified of slipping and touching the wall. I imagined that I could hear my mother screaming, "Pauli, Pauli, my child . . ."

Close to the rocky summit of the mountain the barbed-wire wall suddenly stopped, and what I had imagined to be a very steep precipice turned out to be a watchtower with the snow-laden forest running behind it as if it held a secret in its depths.

As I drew nearer, the watchtower changed its shape slightly and I could make out a rural cottage clinging to its side, perhaps as camouflage, with both structures composing one unit of design.

Since I had failed to synchronize my watch with the clocks in this country, I had been guessing the time from the degree of darkness in the sky; the air was still very light, which must have meant that it was still early—on the other hand, I did not know the movements of the sun and the moon in this hostile land of long ago, and so I could not be sure if I were guessing right.

When I came close up, I saw an oak gateway topped with barbed wire and broken glass; also, there were double-silled windows set in the facade of the house with snow-spotted cactus plants in painted pots, shining in spite of the heavy frost, or perhaps because of it. Smoke puffs rose into the air from the chimney in the middle of the triangular tiled roof, drawing the shape of a stork standing on one leg and tucking its long beak under its wing.

With the last vestiges of my strength I fell onto the oak gate, pounding desperately with my fists as if my whole life depended on the chance that someone would open it. But the banging of my fists proved superfluous, since the gate immediately began to creak and swing back on its hinges as it was opened by a little female creature, apparently still a child, whose whole appearance reminded me of a paper doll, as thin and transparent as could be, wearing a deep green dress with a pattern of exotic landscapes and naked girls sunbathing on it, and buttons in the shape of little bells. Owing to the suddenness with which the gate had opened I stumbled against the little girl, and the warmth emanating from her body enveloped me, melting the icicles clinging to my coat and glasses and changing their colors.

When I touched the child a shudder ran through her body, as if the wind had blown into her skirt. The metal buttons on her dress chimed like the sleigh bells that I had apparently heard immediately after getting off the train. Without a word I followed her as she led me into a kind of rustic vestibule, covered from the outside with a creeping vine.

I walked behind her without opening my mouth or, more precisely, without being able to open it because of the cold, while all the rest of my body cried silently for help—after all, I had left my mother in a shelter open to the four winds and the snow, next to the railroad tracks, beneath two clanging horseshoes.

Accordingly, it vexed me grievously that at this moment all I could think about was myself, as if I had forgotten my mother; however, there was nothing I desired so much at this moment as something hot to drink and a heated room where I could recover my strength.

And, in fact, there was a fire leaping in the open stove of this rustic vestibule, with a pot as big as a caldron standing on top of it. But the vestiges of the chill refused to leave my body nevertheless, and even grew worse.

I stood still as if I were asking for help, with the world outside the glassed-in vestibule impinging itself vividly upon my senses, able now to encompass the entire area of the deserted death camp at a glance, including additional watchtowers soaring into the harsh winter sky.

And suddenly I thought I saw my mother sinking into the snow, deeper and deeper, at the foot of the death camp, while the wind heaped lumps of frozen whiteness onto her body; and soon all that could be seen was the woolen scarf I had tied around her head, waving at the deserted landscape like an arm signaling desperately for help.

Choking, I tried to banish this mirage from my sight and concentrate my thoughts on what was happening around me.

The little girl hurried over to the stove and threw coals into its maw to feed the fire, and as the flames played on the grill like burning, dancing dolls she let her eyes rest on them greedily, until her sallow face blackened.

In the sudden purple radiance that flooded the vestibule I made out an old man sitting on a goatskin and sorting plants. From the sack lying next to him he extracted handfuls of dried chamomile leaves and flowers, and with a monotonous movement he crushed them finely with a pestle in an iron mortar gripped between his knees, which were sticking out in front of him on the floor. He pounded away with the pestle, as if he had been doing the same thing for years without a pause—and by now he was doing it without paying any attention to the nature of the task before him, which he performed as if in submission to some ancient duty by which he had long ago been possessed. After a while he started rolling a cigarette very slowly between his fingers; then he took some of the pounded leaves and strew them over the paper in order to smoke them—although this was not, presumably, what they were intended for. He stuck out the tip of his tongue and glued the rolled paper with his saliva. Then he raised himself slightly from the goatskin and offered me the cigarette that he had prepared for me with his own hands.

I am not accustomed to smoking at the best of times, let alone smoking dried chamomile leaves stuck together with a stranger's spit, but the chill that had invaded my whole body forced me to stretch out my hand and take the old man's gift. When I drew the smoke into my lungs I was overcome by a fit of coughing, while dense gray smoke billowed around me, making me feel as if I were drunk or drugged.

Afraid of insulting my host, I went on smoking the cigarette as the child watched me with what appeared to be an expression of sympathy on her face. I opened my mouth a couple of times with the intention of explaining my situation, but the pungent smoke kept on making me choke, and it was only with a great effort that I managed to pronounce a few meaningful syllables, stammer a few broken phrases about the need to rescue my mother. All I could do was mumble incoherently, without even knowing what I was saying, when I should have shouted at the top of my voice: I left my mother by the railroad tracks, and she must be freezing to death!

I stood with my back to the stove, almost roasting in the flames crackling in its maw, but my bones went on shivering in the cold flowing deep inside me, in my very nerves. The little girl crouched next to the stove and turned the coals over and over, until they gave off such a glow that I could see the bones of her head reflected through her delicate, quivering skin. Dropping the red-hot coal scuttle she sat down on the floor in order to listen to what I was saying, and she let her hand fall onto her lap, where it lay quivering with attention.

The man who was sitting all this time on the goatskin hid his face in the open neck of the hairy fur jacket that he wore on the upper part of his body, naked but for a pair of ragged old army pants, and went on pounding the chamomile leaves in the rusty iron mortar between his knees, which were stretched out in front of him. But suddenly he lifted his sharp chin and stared at me with his lashless eyes, his lower lip with the moist cigarette stub still sticking to it protuding like a lump of raw meat and dribbling gray saliva. He inspected me from head to foot, his eyes widening in his emaciated, angular face. Then he flapped his fur sleeves above his naked chest and stretched out his bony arms with the intention of helping himself up.

I sprang aside. At the sound of the old man shuffling to his feet in the hybrid costume of soldier's pants and peasant's fur, or the clatter of my own jumping feet, the little girl turned around and her mouth fell open in an expression of anxiety, as if she knew what the old man was about to say.

"Angelus," he said, pronouncing each syllable separately, "he must be informed."

The child crouched on all fours at the man's feet, groaning as if she were expiating her sins before him.

And now the man took up the mortar in his two hard hands and went over and emptied it into the caldron on the open stove, whereupon the room filled with the stimulating smell of some kind of disinfectant. After the water in the caldron had bubbled and boiled he poured the liquid with its suffocating fragrance into a barrel standing ready next to the stove; then he rolled the barrel toward the exit from the almost unfurnished vestibule.

"No . . . Father . . . no!" cried the little girl in an attempt to bar his way, but he pushed her forcibly aside and he was already out the door, shuffling through the snow on the steps and dragging the barrel of disinfectant after him, as sparkling yellow drops splashed onto his faded blue army pants.

The gate creaked loudly shut.

I hoped, against all the logic of what was happening around me, that the man had really gone to fetch help, to relay the message about the need to rescue my mother from her predicament, or perhaps even to get hold of a car or a sleigh himself—although, to tell the truth, the child's behavior seemed unreasonable to me.

I had an evil presentiment that this man, in the ex-soldier's pants, after understanding, after realizing the purpose of our visit, my and my mother's, that is to say, had become suspicious that we were intent on digging up information about the old mass murder, and he wanted to prevent this at all costs; and this was why he had gone out—in other words, to warn the villagers, his accomplices in the crime. He had even mentioned some name, or title, which had slipped my memory in the meantime.

The little girl stood by the door without taking her eyes off me. She had a string of beads around her neck, and she raised it to her mouth and sucked the gleaming pearls.

The sense of danger grew stronger, and now, together with the fear for my mother's fate, I also felt a certain bitterness toward her for having involved me in the journey to this death camp, which up to now had been so far from my heart, and in fact—from my memory, and to tell the truth—had also seemed unimportant in my eyes, since what I wanted was a normal life in the world of the present.

I was aroused from these thoughts by a spark from the fire that jumped out of the stove and began smoldering on my coat. The coat seemed to be made of highly inflammable material, considering the rapid inroads made by the burning ember in the cloth, and I was obliged to take it off quickly in order to avert a catastrophe. I threw it onto the floor and stamped on it to put out the fire.

The little girl sprang toward me and with the aid of the coal scuttle she put the fire out easily and swiftly. Then she picked the coat up and hung it gently on the back of a peeling painted chair. She stroked it caressingly with her hand, as if she were cleaning it.

"You're cold," she said suddenly, as if stating a fact and in a surprisingly adult voice, and she went up to a carved wooden chest standing in a corner of the vestibule under a picture of a blackened Madonna and ancient apostles against an imaginary background of the holy land. She pulled various blankets out of the chest and spread them out on the floor.

At the side of her mouth there was a faint seam, but when she spoke and tried to smile at me an expression of beauty, suppressed and spoiled as if out of some kind of spite, trembled on her face.

She took a samovar decorated with cheerful birds from the side of the stove. The gleaming, ornate utensil looked out of place in the austerity of the room.

She poured tea into a glass. Or, to be more precise, she poured boiling water onto the leaves that the old man had been sorting and drying beforehand.

"Drink." She offered me the steaming glass. Although I was longing for a few sips of a hot drink to restore my spirits, my hand stopped suspiciously halfway to the glass because of the fear in my heart.

She took a step toward me, so that her dress brushed against me, still holding the glass out to my mouth. I felt the warm, trembling touch of a round, feline hand. I could not control my movements.

I drank without thinking, overcome by giddiness. Through the glass, which I held in front of my eyes, I saw the figure of the little girl, who now looked immeasurably older than she had before, as if we were both looking into a distorting mirror. I blew into the glass.

No, she wasn't a child at all, but a woman, a woman who for some reason had not reached her full growth. I wondered how I could have been so mistaken in my first impressions.

She stretched in front of me, as if she were growing breasts.

All my exhaustion seemed suddenly to rise up in me, and with my head spinning I sat down on the only chair in the room, on which she had hung my wet and scorched coat.

I sat with my back to the little female creature and my face to the mountain, upon whose summit loomed the abandoned death camp with its walls and watchtowers, like a miniature model of an ancient towered city on the palm of its designer.

Strange, it was only now that I recalled that the bodies, or the ashes, of my grandfather and grandmother were buried here, only a few kilometers away from me—the grave that had destroyed my mother's world, robbed our family of its peace, and given rise to such hostile feelings on my part toward my mother and her behavior. And how different it was from the place depicted in the photograph that my mother had obtained with such difficulty through the assistance of the official institutions soon after the end of the war.

A delicate chiming of bells came clearly to my ears. I raised my eyes to the little woman, the metal buttons of whose sea-green dress had misled me on my arrival by their tinkling and made me think of the chiming of tiny bells.

She was busy arranging the blankets on the floor, close to the fireplace, going silently about her business. When she bent down to the ground with the back of her neck to me, the hair on her round little head stuck out in hard bristles. It seemed to me that she had deliberately pulled the neck of her dress down in an attempt to catch my eye. And when she caught my glance, she bent her head down to the bundle of rags rolled into a pillow as if she were about to lie down to sleep on it. She let out a little moan of pleasure. From somewhere in the room a white kitten—or so I thought for a moment—jumped on her, but it was only her white hand fluttering next to her head. For a while she lingered on the bed that she had made, then she rose and pointed to me and then to the blankets spread on the floor, as if she were talking in the sign language of the deaf.

Weakly I got off the chair and lay down on the blankets, trying to keep my ears tuned to the din of the sleigh bells drawing nearer through the night in order—so I thought—to take me to my mother. I was afraid that I might suddenly fall asleep against my will.

And the little creature apparently thought that I had indeed fallen asleep, for she dimmed the light and stood at my head listening to my breathing, smoothing the ragged blankets over me; and when she saw that I showed no signs of waking, she began to rummage in the pockets of my coat hanging over the back of the chair. She looked wonderingly at every item that she extracted from the pockets; felt my crumpled handkerchief, passed her fingers over the Yale keys, and lingered over the half-lira coin. Lucky I keep my passport in my pants pocket, I thought. She pressed the coin to her face, slid it over her lips, and then slipped it into her bosom.

The room began to grow dark, not because of the dying light in the oil lamp or the fire in the stove, but because of the clouds hiding the moon outside.

A sudden fall of snow covered the windows, but I kept on hearing the chiming of the bells. It's true, a sleigh is approaching, I said to myself, and was on the point of jumping to my feet when I saw that it was the metal buttons on the dwarfish woman's dress that were making the bell-like noises: She was taking off the deep green dress with the pattern of exotic landscapes and naked sunbathing women. She bent over me and brought her mouth to the big toe of my right foot. She slid her lips over my toes as if they were fingers playing piano keys—she wanted to test me to see if I were sleeping. Then she stood up again. Standing there without her clothes on, she tried—not unsuccessfully—to imitate the movements of the naked girls on her dress, enabling me to think for a moment that all I was seeing before me, through the narrow slits of my eyes, was the portrait of a nude. Then she slipped between the blankets, as if some suppressed female instinct had suddenly come powerfully alive in her.

In spite of the cold, which had already invaded the whole room, I began to sweat. It occurred to me that while I was lying here, in this alien house, next to this pathetic little female creature exuding an alien smell, my mother was lying by the side of the railway tracks, in the middle of the night, in the middle of the winter.

My guilty conscience cut me like the stabbing of a knife.

My limbs shrank as if they were caught in pincers, and with the cold making my whole body shiver I imagined that I was freezing and that the sweat bathing my skin was turning into a thin layer of ice.

"Stop it," I grunted when the hand of the little woman began moving in the direction of my groin. I wanted to take a firm tone, but all I could manage were a couple of weak words.

She pushed her head into my belly.

"I knew it . . . I knew it would happen like this . . ." her lips whispered.

I wanted to get up from the nest of blankets, but she stretched her whole fragile body on top of me and forced me to stay pinned to the ground, to the bed of blankets underneath me.

What a mean trick—the thought flashed through my brain— she's trying to keep me here until her father the old soldier's accomplices arrive to finish me off . . . because they think I've come here with the aim of tracking the murderers down.

But the little woman seemed far too excited to be capable of calculations or scheming tricks.

As for me—I didn't have the strength to get to my feet, and I just lay there, how long I don't know, with my mind clouded over, until I heard her talking.

"I've waited . . . all these years I've waited . . . and now I'm not going to miss my chance . . ." she hissed between her rodent-like teeth, half pleading, half stating a fact.

My elbow brushed her lightly and I asked, without really meaning to start a conversation: "But what have I to do with you?" I blurted this out after the spasm that had seized me a moment before began to fade.

Her brown bird-eyes floated above me. "I want . . . I want to get away from here. . . . I can't stand it any more. . . . I can't. . . ." Her face shone with tears.

"So who's preventing you?"

"Preventing me? . . . I've tried to run away . . . more than once . . . but whoever crosses this border . . . no, it's impossible . . . in any case, not on my own . . . and maybe it's impossible altogether. . . ."

"Aren't you a native of this place?"

"In a way, yes . . . that is to say, I came here with my father a few years after the end of the war . . . after he came back. . . . By the way, my name's Irena."

Now she began rubbing her body with one of the blankets, as if she were cold. My hand brushed against her unwittingly. She was burning. Someone's breath hung between us in the air and I didn't know if it was from my mouth or hers, or perhaps from both together.

Later on I stretched out my hand to her dress lying in a bundle next to me. I wanted to wipe my perspiration with it, and once again the delicate, distant tinkling of bells rose in the air, this time to the accompaniment of light from the camp projectors.

"You won't leave . . . you must promise me that you won't leave here without me! . . ." she sobbed, "because I . . . I have nothing here . . ."

"What about your father?"

She did not reply to my question. Instead, she pricked up her ears and listened attentively to what was happening outside, until in the end she cried out in terror, "He's coming . . . he's coming. . . . He wants to take you to Von Angelus . . . because he has to take you to him . . . and you mustn't . . . you mustn't . . ."

But the projector lights went out again, and the tinkling of the bells faded too.

I stood up wearily from the improvised bed, while the little woman fell helplessly at my feet, where she crouched as if she were tying my shoelaces. She went on in a whining voice, "Year after year he goes on sitting here . . . just him and me . . . and sometimes it seems to me that he himself has forgotten the reason why . . . because this place dulls people's minds . . . and it ruins their bodies too. . . . He came here to atone . . . and because of him I came too . . . I had no alternative. . . . We do all kinds of jobs for the camp. . . . But I want to go away . . . I have to get away, at any price . . . and not be anything. . . . I don't want to be an atonement for other people's sins . . . never mind who . . . I just want to live my own life . . . like other people . . . without any connection to what happened in the past. . . . I was only a baby then anyway. . . . What's it got to do with me? . . . I can't even really remember it. . . ."

She was silenced by her own frankness and dropped her head onto the cold floor, where the sharp bristles of her hair stuck out in the dark room. After a pause she roused herself again, seized hold of me, and began shaking me. "You mustn't go to Von Angelus. . . . He'll torture you . . . I know it . . . I sense it in my bones . . . The moment I set eyes on you . . . And Father . . . it's his duty to take you to the office . . . he can't do otherwise. . . ."

"Is he his accomplice?"

The woman with the dwarfish body was concentrating all her senses in the direction of the camp.

"Here he is. . . . He's coming . . . he's coming . . ." she cried, "and he's going to put you on his wagon."

I pricked up my ears in vain. As the storm outside subsided, all that could be heard was the whisper of the falling snowflakes and the groaning of the trees in the distant forest beneath the weight of the winter.

"I asked you . . . that man whose name you mentioned . . . Who is he? Was he your father's accomplice in the crimes of the past?"

"Crimes? Not at all . . ." She was horrified. "Von Angelus was a prisoner himself in this very camp for years, and now he's the director . . . They tortured him here until he nearly died . . . that's why he's so hard . . . so very hard . . ."

She stared into space for a moment and then said in a scarcely audible voice, "But what have I to do with them?"

She took my coat from the back of the chair, where it had dried in the meantime, and held it out to me, as if she were resigned to her fate.

At that moment the door swung open on its hinges and the old man in the ragged army pants stood on the threshold, holding a long whip in his hand and pointing it at me.

At first she still tried to cling limply to me, but at the sight of the determined glint in the old man's eye she dropped her hand immediately, as if all her vitality had deserted her. He measured his daughter with a scornful look, under which she seemed to grow smaller and resume her childish appearance, and then he spat at me, as if he were spitting out the pit of a rotten fruit, "You're not the first . . . to go to bed with her." And he lifted me onto the sleigh, with all my thoughts concentrated on my mother and the hope of saving her from death in the freezing night.

I didn't even hear the gate close behind us. And as soon as we left the magnetic field of the house the sight of the dwarfish woman too blurred before my eyes. But when we started circling the walls of the death camp it seemed to me, perhaps only for a second, that the little creature was hiding somewhere at the back of the sleigh.

We drove around and around the great walls of the abandoned camp. I noticed that whenever the mules (or perhaps they were ponies—I don't know) drawing the sleigh placed their hoofs on the phosphorescent borderline they became so thin that their skeletons were clearly visible, like X-ray photographs.

I hadn't been in a snow sleigh since I was a child, and but for the atmosphere of fear and the circumstances that had brought me here I might have enjoyed the gallop over the glittering white waves; in a flash I remembered the sleigh that had once belonged to my grandfather, with the driver goading the animals on and the bells ringing and ringing, then as now, and me sitting next to the driver with a big quilt over my knees to keep me warm. And in the background, the pealing of church bells in the distance.

It was later said of this *goy,* the driver who had served my grandfather faithfully for so many years, that he betrayed his master to the murderers.

"Close to the station—that's where I left my mother. . . ." I shouted into the ear of the old soldier who was holding the reins of the mules.

Because of the blanket of snow covering everything around us, I could not tell if he was really driving his mules in the direction I had demanded. He had the animals well under control, and at the same time I was surprised to see that whenever he cracked his whip over the backs of the mules the waving thongs in his hand hit him too, and hard. Despite this, however, he kept on beating the beasts, and the hairy chest peeping out of his fur tunic was already criss-crossed with bloody stripes. But of course it was only the strong wind that was blowing the thongs of the whip onto the chest of the driver, whose shaven head swayed indifferently from side to side.

Once more we passed the entrance to the camp, and I imagined that I heard the strains of an orchestra wafting through it. I saw something written over the gate in Gothic script too—but owing to the pace at which we sped past I could not read what was written there.

"Stop!" I shouted, thinking that I had caught sight of the shelter where I had left my mother when I got off the train, at the beginning of the night.

The sleigh slowed down. Actually, it was only the mules that slowed down, for the old soldier went on whipping them with all his strength. In any case, in the split second during which the two beasts paused in their flight, I was able to take in the whole of the no man's land next to the railway tracks as well as the open shelter where I had left my mother.

There was no trace of her in the place where I had left her, insofar as it was possible to ascertain in the twinkling of an eye from the seat of the sleigh—for just as I was about to slide off the seat and climb down, the mules decided to obey their driver and the sleigh continued on its flight, buffeting my body against the side.

I shouted my mother's name into the white void, but in vain, and I felt a small child coming to life inside me and wanting to burst into hopeless tears, as if he were kneeling still outside the white door behind which his mother had shut herself in—something he had found so hard to forgive her for, for so many years.

Except that now there was not even a wooden door that could lead me to my mother, only the endless snow stretching all around —with no sign of her anywhere.

Crushed, I crouched down on the seat—my alarm mingling with feelings of guilt and anger at having given in to my mother's craziness, her attempts at blackmail, her horrors about the past, the war and the dead—and concentrated on the journey.

Then I was overcome by a kind of temporary oblivion, a paralysis of the will.

The beasts seemed to enjoy the melody accompanying their galloping and brought their hoofs down in unison. But when the sleigh, swaying like a merry-go-round, reached the main gate of the camp and the old soldier tried to rein them in and turn their heads in the direction of the entrance, they recoiled, jerking the sleigh forward and rearing on their hind legs like dancers in the snow.

We had already circled the camp five or six times, with the animals' resistance reawakening every time we approached the gates. Then the driver decided to try cunning and drove the mules to the side of a building that looked from the outside like a hothouse with a clumsy chimney rising above it. The structure was situated in a kind of breach, like a backyard entrance through a gap in the fence. When we passed the point that should have marked the borderline of the camp, the two mules twitched their tails nervously, as if they were trying to rid themselves of stinging flies. A strong smell of wildflowers met my nose, despite the frost. The air was quite warm, considering that it was winter, leading me to suppose that the walls surrounding the camp on all sides acted as a break on the winds blowing strongly outside. And perhaps the projector lights warmed the air a little too, situated as they were in the corners of the square courtyard and shining with an eternal light.

The mules stopped.

Large crows crowded in the circles of light, and their feathers gleamed like well-brushed black hair. Suddenly one of the birds left its companions and flew onto the neck of one of the mules. The beast lifted imploring eyes to the old soldier, who rose to his feet, climbed down from his seat, and took the plump bird from the trembling neck of the mule. Perhaps he wanted to punish it first for its rebellious behavior, for he pressed its beak together as if to muzzle it, but then he stroked its feathers and returned it to the flock, and it hopped about in the light of the projectors.

The old soldier, as one who had done his work well and was now in a good mood, twirled his whip around and cracked it in the air, and the sleigh moved a few meters further into the square courtyard, which reminded me of an army barracks, all spit and polish and painfully clean. We stopped in front of the open door of an office.

The old man cupped his hands around his mouth like a loud-speaker and called, "Master! Master!" and when there was no reply he seized me under the armpit and made as if to lift me off the seat. Perhaps he wanted only to help me off, but the ostensibly polite gesture had a military brusqueness about it.

When my feet were on the ground, the old man stood at attention by his seat and saluted the open office door.

The light encircling the courtyard lay on the threshold to the office too, and as I stepped forward I could see a man bending over a desk made of crude wood—not in the posture of a man hard at work, but as if he had fallen asleep while writing and his head had dropped onto the table, where it lay resting on the arms stretched out in front of him. The hat on his head covered his brow.

The man called Von Angelus moved his hand as if to trap an irritating fly, let out a deep snore, and then stretched and rubbed his eyes.

"So you've arrived," he exclaimed, and pointed to the chair standing next to the desk, inviting me to be seated.

The office was small, or perhaps it only made that impression because of the many urns filling most of its space, urns and slabs of marble in various shades. The place looked like a tombstone-cutter's office.

"I hope you are well, sir," he said, nodding his head, which was adorned on either side with silver sideburns, at me. Rising from his desk he looked as tall and thin and bony as a picture of Don Quixote by Doré. The velvet jacket hanging over his shoulders, on top of his thin shirt, gave him an air of negligent elegance. He stood up, stretched, and shook a few tobacco flakes from the sleeve of his jacket.

"I beg your pardon, sir," he said, "but I must have dozed off during the long wait . . . most unsuitable . . . really."

In the little mirror on the desk he inspected his face and curled the moustache lying like a soft yellow thread above his sunken, bloodless lips.

"In a moment we'll be able to tour the entire area of the camp . . . in any case, I shall be happy to be of service to you, sir . . ." said Von Angelus, rather mechanically.

I sat on the chair that the director of the camp had pointed out to me, staring at his long fingernails with their prominent crescents —his fingers were extremely well shaped.

"The temperature has dropped very low," he remarked, as he went up to an electric heater, with the apparent intention of switching it on. "People unaccustomed as we are to the climate in this camp can freeze here . . . and tonight too . . . but we ourselves don't feel it so much any more. . . ."

I bent over the desk, stopping my legs from trembling with difficulty and thinking that my mother, she too . . . in this winter . . . she too might have . . . perhaps she really had frozen to death and lay buried beneath the snow—I tried in vain to suppress this thought.

"Yes," I said, "perhaps you know, sir . . ." I began, but couldn't bring myself to finish the sentence.

After Von Angelus had finished improving his external appearance he offered me his hand and renewed his offer to accompany me on a tour of the camp.

"Every detail . . . for twenty-three years now . . . we've kept everything up with the greatest of care. . . ." he said, as his eyes roamed the courtyard, which was drowning in the projector-illuminated night. His eyes were as still as two blue marbles. He stood behind my back, toying with a box of matches and a pipe that had gone out. He kept on lighting matches and blowing them out again distractedly, and seemed to be looking for words in which to express something sad or unpleasant.

In the end he said, "Yes . . . your mother . . ."

I looked at him in astonishment and said, "Next to the railway station . . . I left her there; she wasn't feeling well. . . . I tried to drag her with me, but I was too weak . . . and I ran to get help . . . and now too . . . Yes, I looked for her and I couldn't find her . . . but perhaps you know . . ."

"I'm very sorry . . ." muttered Von Angelus incomprehensibly. Then he raised his voice and asked in a louder tone, "Would you like to see your mother?"

"What?" I cried in excitement, but Von Angelus had already opened the side door to his office, saying in a low voice, "Excuse me, sir, but I have to get your mother ready for the meeting," and he left the room.

I remained alone in the director's office. My mood wavered from hope to despair, as the intention behind the man's words remained unclear.

I wondered at the many urns standing on the shelves and in the corners, and contemplated the various kinds of marble slabs, and reflected again that this was the entrance to the place that had made my mother ill, robbed her of her peace of mind, and caused her to cast a gloom over my childhood years. Her deepest longings, her pleas, and her tears were all directed here: It was because of this place, after my father's death, that she had conducted that weird mourning ceremony opposite the photographs of the dead. . . .

And all I had to do now was shut my eyes in order to see my mother's memorial candles and my mother leaning over them and whispering, "Pauli, come closer . . ."

And the row of candles burst into flame, a candle for every photograph, a candle for each picture of her dead.

And the flames leapt and stretched as if they were being miraculously transported from one place to another. The air filled with a smell of wax. In the middle of the room stood the pictures of my mother's parents and all the dead members of our family, and the candles with black ribbons tied about their waists stood around them like acolytes in their habits officiating at a funeral.

The mourning bands were also tied to the two big photographs, in the center, of my grandfather and grandmother.

My mother stroked the portraits with her fingertips, as if she were lightly caressing the face of a sleeping man, and each finger was separately cherishing the object of its touch.

She sat with her back to the window, to what was outside the window and what was inside the window, and only her loneliness seemed to draw a circle of chilly radiance around her, into which she both yearned, and feared, to be drawn.

Afterward she spread her hands above the flames and her lips moved. The sounds dropped heavily from her mouth, with the rhythm of slowly closing eyelids. One might have thought that my mother was singing to herself, or blessing the candles—except that I had never once seen her doing so.

She put her head to one side, half her face turned upward, in the direction of the sparks flying from the candles. Then she touched the coil of hair gathered at the nape of her neck, and her tresses shook and fell to her shoulders. The loosened hair flooded her eyes, her nose, and her lips, floating above the flames. A fragile, burning lizard twisted in the air and fell to the table. And another thread of her hair, and another. And my mother's lips trembled at the touch of the words, although she herself had long ago fallen silent.

"Forgive me, my dear ones!" The words went on trembling in the air. It seemed as if my mother wanted to gather both the pictures and the flames beneath the tent of her hair. But her magnified shadow on the wall cast darkness over everything. And only her hands resting on the table seemed to be conversing with each other, telling each other their troubles.

Then her right hand rose and took one of the candles, brought it close up to her left hand, and trickled drops of wax onto it.

My mother's face twisted in pain, shone with pain.

The smell of mourning crept through the room, whipped and seethed, and turned to silence. . . .

The director of the camp stood above me. He touched me lightly, saying, "Come with me, sir," and he turned in the direction of the courtyard.

I walked behind him, trying to shake off the sudden numbness that had taken hold of me again.

The courtyard had been well swept and cleared of snow, but still the wind dashed grayish-white flakes against my lips. I was afraid to open my mouth in case the snow came in, mixed with the feathers of the crows. As I placed my feet on the paving stones, I felt the earth shaking and quaking, as if it were made of bones.

The camp was built in a horseshoe shape in order to facilitate the access to each separate hut, but nevertheless we kept going in and out, in and out, through doors within doors.

I did my best to keep in step with Von Angelus.

We went down a corridor, at the end of which stood a barrel of yellowish disinfectant, one of those that the old man had been preparing in the vestibule of his house—and once I had brought him to mind, the image of the little female creature called Irena appeared before my eyes, too . . . and a certain thought connected with her flashed through my brain, giving me a disagreeable, stabbing sensation in the region of my groin—but the thought eluded me before I could grasp it clearly and bring it to consciousness and vanished as if it had never been.

We began descending, Von Angelus and I, down a spiraling staircase illuminated by a fluorescent light. There was a strong reek of mold. Von Angelus walked ahead, like a man taking the measure of his own private estate, pausing by this or that alcove displaying and classifying articles of worship, valuable old paintings, and moldy holy books in glassed-in cupboards.

Von Angelus had a cane, a kind of walking stick with a knob at the end, with which he pointed out the various exhibits, making explanatory comments as he descended step by step, explaining or tapping lightly with the knob of his cane on the wall, which was painted with green oil paint. From time to time there was a slight echo, which sounded as if it came from little air bubbles trapped beneath the plaster and the paint.

The wall was smooth and well-washed, with a tiny stain or crevice here and there. On a sudden impulse I slid my fingers along the wall, taking care not to slip on the narrow, spiraling stairs. Here too the smell of disinfectant stuck to my fingers.

At the end of a row of stairs the wall grew very damp and spotty. I noticed rash-covered areas within the layer of plaster, like pustules on sick skin. I may have lingered a little, for Von Angelus turned his head toward me and made some critical remark about the sanitary workers of the camp, who had recently begun to neglect their work. The people who worked here as volunteers—so he said—were few, very few indeed, working sometimes with their entire families, some of them in order to atone for the "little sins" of the past; it was only these vounteers, and precisely the most simple among them, who still cared about the upkeep of the camp.

He twirled the knobbed stick impatiently between his fingers and continued his way down the spiraling staircase with practiced steps.

The "rashes" and "pustules" on the wall spread and changed their color from a moldy green to a rotten pink, sunk deep into the wall. Bristles from the painters' brushes seemed to have stuck to the wall here, for they protruded from the paint like white hairs sticking out of a malignant sore. I stumbled slightly and pressed my fist to the wall. Suddenly I felt a layer of plaster crumbling under the pressure of my hand and my fist crashing into a crevice swarming with life —and a kind of slime spurted into my sleeve.

I almost fell down the stairs as I tried in horror to tear the infected sleeve off me, as if at that moment I would have torn my right arm out of its socket if only I could have rid myself of the pollution of that decomposing wall.

Von Angelus gave me a disapproving stare, as if I were causing an unexpected nuisance, and after a moment—without having to look too hard—he found a spray gun and sprayed disinfectant over the wall and me, after first dipping his finger into the liquid to inspect it.

"I can only apologize to you, sir," he said in a businesslike tone. "As I have already explained to you, we are experiencing difficulties in finding sanitary workers," and he continued leading me down the stairs, while I composed myself with difficulty and tried, despite the cold, to take my coat off, or at least pull my right arm out of the infected sleeve.

We approached a shining white hermetically sealed door, which reminded me of the door of an operating theater in a hospital.

Von Angelus waited patiently until I caught up with him, as I giddily descended the last of the winding steps. While he waited he struck a pose with the knobbed cane on his shoulders. A curious mirthfulness came over his face, like a person whose only remaining happiness lies in the discomfiture of others.

"This is where they tortured me. . . . For three days and nights they tormented me in there. . . ." he remarked with apparent indifference, as if he weren't talking about himself, and only the excessive dryness of his voice indicated his suppressed emotion.

Here too the sharp smell of Lysol and chamomile came to my nostrils; the gloom blurred everything into almost total shapelessness.

"Would you like to see, sir?" he asked, pushing the handle down without waiting for my answer.

My mother . . . I want to go to my mother, I wanted to whisper, to scream, but Von Angelus wasn't in the least interested in what was going on inside me. He was preoccupied with his own concerns and feelings, or so it seemed.

Something was wrong with the electricity, and Von Angelus was obliged to switch on a flashlight, making a lot of noise as he did so. The everlasting light in which the upper structures of the camp were bathed did not exist on this underground floor, and the director of the camp was obliged to fiddle about with the electric wires by the light of his pocket flashlight. He manipulated various switches with great dexterity, as if he were very well versed in the lighting system of this part of the camp, muttering to himself or to me, "The visitors are getting fewer . . . their numbers are decreasing year by year, especially the Jews . . . and those who do come—official delegations . . . people coming to collect reparations . . . the lowest kind of logic . . . and in the circumstances I can't get the proper budget for maintenance," he complained.

After a few moments he succeeded in fixing the electricity and a fluorescent bulb went on in the front of the room, creating a dazzling light as on a stage. The light picked isolated objects out of the darkness: a footstool, a table covered with a black silk cloth, upon which lay a thick book.

I had the feeling that we were in a spacious hall, that the screen of dazzling light—or so I imagined—erected a barrier between me and many other implements that were there, swallowed up in the darkness.

"Cat and mouse," exclaimed Von Angelus, as if he were naming, somewhat strangely, one of the implements in the room, while I remained standing not far from the table upon which reposed the thick book where visitors to the camp were invited to sign their names. The dazzling light bulb hung beneath the door, where it swung slowly from side to side like a huge eyeball.

"Would you like an illustrated lecture?" asked the camp director. And I heard a warning cry inside myself, the warning voice of the little woman from the watchtower house, warning me of the danger threatened by Von Angelus.

I stepped to the side of the table, as if I were about to turn my back on him and beat a hasty retreat from the room.

As the light bulb turned, I saw that I was indeed standing in a large hall. It was completely empty, so that there was nothing to which I could relate Von Angelus's curious remark. Or perhaps he had been referring to an implement that had once stood somewhere in that hall, which had been removed just before the end of the war by the murderers themselves, and he was the only person who still remembered it and spoke of it.

In order to hurry him up and in order to make some sort of gesture, however empty, toward the place—and especially simply in order to do something, no matter what—I opened the guest book and after a slight hesitation I signed my name, wrote the exact date, and added the words: "On the soil of Germany," but before I could finish writing Von Angelus stopped me and took the pen from my hand: He drew two lines through the word denoting the geographic location of the place, and crossed it out.

I stared at him in astonishment.

"Don't you know, sir, that there is no such place on our planet?" said Von Angelus.

I was almost ready to laugh, but the camp director squeezed my wrist until I let out a groan. He looked at me—or rather, through me, toward the light glaring beneath the door.

"You must remember, sir, that Germany does not exist . . . in any case, not on our globe . . . in which case you cannot, sir, now be standing on German soil . . . For Germany—Germany is a condition and not a country. . . . Yes, Germany is nothing but a condition. . . ." He paused for a moment and continued in a low voice, "And that is the reason why I stand here on guard . . . in order to preserve the night of this camp . . . to stop the process of turning Germany into a physical reality . . . and only you Jews . . . in your pursuit of the present . . . of material things . . ." Here he came to a sudden halt.

His excitement finally broke out of his body, and he dropped his cane to the ground, sweeping the fountain pen, visitors' book, and black silk cloth down with it.

I stood there in embarrassment. I let him pick the things up without offering him a hand.

There was no doubt in my mind that there was a measure of insanity in his words, for obviously a man who had chosen to spend his life in an abandoned death camp, a camp in which he himself had been incarcerated . . . it was inevitable that conditions such as these would leave their mark.

Von Angelus put everything back with a nerve-racking slowness. Then he turned off the electric light switch, and the blinding glare gave way to darkness.

We turned on our heels and continued our descent down the winding stairs, down, down, until finally we emerged in a snowy courtyard, resembling the upper courtyards except for the fact that it was full of countless slabs of marble.

The sight of the snow stung my eyes, and for a moment the unexpected radiance hid even the figure of the camp director from my eyes, and all that I heard was his voice. He was singing to himself. It was very strange to hear the sound of singing in the depths of the earth, even if the song itself was very melancholy, like a funeral dirge, and the words, I think, were in Latin. As he sang I heard a delicate chiming, as of sleigh bells.

"And now, sir, I shall lead you to your late mother," said Von Angelus when he had finished singing, and his voice reverberated with a fatherly tenderness and sorrow.

I pulled my coat tightly around me.

My teeth chattered.

I heard and did not hear what he said.

We were standing in front of a structure surrounded by a glass dome, like an inverted sky, or like the "hothouse" with the clumsy chimney I had seen when the old soldier brought me to the camp, after I had discovered my mother's absence from the shelter where I had left her next to the railway tracks.

Through the glass dome I could see many flowers reflected— petunias and geraniums, lilies of the valley and Easter lilies, crowds of Easter lilies waving their heads at the snow below.

Von Angelus walked slowly over the white wintry expanse as if he were stepping on tiptoe for fear of waking a sleeping man. The courtyard, as I have already mentioned, was crowded with marble slabs, like memorial stones, and on them thousands of names were carved in miniature letters.

It was like a labyrinth in which we went on walking around and around.

"If I understood you correctly, sir, you are now taking me to my mother?" I asked in a voice made weak with fear.

Von Angelus nodded his head but avoided turning his face toward me. The smell of the flowers was choking me.

The strains of the orchestra music, which had reached my ears when I first approached the gate of the camp, now burst forth and filled the whole space, doubled and tripled in volume because of the enclosed architectural design of the courtyard, until even the steel and glass structures in the nether regions of the camp were forced to respond, shaking and clattering.

Even the Gothic letters that had flashed before my eyes flicked on again, and I imagined that there were two words written there: "*Toten Lager.*"

Before we reached our destination I heard Von Angelus say again, "You must prepare yourself, sir."

"So, this is the place . . ." I said.

At first I still tried to take in the details belonging to this nether camp, about which I had had occasion to read from time to time in the wake of my historical studies, but the moment I arrived at my destination, all I could see was a square frame like a door set at my feet in the floor, and when I drew nearer with a pounding heart, I saw that the square shape was that of an iron bed.

I cannot describe the walls surrounding me, for the moment I cast my eyes in the direction of the iron bed upon which the body of my mother was lying, the bed seemed to grow in size and banish everything else that might have been there, taking up the entire space as if it were floating detached in a vacuum: the snow, the stars, the roads both visible and invisible, and the entire deserted camp—everything shrank and turned into one poor iron bed, upon which lay the frozen body of my mother. The flowers went on exuding their suffocating scent, surrounding the inner part of the chimney, with the twisted stems of the masses of blooms, purple- and scarlet-hued, flickering from time to time as if they wanted to set themselves alight in the shadow of the inverted glass dome.

My mother's shrunken body lay on the bed, scrupulously covered with a white sheet. Her hair was all loose and her eyes were slits. They flashed metallic sparks.

I ran up to the bed. I bent over it. No—I must have breathed on her, for her eyelids rose and fell like those of a doll.

"Mother," I cried in dread, my hand reaching out to touch her.

"Don't do that, please!" I heard Von Angelus growl behind me. "You must not touch a lifeless body, sir!"

I stepped back unwillingly, and overcome by a sudden weakness found myself obliged to sit down on the floor next to the iron bed and bury my head in my hands.

"I . . . you know yourself . . . all I wanted was your own good. . . ." The words broke with difficulty out of my mouth, "I only left you in the snow so that I could run for help . . . and I was delayed. . . . and if I was delayed in the house of strangers, it wasn't any fault of mine. . . ." I spoke to my mother pleadingly. And she moved her head slightly, as if in a breath of wind.

But even as I spoke, the figure of the dwarfish Irena rose before my eyes, and with her image came a prickling sensation in my body.

My mother's face was covered with spots of frost.

After I had recovered I rose to my feet, and despite Von Angelus' prohibition I put my arm around my mother's meager body, which was wrapped in a white sheet. I tried to shake her body, to warm it with my breath.

"Now that I've found you . . . I'm going to take you home . . ." I whispered.

My mother tried to open her mouth, but all that came out of her sunken lips was a sound like a sigh.

I wanted to sit at her head, but Von Angelus seized hold of me and pushed me roughly away from my mother.

"You have no right to remove the woman from here, sir, and you have lost all rights to her after abandoning her to the mercies of the winter . . . yes, sir, you abandoned her . . . you deprived her of the natural state of identification, and but for the fact that I happened to be in the area of the railway tracks on that stormy night, the poor soul would have died of cold, and been buried beneath an avalanche of snow, without leaving a trace . . ."

I said, "My mother will decide on her own fate." I tried to make my voice sound firm and aggressive as I felt the blood rushing to my head.

But my mother only stared into the air, at the halo of light trembling on the glass dome closing her in, and I could not discover what she wanted.

Von Angelus stood forcefully between me and my mother and prevented me from reaching her.

I wondered how it was that my mother was not afraid of this man with his eroded flesh, whose whole being exuded a chill. I sensed, despite her frozen state, that the moment the man approached her bed, a certain sign of life awoke in her eyes; he really had taken care of her devotedly, to judge by the appearance of the bed he had made her, and the white sheets wrapped around the low iron bed.

My mother lay mutely on her bed with two people standing watch over her, staring at each other with hostile eyes.

And then the sounds of a commotion broke in from outside, from the direction of the gate, and loud human voices were heard. Von Angelus pricked up his ears alertly, put out his hand to straighten the bow tie around his neck, and exclaimed, half in anger and half in pleasure, "They notified me of their arrival three days ago, and it's taken them up to now to show up."

Very tense, he added nervously, chewing on the denture in his mouth, "Yes, yes, certainly . . . I'm not mistaken . . . the deputation has arrived." He was beaming, despite the slanderous things he had said before about the nature of the visits to the camp. He turned on his heel and hurried away from the "hothouse" area to welcome the new guests, as if my mother and I had ceased to exist.

Saying to myself, The moment has come! I bent over the bed, took my mother in my arms, lifted her up as if she weighed no more than a feather, and hurried off with her through the labyrinth of the courtyard, between the heaps of snow and the memorial stones.

I covered my mother well in the folds of my overcoat on top of the sheet in which she was wrapped and ran around and around, as if I were afraid of being trapped in the labyrinth, coming back again and again to my original point of departure, my ears ringing, for some reason, with the tinkling of tiny bells on some invisible sleigh.

When my mother saw her deathbed receding she let out a tearful cry, as if she wanted to cling to it, as if she refused to be separated from the blue radiation of the glass dome above her head and the reflection of the profusion of "hothouse" flowers all around her.

In the end I pulled her by force out of the magnetic field of the nether camp and ran as fast as I could, hoping not to encounter the shadow of Von Angelus, or any other camp guards, or the deputation that had just arrived on a visit.

It was a groundless fear that had taken root in me, since no one tried to prevent me from leaving the camp; even the gardener, staking the exposed trees somewhere in the distance, avoided looking at us, despite the noise made by the clumping of my feet in the snow.

Nevertheless, although there was no one to be seen in the entire area of the camp who might prevent my flight, I still thought that it would take superhuman strength to burst through the phosphorescent line marking the border of the death camp, revolving as if around its own axis.

I went on running, even when I was already outside in the snow.

And suddenly—"Irena! Irena!"—a voice called from somewhere in the winter landscape the name of the dwarfish woman from the watchtower house, as if in mockery or complaint, and I did not know to whom the voice belonged, or what the reason could be for this mocking call, which seemed so detached from time . . . or perhaps it was only inside myself that some voice was crying, mocking, for a reason I did not know, while drawing ever nearer, thundering and blackening as it descended from the mountains, like a revolving, expanding dot, I heard the dawn train approach.

As the round disc of the sun was trapped between the peaks of the alien mountains, I was already standing on the steps of the train coach. Then my mother was lying on the floor of the coach, and I was shutting the door with one hand and lifting my face to the moving window.

Like a block of ice my mother lay at my feet.

I bent over her and said, "We're going back to the sun . . . and we won't remember anything any more . . . this whole journey . . . I promise you. . . ."

At first I thought the snowflakes clinging to my mother's body were melting, for she was quite wet, but it was the frosty tears that were dropping from her eyes—and they weren't tears of happiness, of that I was quite sure.

"Nothing will remain, no trace of all this place . . ." I persisted foolishly, laying my mother down on the spacious seat of the empty carriage.

"First I'll take you to the hospital, and after that . . . after you've recovered and gotten back your strength . . . we'll get on a ship and sail for home. . . ."

I rested my head against the winter-padded windowpane, where the reflection of the sun blazed in its efforts to resurrect itself, and counted the telegraph poles falling flat on their faces by the side of the train.

The wheels thundered.

I saw the mountainside through the window.

And perhaps I saw too a little figure, the figure of a child, or of a woman who had not reached her full growth and who now, in the depths of the winter, was dragging herself along with difficulty and pain.

She climbed onto a sleigh that was waiting for her, with an old man sitting in the driver's seat. The sleigh was drawn by two mules (or ponies perhaps, I don't know).

At that moment a horrifying thought flashed through my mind together with the painful, prickling sensation that came back to attack my body in the lower region of my abdomen.

Irena! Irena! . . . And what if this dwarfish woman . . . that night . . . I don't know when . . . in the house attached to the watchtower . . . then . . . when she hung her burning body above mine . . . and I seemed to lose my senses . . . my orientation . . . what if this pathetic little creature . . . the offspring of a lost generation . . . because of the contact of a moment . . . a contact of whose very existence I was not even sure . . . what if she had infected me . . . by the touch of her body . . . with some kind of disease . . . like a curse . . . in me too . . . and from now on . . . like all the sons of this place . . . I too . . . would be infected with a slow, creeping destruction . . . perhaps incurable . . .—the absurd thought trembled in me; but the prickling in my groin died away with the swaying of the railway coach in which I stood.

I blew onto the windowpane and wiped the glass to gain a clearer view of the mountainside and the sleigh, which had already begun to move along the enormous wall of the camp sleeping its eternal sleep, its sleep of death, while I traveled in the opposite direction, farther and farther away, longing to rid myself of it forever.

My mother had fallen asleep on the broad seat, or stiffly shut her eyes—since owing to the numbness in all her limbs I could not really tell what was happening inside her.

She's fallen asleep, I thought.

The train rolled on, rushing ahead.

But I could still see the camp clearly, albeit in miniature, like a scaled-down model of an ancient city in the palm of the hand of the designer, soaring high on the peak of the mountain surrounded by the halo of an unearthly morning there on the blackness of the mountain which was already whitening, and refusing to melt away, just like the spot sticking to the windowpane, which I breathed on and tried to wipe away—but in vain.

Translated by DALYA BILU

MRS.
ECKHARDT'S
STORY

David Schütz

"... Are you sure I'm not boring you, young man, with all this ancient history? You ask about the woman, Lotte-Miriam, and the people surrounding her in those bygone days. When was it exactly? Nineteen thirty-four or -five, I don't remember any more.

"And what remains today of that enthusiastic little band, who turned their backs on the false way of life spreading through our big cities and the rottenness festering in them, and went back to nature? It's hard to believe, young man, how full of faith we were then, and how young. We built our houses with our own hands. We ploughed the virgin lands we bought from the farmers. And then, very slowly, almost imperceptibly, things started changing. Gustav, for example, Lotte-Miriam's husband, was in love with his cello. In the evening we would listen to its deep, sweet sounds—and we could tell, just by listening, that Gustav's heart was far away, in some other place. Believe me, it was impossible not to be swept away in the sadness emanating from that house. But you want to hear about the woman, about Lotte-Miriam.

"In the winter winds her long locks would coil themselves around her neck like snakes. I remember her laughing into the wind, exposing her white teeth. On fine days she would take off and disappear. Anyone following her, as I did, would see a shadowy figure plodding over the ground, bending down to pick all kinds of plants and mushrooms, mosses and berries. Later on strange, heavy smells would spiral from her chimney. Sometimes, when she went off for a few days at a time, she would ask me to keep an eye on the children. The poor little ones would hide between the pillows and blanket, blue with cold, wailing like a pair of abandoned kittens. Especially Michael. He would cling to my neck with his tiny hands, kiss my face, and cry. They were two poor little puppies, those two. And she, Lotte, would take off for those hills you can see through the window, trudging along in her heavy boots and dark raincoat —a single living creature against the low sky.

"I think that she liked listening to the rustling of the trees in the wind, the murmuring of the rivers. She followed her instinct and roamed far afield. The smell that clung to her was the smell of distances. The peasants would come to ask her advice. Cautious and suspicious, they would ask her for remedies for rheumatism and indigestion, or for help with a woman in labor. Little by little her fields were neglected. And from the day that Gustav—who worked the land alone while Lotte was wandering in the hills—disappeared, she avoided her fields until most of them reverted to marshland and thorns. The peasants believed in her. In their hearts they were sure that she was a witch and communicated with the spirits of darkness. And they weren't the only ones who thought so. Lotte seemed to entertain some such notion herself. In any event, she did nothing to clear the air. She enjoyed the clumsy awe she inspired in the peasants, she cultivated it deliberately. She delighted in the circle of dread being drawn around her, and perhaps—who knows?—she really believed that she could make the rain fall at her command, or kill a man with a curse.

"Eckhardt didn't like her. My husband couldn't understand what she thought she was up to, roaming about the hillside while her children crawled in the mud in front of the house. He was sure that it was because of her spells that Gustav ("the faithful," Eckhardt called him) had left, simply taken his cello and gone off without so much as saying goodbye.

"In addition to this, Eckhardt was one of the first to join the Party* in our district. I'll never forget the tension in the air when Eckhardt came back one evening and dropped in on Lotte and Gustav—the others were already sitting there arguing—all spit and polish in his uniform, the symbol on his sleeve sticking out as aggressively as a slogan on the wall. Franzl was horrified (he was close to the Communist Party) and stood up to leave as a sign of protest. Tauber's jaw dropped. Only Gustav was pale and quiet. It was clear that something important had happened. We girls were indifferent, although I, for one, was vaguely aware of something or other about Lotte-Miriam's Jewish descent.

*The Nazi Party.

"I hope I'm not boring you with all this ancient history. Anyway, Franzl and Tauber left the village soon after that evening. And to this day I don't know whether there was any connection between the two events. In other words, if they left on account of Eckhardt's ideas, or not.

"As I've already told you, Eckhardt didn't like Lotte. And after Gustav disappeared, my husband stopped greeting her. And so did the other farmers, who were all flocking to join the Party. But at night, in secret, I would see them stealing softly to her door. Until the morning when Lotte came knocking at my door.

"It was early, just before dawn. Eckhardt was still asleep. I went outside, I remember, in my pajamas, with a coat around my shoulders. Standing next to Lotte were her two children, Ingrid and Michael. They were dressed in their best, unusually neat and clean.

" 'Mrs. Eckhardt,' she said to me, standing there on the threshold, with a formality we had abandoned long before, 'Will you look after these children for me until I come back?'

" 'Until you come back?' I asked. 'Are you going away?'

" 'Yes,' she said.

"I was rather taken aback, and to give myself a chance to recover I said, 'Come in, Lotte, it's cold outside.'

" 'No, thank you,' she replied. And it was only then that I noticed the red bag lying on the ground between the two freezing children.

" 'I'm in a hurry to catch the train,' she said. 'Will you take them or not?'

" 'That's something I'll have to consult my husband about,' I said.

" 'Good,' said Lotte, her eyes hard on my face. 'Good, you consult him. The children are staying here.'

"And off she went. Just like that, without even waiting for an answer. She picked up her red bag, kissed the children, and left. They cried and clung to her skirt. She pushed them away and ran through the morning mist toward the railway station. I went on standing there for a while, watching her red bag vanishing into the white dawn vapors. When Eckhardt woke up he washed his face in cold water and sat down to drink his coffee. I pointed to the children standing on either side of the table, miserable and awkward in their finery, and said, as calmly as I could, 'Lotte has left them with us for a few days.'

" 'Has she, indeed?' said Eckhardt, slicing the bread with his sharp knife. 'The poor little bastards.' And without another word he beckoned me to seat them at the table and feed them.

"For four years I fed them, sir, and Lotte didn't even take the trouble to send us a message. Gradually I got used to the idea that she had disappeared or died. The children grew, went to church on Sundays, and celebrated the potato feast in autumn with the others.

"Four years later she came back. She came in the evening—it was already dark outside and the children were sleeping in their room—and she had another baby in her arms. You may well look surprised, sir, but in those hard times we had grown accustomed to every kind of craziness. Lotte gave me the third child too—her name was Helena, a pretty baby with wide-open gray eyes. We sat huddled together like a pair of thieves, warming our hands by the stove. Lotte was afraid of waking her children, afraid of their embarrassing questions. Rather incoherently she told me that she had lost track of Gustav Kleinman somewhere in the east. He and his cello had been swallowed up in the hordes of people hurrying through the streets of the big city, Berlin. On the other hand, she had found Tauber. The same old Tauber, not quite all there, lost in dreams of glory. At first she had shared a little apartment with him. When their situation deteriorated they were obliged to give it up and move into one of the rooms. In the end, or so I understood, they couldn't even pay the modest rent for the one room and lived in fear of being thrown onto the street by the landlady. After a lot of pleading and begging, she agreed to let them sleep in the passage leading to the rooms.

"All this time Lotte was running around the streets of Berlin, ostensibly looking for her husband Gustav. Tauber, on the other hand, was on the point of completing his great work, a novel about the Crusaders. He would sit in the passage in his red dressing gown, recording, on sheets of yellow paper, the adventures of the knights on their way to the Holy Land and what happened to them when they got there. According to Lotte he had already covered six hundred and fifty pages with the description of their sufferings and exploits, and the great work was approaching its end. 'One more proof, clean and final,' he would say, 'and the novel will be published.' But all kinds of digressions and additions kept on cropping up, little subplots that needed further development, obliging him to postpone the completion of the final draft until all the adventures of the various heroes could be tied together and the entire collection of episodes united in one stunning finale, one mighty crescendo that would illuminate everything that had gone before in a single flash of sublime and miraculous light.

"God only knows what the pair of them lived on. From everything she said it remains a mystery to me what she was doing all those years and how she supported that man sitting in the passage in his red dressing gown and writing the history of the Crusades. I expect she was selling love potions on the sly and divining over concoctions of herbs. (Don't laugh, sir. If you knew Lotte like I do, you wouldn't laugh.)

"I was always secretly jealous of Lotte, I won't deny it, on account of her looks. She didn't look in the least like the farmers' daughters, all their beauty withered after one brief bloom. I have to confess that when Lotte was sitting there in my warm kitchen I hated her. Showing up out of nowhere, a beautiful woman chattering and laughing, sitting in my kitchen and scheming to take my children away—the children I had brought up. When I saw her coming down the path, slipping through the dusk like a phantom, I was filled with dread. I felt as if I was seeing a ghost. And afterwards, I won't deny it sir, you might as well know the worst —I felt suffocated by hate. Worse than hate—loathing. I wanted to be sick. And the lump sticking in my throat was so big I couldn't open my mouth. Surprised by my silence, Lotte kissed me joyfully; I suppose she thought I was too excited to speak. How can I describe my relief to you, sir, when I realized that she hadn't come to rob me of the children, but to give me another one?

"Lotte, as I've already mentioned, was busy looking for her husband. And Tauber was far away in the Promised Land with his crusader knights. And thus Helena was born. Yes, Helena's father was none other than that wretched Tauber. Of that, at any rate, there can be no doubt.

"Tauber went on sitting in the passage in his filthy gown, putting the finishing touches to his portrait of those bold-hearted seekers after God and loot. And he didn't stop even when the streets of the city were full of marching men kicking their boots into the air, drunk with pride and idolatry, or when the flags and loudspeakers saluted the victory parade. You know something about those crazy days, I suppose? Many people have written about the events that brought Hitler to the pinnacle of power. People were delirious with excitement. Contracts were torn up in broad daylight, and new, unmentionable ones were signed in secret. Of all this Lotte said nothing, as if it wasn't all happening right under her nose, as if the changes had simply passed her by. Instead she told me enthusiastically how one morning she just couldn't stand it any more, she dragged him out of bed, pushed him out of the house, and locked the door behind him. When Lotte was fed up with Tauber, she sent him to work in a munitions factory.

"In those days Tauber was in a state of peculiar excitement. He would suddenly burst out laughing for no apparent reason, walk the streets alone, go without sleep at night, and neglect his regular affairs. At last he seemed on the point of finding the solution to his giant puzzle. All his heroes and their exploits, their women and their horses and their loyal retainers, had come together and united in one spectacular climax. About one week after he had begun work in the munitions factory—it was a Sunday and Tauber had volunteered to do overtime for the Reich—there was a big demonstration in the city. The yards and houses were festooned with brightly colored placards, crowds of people blackened the streets, flags waved in the wind, loudspeakers blared, and the shouts of the crowd were drowned in the thunder of the flying Party cars. Tauber, emerging from the dark factory into the brilliance flooding the streets, made his way slowly toward a group of people gathered around a huge placard. And then one of the crowd pointed at the poor wretch and shouted. Before he realized what was happening he was grabbed by a multitude of hands, and right there in the street, under the blaring loudspeakers, they lynched him. His broken, mutilated body was exposed to Lotte in the morgue. The orderly explained to her patiently that someone had mistaken him for a Jew. ('Absolute rubbish,' said Lotte.) The official notice ascribed the cause of his death to a 'street accident.'

"Lotte returned to the passage, forcing her way in past the protesting landlady, rummaged in the chest next to the bed, wrapped the six hundred and fifty yellow pages in Tauber's red dressing gown, and bore her precious burden outside. It was a surprisingly hot, summery day, with a harsh glare in the streets. Lotte swayed in the dazzling light. She walked uncertainly, as if she was drunk, or didn't know the way. The landlady peeped cautiously through the window. When Lotte reached the round billboard, one of those solid concrete columns they used to paste their giant placards on, she laid the bulging dressing gown on the pavement, a sacrificial offering, and continued on her way. The passersby paid no attention to the curious bundle at the foot of the column. The sole spectator was the landlady, who shrugged her shoulders and shut the window behind her.

"Three years slipped by unnoticed. You know yourself, sir, how swift that silent journey is. Three difficult years, like a few moments. Ingrid was already twelve years old. To my astonishment she was drawn above all to the church. She went there whenever she could, pale with excitement at the sight of the priest performing his secret rites. I won't deny it—on that very chair where you're sitting now, she would sit transfixed, still as a statue, staring into space and dreaming with her eyes wide open. Once or twice I saw her hurrying late at night to the old graveyard next to the church. But apart from these little eccentricities she was a good, hard-working girl, and who knows what would have become of me without her help during those dreadful years. While she sat staring at the window Michael would sit at her feet carving his wooden women. Always the same awkward figure, with breasts sticking out and arms spread over the body like wings. He would sit carving while Eckhardt was busy organizing his Party comrades and I was making supper. He had a knife that his father had left behind. A sharp, heavy, farmer's knife. Michael refused to be parted from that knife. He would walk around with the knife sticking out of his pants pocket.

"Helena was already three by the time those three years had passed and Lotte appeared again. You won't believe it, sir, when I tell you that there was a baby dangling from her arm again—the child of her old age. But this time she was hunted, afraid. She was pushing a carriage piled with household goods and a sewing machine with one hand. And in the other arm she carried the baby. The baby was plump and quiet, a big, fair creature, like the babies artists once painted in the arms of the mother of God. But Lotte herself was so shrunken it was almost impossible to recognize her. The skin hung from her face like a rag on a washing line. She was so thin and worn. There were gray rings under her eyes, and their brilliant turquoise color had finally dulled. With a weak, apologetic smile she complained that the baby, Emmanuel, was exhausting her strength.

"I said to myself that I already had enough of her children. Eckhardt was worn out with work. After the war broke out most of the Party members had been conscripted and Eckhardt had taken on their duties, one after the other. He had even taken charge of the Party funds. The children took care of the farm and their baby sister like adults. And I said to myself that I had enough children already. This pretty baby sleeping on his mother's shoulder would stay with her.

"Lotte made no attempt to persuade me. She stood there, here in this very room, with the baby sleeping on her shoulder, and told me that her identity had been uncovered in Berlin. One of her old acquaintances (Franzl?) had informed on her to the authorities, reported that she was Jewish. And they were already hunting her down. She had abandoned everything, her home and her job, and escaped. Naturally the first one she came to was Mrs. Eckhardt—me. And don't be surprised, sir, if I didn't take the opportunity to ask her who the father of her child was. In the face of her flight and panic the question seemed trivial.

"Anyway, as I said, I was about to reject the baby when the door of the room opened and Eckhardt came in, half asleep and wearing his dressing gown.

" 'Lotte,' he said, and put out both his hands. He bent over the sleeping baby and gave it a long look. Neither Lotte nor I said a word.

" 'Well,' said Eckhardt in the end, 'are you abandoning him to us too?'

" 'I beg you,' I heard her whisper.

" 'I can't understand why you keep having them,' grumbled Eckhardt.

" 'I'll come back for them one day,' said Lotte.

" 'They'll be loyal sons of Party and fatherland,' shouted my husband, Walter.

" 'It's better that way,' Lotte quickly acquiesced.

"Walter Eckhardt turned around. He laughed grimly. Lines of laughter appeared between his pale eyes. 'Lotte,' he said, amused, 'so you of all people are swelling our ranks.'

"I couldn't restrain myself. I asked to speak to him in private. Lotte remained alone in this room. Walter and I went into the bedroom.

" 'Well,' I said to him, 'I think the three we've already got are enough for me.' Walter nodded and went over to the big wardrobe you can see over there. He rummaged in one of the bottom drawers and pulled out an iron box. I reminded him of her irresponsibility in the old days, of how the faithful Gustav Kleinman had abandoned her and her children because of the way she would slip away on foggy nights and wander around the countryside, howling with the stray dogs. I sat on the bed, supporting my head on my hands, and Lotte giggled behind my back, showing her beautiful teeth. Enjoying herself with men in the city while I spent sleepless nights worrying about her children.

" 'Have you got the key?'

" 'What key?'

" 'The key to this box,' said Walter.

" 'No.'

" 'Pity,' he said, looking at his bunch of keys, 'I must have lost it.'

" 'I want to make it quite clear,' I went on, 'I'm not the woman I used to be. I did what I could to the best of my ability. On no account do I owe Lotte my life. It's time for her to wipe that grin from her pampered face, it's time for her to start worrying about a thing or two. She's not a cat to drop her litter wherever the mood strikes her and walk elegantly away, wagging her backside and leaving the worry and the mess to others. And another thing, Walter,' I said to him, 'the time is coming when we'll have to look out for ourselves. And ourselves only.'

"Walter sat down on the bed beside me and shook the iron box in his hands.

" 'What's happened to you,' he said, 'that you've got so much to say for yourself all of a sudden?'

"I thought to myself: Am I talking too much? But I couldn't keep quiet. I told him that we had been at war for three years now —and where would it end, I said to him. Where would it end?

" 'You're right,' said Walter meaninglessly, going out of the room and coming back with a hammer and a screwdriver. 'You're right.' And with two well-aimed blows he opened the lid of the box and extracted a few bank notes from it.

" 'What do you think you're doing?' I cried.

" 'She needs money,' he replied, and went into the other room. I hurried after him. Lotte had fallen asleep on the chair, one hand folded under her head. And truly, she was pitiful—an ugly, deflated bundle slumped on the chair. Walter shook her shoulder. And even before she stretched her arms and apologized, he had put the money into her hand. When she tried to say, 'But . . .' Eckhardt put his hand over her mouth.

"It was only after she had gone that I discovered the money belonged to the Party. Perhaps you don't know, sir, that my husband, Eckhardt, was killed defending Berlin in 1945. He was found crushed next to our anti-aircraft guns, together with another boy from our village, Rudolf, who had volunteered with him. Both of us knew that the end of the Reich was inevitable. But despite this knowledge, and despite all my pleas, he made his way into the dying city. No, I don't know why. The children were no longer with us. The house was empty.* Lotte had kept her promise. A year and a half before the end she came and took her children away. All four of them. We both wept. Actually, I don't know if she wept. My own eyes were too full of tears to see. We fell into each other's arms and couldn't let go. The children cried, too. Even little Emmanuel wailed and whimpered as if he understood everything. What a sight we must have made, the two of us standing there in the doorway with the children, unable to tear ourselves apart, until we heard someone shouting: 'The train's arrived!'

"Lotte-Miriam came to visit me once after the war. Ingrid came too, and we went to the church together to pray. It was good to remember her again, to feel her dear face. Helena, as you know, lives here now, in Lotte's renovated house, right next door. But she keeps silent most of the time and hardly ever takes the trouble to visit Mrs. Eckhardt, a half-blind old woman. All the others have scattered. I heard that they went to Palestine. And I sit here alone, sinking like a stone. Sit and watch all those distant memories fading away. And my memory fails me too sometimes, and everything gets blurred. It seems to me, young sir, that I told

*Mrs. Eckhardt seems to be hinting quite clearly here that her husband volunteered for army service at the end of the war because of the emptiness of the house. But this, of course, is only speculation.

you as soon as I invited you in, and I must have mentioned it again more than once while we were talking, that if you hadn't announced your name so firmly I would never have recognized you as Lotte-Miriam's younger son."

Translated by DALYA BILU

LANDS OF PEACH, APRICOT, AND BREAD

Ben-Zion Tomer

Mile after mile after mile. A day and night? Many days and nights? Everything becomes blurred and confused in the monotonous rhythm of the wheels turning round and round on themselves, lulling you to sleep and waking you by turns. All you know now is that you're traveling, that it's night—a dull, waxen light; that you're crossing a bridge—the hollow echo sending shivers through the coach and terrifying you with the picture of the bridge collapsing, the train hurtling down, your mouth filling with the sound of water as you open it to scream. Suddenly you're inside a tunnel. You can always tell when you're in a tunnel, even when you're sleeping. Fears that have never died in you come to life: The mountain caves in, blocking the mouth of the gaping hole; you're trapped in the bowels of the dark. You remember the miracle of Jonah. He in the belly of the fish, you in the belly of the earth. The suffocation, the approaching end, and then, when all is already lost, beyond the last scream—the redeeming emergence from the depths.

Mile after mile after mile. From time to time my head falls onto my mother's shoulder, and from time to time I wake to find the skull of a stranger, yellow-skinned and foul-smelling, on my shoulder. His eyes, darting like mice, and the panic on his face when I shake him off show him to be an inmate of the camps, not yet accustomed to his freedom, uneasy in it as a man with his feet in a pair of new shoes. Something in their faces reveals their histories without their having to say a word, that same something that has always helped you tell domestic dogs apart from strays. His faded gray coat is buttonless, belted with a thick piece of forester's rope, as frayed and disintegrating as its owner. Criminal or political? Political, I decide in his favor, but caution is called for nevertheless.

"Refugees?" he asks.

"Refugees."

"So."

"Yes."

"Where to?"

(Warning bells go off in all the cells of your brain and heart, alerting you to the danger of ambush, but his voice is gentle and melodious, denying his skull-like appearance.)

"Where to . . . with a war on in the world who can tell?"

"True," the man agrees.

"In the meantime we're traveling," Father says, and he sounds reassured.

"Indeed."

"To the south, perhaps."

"So . . . to the south . . . everyone seems to be streaming south."

"And you, where are you going?"

"Somewhere," replies the man, with a faint smile illuminating his cracked lips. "I'm on my way to the south too . . . see you in the south, neighbor," and he closes his eyes and falls asleep.

Mile after mile after mile. An insignificant little bridge, and the coach suddenly jolts the skull, with its nauseous odors escaping from its gaping, toothless mouth into my face.

"Maybe you know Andzey, Andzey is also politi . . ."

"Shut up!" my mother interrupts.

"It's worth asking."

"And worth more keeping quiet!"

This last exclamation of Father's was sharp and final, and in order to demonstrate to me that the argument was indeed over, they both let their eyelids drop at once, as if at a prearranged signal. I too closed my eyes, but Andzey, once having come into my mind, refused to go away. He stood there in our workshop, once with his father and once with my father's apprentice, Shmiel, conferring at length, and in whispers. Angry at being excluded, I tried to eavesdrop, and they went into the park opposite the little church. Shmiel's wooden leg clickety-clicked over the cobblestones and with every click doomsday came closer and an obscure terror filled my heart.

When I entered the park a strong wind rose and flocks of yellow leaves flew at me. I took shelter behind the trunk of a tree and a hail of chestnuts suddenly fell onto my head. Someone laughed at the top of the tree. I lifted my eyes and saw—Andzey. Before I could pick up a chestnut or two to throw back at him, a thick mist came down on me like a blanket. Shmiel's leg went on clicking in the caverns of my ears, where it was joined by the sound of wheels clattering against steel, of whistles cutting through the living nerve.

The smell of fresh bread tickled my nostrils. I wanted to awaken, but my eyelids seemed welded together. My hand groped in the direction of the smell. I stuffed the bread into my mouth, dimly aware of my father's muttering. Someone gave me boiling water from the samovar to drink, and either because of my haziness or because of the jolting of the train a rivulet of water slid down my chin and into my collar, its cold slipperiness on my skin as nauseating as the touch of a snail. All at once I was awake. The train went on racing between the two walls of darkness, and the rocking coach jolted the sleeping heads like huge puppets. There was a foul smell in the compartment, and it came chiefly from the "political." His mouth hung open and emitted a jumble of grunts. My mother, too, grunted something in her sleep. I stood up, went over to the window, and leaned my forehead on the damp glass. Tidal waves of darkness pulsated beyond it, covering the iron chariot in floods of black ink as it puffed and panted like a tired swimmer in deep water. Suddenly, like candles in the sea, the dim lights of a lost little village, and after it, so unexpectedly, the darkness was transformed, becoming milkier from one moment to the next. The landscape on the other side of the windowpane, beyond the whitening mists, went on hiding, but gradually the mist retreated and the sun, rising somewhere in the east, began to fly like a big golden ball across the playing fields of the sky.

"The horizon, my boy," said the "political," who had risen from his seat and joined me at the window, "I haven't seen the horizon for ten years. Do you understand, my boy?"

"Yes," I said.

"Not really. You'll never really understand the meaning of ten years without a horizon, with nothing but forest around you, forest and more forest, above you, behind you, in front of you, forest wherever you look."

"You seem to have forgotten that I've come from Siberia too."

"True . . . in our country everyone grows up quickly. How old do I look to you?"

"Let's say—fifty."

"And can't you count any higher than fifty?"

"Maybe fifty-five."

"You're a poor marksman, my boy . . . I'm thirty years old."

"Impossible!"

"I agree with you, but for reasons the opposite of yours . . . the truth is that I'm a member of the generation of the Flood. . . . Have you ever heard of Noah's ark?"

"I read about it."

"You'll find all the animals in the ark, but not one single man."

"You forgot Noah."

"Ah, the saintly Noah . . . his presence in the ark is nothing but a fairy tale."

"I don't understand."

"It's quite simple. Saints, my boy, don't captain ships. Remember what I say . . . saints are the first to drown in the flood."

"You have a way with words."

"It's my trade, my young friend. I was once a writer."

"A writer? Really? . . . And what do you mean, 'once'?"

"I mean that I gave it up."

"Willingly?"

"Yes and no."

"I don't understand."

"At last, something you don't understand and don't pretend to understand. . . . Do you read a lot?"

"Yes."

"Poetry too?"

"Yes."

"Does the name Pasternak mean anything to you?"

"No."

"A poet. A real poet. You want to hear?"

"Yes."

"Then listen:

"Oh, had I known that's how it happens
when I made my stage debut,
that lines, when mixed with blood, do murder,
will rush into your throat and kill you!

"I should most flatly have refused
to jest with such a private matter.
It was so distant at the start
and my first interest—so half-hearted.

"But old age is like Rome, demands,
instead of wisecracks and of tricks.
Actors must give no easy readings
but death outright in sober earnest.

"And when the heart dictates the line
it sends a slave onto the stage
and there's an end of art and there's
a breath of earth and destiny.*

"Wisecracks and tricks aren't dangerous; on the contrary, they'll even pay you well for them . . . prizes, *dachas* . . . But to write what the heart dictates? For that, my young friend, you'll get a luxury *dacha* in Siberia . . . And who needed it, my learned friend, who? Perhaps you can tell me, eh? That's it, my young friend, 'If I had known that's how it happens/ when I made my stage debut,/ that lines, when mixed with blood, do murder, . . . I should most flatly have refused/ to jest with such a private matter . . .' "

"I don't understand what you're getting at, but in any case you don't seem to understand the need for caution . . . it's dangerous . . ."

"When it could still have made a difference, my son, I threw

*Translated by J.M. Cohen, in Stefan Schimanski, ed., *Boris Pasternak: Prose and Poems,* London, 1959.

caution to the winds, and now it doesn't make any difference any more. . . . My lungs are rotten anyway; they can't take any more."

"The southern climate, they say, is good for diseased lungs."

"And supposing it is, will the climate reconstruct my diseased soul, eh? . . . The soul, my son, is not a building to be reconstructed and engineered, whatever *he* may say. . . ."

"Who is *he?*"

"He, of course, the chief soul-engineer in our country. . . ."

"I think I'll go back to my seat; I'm feeling tired."

"Are you afraid of his name?"

"I'm afraid of *you* . . . . For both our sakes I think we'd better change the subject . . . for my sake anyway. . . ."

"Oho . . . I was wrong, it seems, when I said the soul couldn't be engineered. . . . Yours has been engineered already—weighing your words like a huckster in the marketplace . . . we've managed to turn even little boys into businessmen calculating profit and loss. . . . But you're right, of course—if you don't live to see the Sabbath eve, how will you ever be able to sing the Sabbath songs?"

"Are you a Jew?"

"No. But I heard the saying from a clever Jew I once knew. . . . The day before his prison term was up he died. . . . Pretty stories we produce in our country, no? . . . You see, my boy, writers in this country don't need to use their imagination at all; everything they need is concocted for them by our illustrious Russian reality. . . . But when they forbid you to dip your pen into the concoction, it cooks up lies instead . . . and that's why our literature is so dreary. Do you understand?"

"No."

"Congratulations!"

"I don't understand."

"Which is exactly why I congratulated you . . . It's not easy to advance to non-understanding, and especially to admit it. . . . Hey, citizen, that seat is already occupied!"—and the "political" turned toward a squat peasant who was trying to take his seat—"Yes, by me. . . . For how long? Until it stops being occupied. . . . You see, my boy? It's not enough that a man hasn't got a permanent home in the world, he even has to keep guard on a temporary seat in the train to see that nobody takes it away from him. Well, I'm tired now, and I'll bet you are too from all my chattering."

"No, no, not at all."

"But I am," and so saying he returned to his seat, lowered his head, and fell asleep.

Mile after mile after mile of rolling yellow plains, without a speck of green. Only here and there, few and far between, little desert trees, low-trunked and flat-topped, raise their heads like yellowish-green umbrellas. The wind lightly brushes their prickly hair, sends bouncy little balls of thistledown spinning madly over the vast expanse of the infinite plain. The farther south we travel the more the dark-skinned, narrow-eyed faces multiply. They look at you with watchful suspicion, and you return their stares with an uneasy wonder. At one of the stops (a whitewashed mud hut) a balding camel fixes me with vague, drugged eyes, as if to ask: What are you doing here?—I don't know, someone inside me replies, I don't know. Everything is so strange, camel: you, me, spinning through your desolate kingdom like a ball of thistledown. The sun in your country burns me. Siberia froze me and you're burning me.—Run for your life, boy, run!—And the camel kneels, as if he has done his duty and from now on the responsibility is yours, not his.

"Father, where are we going, Father? Everything is empty here; we'll starve to death."

"What are you talking about, my son? We're going to the lands of peach, apricot, and bread."

"You forgot to add raisins and almonds. . . . Why not? We're going to feed on *rozhinkes mit mandlen** . . . roasted doves and bull Leviathan," said Mother sarcastically, coupling the legendary ox with the mythical whale in her sudden fit of rage. Even though I knew, to my sorrow, that she had a way of always being right in

*"Raisins and almonds," in Yiddish.

the end, I preferred to cling to the lifeline of delicacies my father had woven for me from the fragrant words: peach, apricot, bread.

"You see?" I jumped for joy. "What do you say to that?"

"To what?" My astonished mother joined me at the window to verify my discovery with her own groping eyes. The engine slowed down, as if it too wanted to fill its sooty lungs with the scent of the gardens of the town famed for its apple orchards. Green boughs laden with red fruit bent to the ground with the weight of their sweet burden. The warm air made my body drowsy and woke forgotten longings in my heart, and only the metallic voice of the war, raucous in the loudspeakers, spoiled the vision of the dreaming summer town with the gathering dusk falling in golden showers onto its head. Under the canopy of branches made by two intertwining trees stood a white horse, staring with its horse's eyes at the puffing iron monster. The rider, a boy of about thirteen, giggled into his horse's ear without taking his eyes off me. His horse, his giggle, his whole green, blooming world stuck in my eyes like thorns, and the thorns lit a fire in my chest. A sudden hoot sent a shudder through the horse, but the hand of the rider immediately restored it to its obedient calm. A second hoot startled the horse to its hind legs, wild with panic. I prayed to see the rider flung from his saddle, but his practiced hands kept a firm grip on the reins, and the moment the engine sounded its third and final hoot he began to gallop. At first the living horse outstripped the dead one, but gradually the dead overtook the living as it penetrated ever deeper into the caverns of the night darkening on the horizon.

When I turned my face to trap the town one last time in the camera of my eye, the summer town in the golden evening dusk, I saw them turn and go back the way they had come, like a man walking slowly home at the end of the day, until they were swallowed up in the sun setting beyond the gates of the garden city as they closed behind us.

Mile after mile after mile. The "political" opened and closed his eyes, but he no longer paid any attention to me or anyone else. He sat silent between my mother and myself, his head hunched between his shoulders like the head of a sleeping bird, looking as if he had flown far away from himself and his surroundings. And when I tried to catch his eye, it looked back at me as smooth and glassy as ice. Nevertheless, I would not give up. As if by mistake, I trod on his foot; then I apologized and he raised his thick eyebrows slightly, as if to say: Well, I forgive you, and now do me a favor and leave me alone. My other attempts to break the ice met with a similar failure. There was something insulting about his capriciousness toward me: Hadn't he, just a little while ago, confessed his innermost thoughts to me, played me like a flute?—And now I was superfluous, a flute nobody needed. Hunger drove him from my thoughts and reminded me of the two apples stored in my pocket. As soon as I bit into the sweet, winy flesh, I realized that I hadn't seen him take a bite of food since entering our coach.

"Here," I said, offering him the other apple.

"Thank you," he said, "I'm not hungry!"

"As you wish," I replied, stung by his exclamation mark.

"Nice of you to offer, anyway," he concluded on a conciliatory note, and closed his eyes.

"Have you gone mad?" said my mother after a moment or two," and my father added: "Madman! The boy's a madman—playing the saint in Sodom . . . just like your mother"—he turned to Mother.

"Lucky he's not like your mother," she rejoined.

She had never forgiven him for the forced parting from Grandmother. For the most part he was careful not to mention her, and now too he quickly shut his eyes in order not to give my mother the chance to say, as she did in every argument between them, "It doesn't matter what your mouth says, what matters is what your eyes say."

The "political," who my parents imagined to be asleep, rose from his seat and went over to the window, where I soon joined him. A cold, moonlit desert night lashed the windowpane with whips of sand and wind. For a long time we stood listening in silence, I not daring to open my mouth and he as still as a dummy

in a shop window. Not by so much as the slightest twitch of his
frozen limbs did he show any sign of noticing my presence. What
a well-trained body, I said to myself, and stomach too, apparently
—never hungry unless commanded to be so.

"They're right," he suddenly blurted out, motionless as before.

"What are you talking about?"

"Don't pretend to be so naïve."

"I'm not pretending."

"Then don't be smart."

"I'm not being smart. I simply don't understand what you're
talking about . . ."

"You understand very well. . . . I'm talking about the apple, of
course."

"I offered to give it to you, that's all."

"And you were given a cold shower instead, that's all."

"So you are Jewish after all. You understand Yiddish."

"You're wrong on both counts, but I understand something
about people. I've acquired quite a good understanding of the family
of predators called two-footed mammals."

"The apple is still in my pocket."

"A good, safe place. You keep it there."

"Are you really not hungry?"

"None of your business."

"But why are you so angry?"

"That's my business!"

"I don't understand."

"I fully confirm your self-diagnosis, but in return for your
honesty and generosity, I'll tell you a little story, although only God
or the devil knows why I should choose to tell it to you, of all
people. . . . Our modern fairy tale begins just like any other fairy
tale, with the words 'Once upon a time.' Once upon a time, there
were two brothers in our camp, well-brought-up boys who loved
one another and were devoted to each other, a David and Jonathan
warmed by one womb. You know who David and Jonathan were,
I suppose? They're from your Bible. . . . Their parents died in the

great famine after the revolution and the two of them joined hands against the rest of the world.

"One evening, at a party, the younger brother, Dimitri, got drunk and made up a poem lampooning our national poets for their sycophancy. That same night, in the small hours—as usual—they knocked at his door, confiscated every scrap of paper with writing on it, and arrested his elder brother. Dimitri himself wasn't at home. He was too drunk to find his way, and when he sobered up at sunrise he realized that he had been sleeping soundly in the public park. He found them waiting for him at his front door. Under interrogation he did not deny that he was the author. They laughed, especially one of them, a bald man who kept clapping his hands and saying, 'Oh that's nice, very nice . . . nice of you to cover up for your brother and of him to cover up for you. Both of you confess to having written this bourgeois crap, which means that we've trodden on the tail of a proper cell here, an organization . . . and what about the rest of you, eh? . . . Where are the names of the others?'

"The brothers were lucky; their 'cell' wasn't broken up in detention, and they were able to sweeten the bitter pill of exile for each other. Noble creatures, in short. They succeeded in bringing a smile to the lips of the most despairing of the prisoners, they softened the hearts of the most hardened of the criminals—the 'kings' of the camp.

"The commandant of the camp saw what was happening, and he saw that it was good—and so he decided that it was bad . . . and don't be too quick to blame him for it, either. If you try looking at things from his point of view, you'll see that he was right. Absolutely right. Why? Quite simple: Was the commandant the God of our camp, or wasn't he? Yes, of course he was! And in his capacity as God, in control of the whole show, was it up to him to keep order or not? Yes, it was! And if that order was founded on fear, on suspicion, and on the necessary brutalization of the prisoners, and if those two brothers were subverting and disrupting that order, was it up to him to punish them or not? Yes, of course it was! Punish them and brutalize them, at all costs. He could, of course, have had them separated by administrative means—but the commandant of our camp, like any other ruler worthy of the name, was a brilliant psychologist, and he decided to break them instead. 'What did he do?' you ask. Nothing special. All he did was to give them work quotas they couldn't possibly meet, and food rations in the camps, as you know, are tied to production quotas. From week to week he raised the quotas and lowered the rations. At the end of four months, they began to crack and accuse each other of slackness, of parasitism, and God knows what else. But still, they were scrupulous in dividing their dwindling rations equally.

"A couple of months later they were well on the way to brutalization. Angry words gave way more and more often to blows. One evening the elder brother presented himself to the commandant and said, 'I beg you, separate us!'

" 'Oh no, Comrade Prisoner,' replied the psychologist, 'if your brother is slack on the job, it's up to you to teach him a lesson!'

" 'I can't do it,' replied the elder brother, 'and I won't.'

" 'We'll see,' chuckled the psychologist, and sent him away.

"The next morning their quota was raised again, and that evening, when they came back from the forest, the elder brother presented himself to God again.

" 'I'll do it,' he said.

" 'I knew you would,' said God.

"From then on, as a foreman, he was entitled to beat his brother without being beaten in return, not to mention the extra rations due to him by law. And apropos the law, it's a funny thing that it's only in our jails and concentration camps that our rulers are able to enforce it properly. . . . In any event, the elder brother bullied Dimitri and beat him up, but he went on sharing his rations with him. But before long he stopped that, too. Our psychologist celebrated his victory, but even this victory wasn't enough for him. One day he called them both to his office and made Dimitri the foreman. . . . 'How did it end?' you ask? The end, my young friend, was very Russian. One frosty day, when Dimitri was beating his brother, his brother began to encourage him and spur him on: 'Hit me harder, Dimitri, I deserve it. Ah, how I deserve it, brother!' At which Dimitri cried out from the depths of his heart: 'If I go on beating you, I'm a swine!' To which his brother replied: 'No, brother, it's your duty to beat me. If you don't beat me, it'll be a sign that you haven't forgiven me. Beat me, brother, beat me without mercy!'

"Dimitri saw his brother's distress and groaned: 'No, no, brother, I beg you, it's not you who stand in need of forgiveness, but I. The whole thing was my fault from the beginning; it was I who got us into this mess.'

"And like true Russians they kneeled down, bowed to each other, asked each other's forgiveness, and embraced. In good spirits they returned to the camp. The elder brother told Dimitri to go into the hut and rest, he had something he had to see to in one of the other huts. An hour passed and he still hadn't returned. Two hours passed. Dimitri got up from the bunk he was lying on and went to look for his brother. He looked in all the huts, but he didn't find him. Suddenly he heard a burst of machine-gun fire and he ran in the direction of the shots. His brother was lying on top of God's corpse, his hands still gripping the thick neck . . . 'And Dimitri?' you ask. A difficult question. . . . Dimitri is the man who told you this tale . . ."

I wanted to say something, but I didn't know what to say. In the end, after an age had passed—an eternity or a few moments, I don't know how many—I begged him to take the apple.

"Thank you, my son, but not here," he said, and went out into the corridor. He bit into the apple with his eyes shut, all screwed up, as if he were praying.

The night finished dying and a hell of light and sun flooded the plain.

Translated by DALYA BILU

BERTHA

Aharon Appelfeld

In winter, he would return. Perspiring, a knapsack on his back, he would bring with him the fresh scent of worlds unknown here. His comings and goings were quiet. You never knew whether he was happy to leave or happy to return.

Inside, in the small room, life remained unchanged. Bertha would sit on the floor, knitting. It seemed as if the passing of years did not touch her. She remained just as he had left her in summer, small, dwarfish even, and quite unaltered.

"Maxie," she would exclaim, as a crack of light came through the door. Throughout the long months she had waited for this light. As the door opened her gaze would fall on him, helplessly.

Very slowly, with studied caution, he would unpack the knapsack. There were clothes and household articles that he had brought with him from his travels. At the sight of them, tears of joy welled up in Bertha's eyes. "That's for you, for you," Max would say, stroking her hair.

The first days after his return were delightful. Bertha sat beside Max, talking. She told him the various details that had accumulated in her memory, trivial experiences, which in this dark room became objects of childlike admiration. Max also talked. He had little to say; what had happened had frozen somewhere on the way. Of course, it was not possible to tell her everything. During the long summer months, on the floor among the skeins of wool, the gaps that he had left between the stories provided her with food for fantasy with which to amuse herself.

Bertha would light the stove, and Max, like a weary traveler, would sink into a long slumber that lasted through the winter. Only in early spring would he stretch himself, saying, "Well, Bertha, it's time I was on my way."

Between naps he would try, half maliciously, half affectionately, to discuss his plans for her. The conversations were full of tears and laughter, and in the end everything remained as before. Max would leave on his travels and Bertha remained behind. And so, the seasons changed, one year followed another, a sprinkling of white appeared at Max's temples, stomach pains began to trouble him, dysentery, a harsh cough, but Bertha remained as she was, small and dwarfish, these qualities becoming more pronounced, perfected as it were.

At first, he had tried, firmly enough, to put her into an institution for girls. He had even had a few preliminary meetings with the headmistress of the institution, who had turned out to be a strong woman with piercing eyes whom he couldn't stand from the very first meeting. The plan, of course, came to nothing. For several days she roamed the streets, until they found her desolate, and brought her back. No amount of persuasion on his part did any good, he did not have the courage to force her to go, and so she stayed on. There had been one other serious attempt to find her what might be called a suitable living arrangement. This was with a woman, an old woman whose children wanted to find her a companion. Bertha returned the next day, her eyes full of tears, and the matter was closed.

Soon afterward, he began to travel.

Max left, hoping that within a year people would make some arrangement for her, or that she herself would find some way out, but when after a year, upon returning to his room, he found her sitting on the floor among the skeins of wool, half knitting, half playing, he simply couldn't be angry with her.

Several years passed—five years, or more. The passage of time became blurred, especially since there were no innovations. Life went on its lazy routine, devouring time. The coming of winter left a stale taste, something like the sourness of a cigarette. Little by little he began to take the fact of her being there for granted. Even when he made far-reaching plans for her, he made them good-humoredly, for he knew with growing certainty that he would never be able to get rid of her.

Between naps he would sit and watch her, as if he were observing his own life.

Sometimes, he went haunted by the old question of his purpose in life. What was he to do with her, or what was she going to do? It was her duty to think of it—she must not be a perpetual burden on him.

Bertha would stand up, looking at him helplessly with her big eyes, unable to understand. When he nagged her, she would burst into tears. This weeping was deep and bitter. It wasn't she that wept; some sleeping animal wept inside her. Sometimes it was a high-pitched wail. After words of reconciliation, everything returned to normal. Bertha would go back to her knitting and Max would cover his head with the blanket.

Sometimes he teased her with riddles. "Don't you ever feel any change; don't things weigh upon you?" Or, in another direction, "What would you like to be someday?" The questions were venomous, aimed at her most vulnerable feelings, but she did not react. Closed, encased in a hard shell, she dragged after him like a dead weight, and sometimes like a mirror wherein his life was reflected.

She was stubbornly loyal, another quality that was not quite human. All summer long she would sit and knit fantastic patterns in strange colors. "I'm knitting for Maxie," she would say. They were not sweaters. A dumb smile would appear on her face at the sight of the patterns. In the end she would unravel them and then the same wool would appear again on the needles, year after year. The tape measure he brought her was no help, since she did not seem to understand what it was for.

But sometimes she, too, asked questions.

They were not the sort of questions that one person asks another, but a sort of eruption, not entirely irrational, that would claim his complete attention. These questions drove him out of his mind; at those moments he was ready to throw her out, to hand her over to the welfare authorities, to denounce her, even to beat her, something that he, incidentally, never did. At these moments, he felt the whole weight of this human burden that had been thrust upon him.

Sometimes he would let her ask her questions and she would sit and drift along with them, like a ship tossing in the wind. Then came the time when he reconciled himself to his fate. Now he knew that he would not leave Bertha, and Bertha knew that she was to stay with him.

Bertha would remain with him . . . some day she might change . . . medical care might cure her . . . she was a girl like all other girls. They were great thoughts, and they surged up within him. At those times everything seemed pleasantly near. "I'll wind up my affairs, Bertha, and I'll come." The feeling was powerful, leaving no room for doubts. "Isn't it so, Bertha?" he would ask suddenly.

At the moment she was that same Bertha who had been handed to him during the big escape when the others couldn't take her, when the only thing they could do was to give her to him. He hadn't been able to carry her either, but he couldn't throw her into the snow.

At the same moment, he conjured up the snow, those thick flakes falling from the skies, soft as a caress, but sometimes swooping down on you, hard, like the beating of hooves.

From the day that they had reached this country, oblivion had overcome her. Her memory froze at a certain point. You couldn't make her disclose anything from the past, nor was she capable of absorbing anything new. "Some pipe is stopped up." This feeling, oversimplified as it might be, remained a sort of certainty that he could not doubt, feeling as he did that something was clogged up in him, too. This had been so several years ago, but perhaps now as well.

When spring came he didn't go out to work. He took Bertha with him to the Valley of the Crucifixion, opposite the monastery. At that moment they were close to each other as they had never been before.

"The sun is good," said Bertha.

"It's a beautiful spring," said Max.

And there was a feeling that the pipe had become unstopped; there was communication, they weren't suspicious of one another any more, they had left their experiences behind them. Now the words, half-syllables, groped toward their hearts. Something was happening to her as well.

The future became misty and sweet. The way it had been in the first day of the liberation. Open roads and many wagons full of refugees, and an inexplicable desire to walk, to take Bertha and to walk with her to the end of the world, just the two of them, and to swallow up the beautiful distances.

"Isn't it beautiful today . . ." he tried.

"Beautiful," she said.

"Isn't it beautiful today . . ." he tried again.

"Beautiful," she said.

Exposed to the spring, to the good sun, the thoughts welled up in him until he could almost feel their physical movement. He was only slightly annoyed with Bertha for not feeling the change.

He bought food; as long as he had enough money, no one could force him to go out traveling. It was a moment of sweet abandonment that would sooner or later bring some sort of whiplash in its wake. Soon he would have to go back to work, but in the meantime, there was something festive about this walk, in the glittering olive trees, the comfortable warmth, the light playing on his shirt.

This sweet indolence lasted a few days. Not many. A letter arrived reminding him that he must be on his way. The letter was brief and unequivocal, with a sufficiently firm conclusion and certain threatening overtones.

Now he didn't know how these months of his vacation had gone by—or perhaps they had never existed at all. The cars, the refrigerator, the workers, the whole atmosphere of busy commerce suddenly came to life and seemed so near that you could smell them. The signboards flashed vividly before his eyes.

His pity was aroused: pity for himself, for the room, for Bertha, for his belongings, and for a small body that made him, too, bend his head a bit, surrender, and also love a little.

The parting was difficult for Bertha this time; promises did no good. She begged him to take her with him. The next day he saw her packing her belongings.

"Where are you going, Bertha?"

"With you."

In the evening he managed to get away. At the station, when he turned his head, he saw the flickering of lights on the road. A car was being towed to the garage. The trip was slow, as if they wanted to delay him, to prolong that which cannot be prolonged, perhaps even to bring him back. He saw that he was mean, so mean, that he felt the heaviness of his shoes, even the dirt at the roots of his hair, the sweat in his armpits. "It's not the first time I've left her, but I have always found her again—I left her enough to live on." Thus he stifled his thoughts.

That night, when he arrived at work, Frost greeted him warmly. "Well, how was the vacation, Max?" He was glad that he could go out with the first truck, unloading the cold drinks all over the city, feeling the cases on his back, full of good foaming beer. For some reason, he didn't feel like any now. He felt fresh and vigorous, ready for any load.

Late that night, after two whole rounds, he was still as fresh as he had been at the beginning. Only his thoughts pounded inside him, as if they had disengaged themselves from him, leaving him incapable of directing them. He didn't really grasp what they demanded of him, he only felt them revolving in his head.

"You've left Bertha again"—he heard this clearly; the voice resounded like the ceaseless ringing of a bell.

Then came the time that seemed ordained to bring this feeling to a head; a decision had to be taken. His fellow workers saw the need to interfere. Max needed a wife. It started, as these things usually do, as a joke. Later they fixed up a date for him—with a typist at the plant.

He didn't have much to offer her. They didn't speak about Bertha. But with her feminine intuition she discovered it in a roundabout way.

He could have said that she was retarded, that she would soon be put in an institution. This was an accepted way of speaking, even to Mitzi. But he couldn't put it that way; something stopped him from saying the words. Sometimes your cunning betrays you, and you are suddenly left naked and ashamed. At those moments you are as vulnerable as a bare neck at the change of the seasons. Mitzi delved deeply into the matter; she too, had been hurt enough in her life.

Max was called upon to clarify matters, so that, for the time being, her own affairs were pushed aside.

"This Bertha," she said, "I don't understand why she hasn't been put into an institution by now."

What could he answer? Her questions were direct, going straight to the heart of the matter; they showed up all the contradictions, and even contained an element of mild reproach.

"She didn't want to." Max tried to shake off his embarrassment.

"What do you mean, she didn't want to?"

They met every evening; it was as if she were trying to exhaust the matter completely. In order to ease the confession, she invited him to her room.

The problem was not dismissed in her room. It kept floating up to the surface like a buoy.

"It's only a question of making the arrangements," he tried to defend himself.

"Then why has it been going on for so long?"

One day he felt that something had happened to him, something physical—something that had to do with the way he handled the crates. He moved differently, and once he even dropped a crate of bottles. "Take it easy there!" cried the foreman, who liked him.

His thoughts fumbled, as though he were tipsy. Late at night he felt the fire burning in his head.

He tried to clarify the matter to himself logically, drawing the thread of Mitzi's questions to himself. In his dreams, the stark mystery took hold of him—Bertha's knitting needles, toys, hell and paradise, a strange combination of rudimentary symbols and objects.

"Does Bertha dream of me, too?"—Now he did not doubt it.

If she knew how to read, he would write her a letter. He would clarify, explain, enumerate all the reasons, one by one. Distance made it easier to hide one's facial expression. One day during the noon break, between loading, he tried to write, but in the end, when he was about to fold the letter, he realized how idiotic it was.

Mitzi asked him no further questions, as if waiting to see the impact of her words. The silence was hard for him, since he knew that it would only lead to new questions.

The movies became his most comfortable refuge.

But the secret weighed on him. Was it still a secret? He had told everything. He thought he had exhausted the matter. That is how it seemed to him as they sat in a small café once, after the movies.

Late at night, during the second shift when the storehouse was empty, he suddenly felt that he was still carrying the secret within him. If only he could give it a name, he would feel easier; but the name eluded him.

The days were as flat as the cement floor of the storehouse. He felt that the light that protected him was being taken away. Sometimes a feeling of nakedness overcame him. He tried in vain to glean something from Mitzi's eyes; they were watery eyes, the color seemed to melt in them; something was melting in him, too, but he didn't know what it was.

If there were a starting point, it would make things a great deal easier—to say, "I will begin from here," to take a day off and go up to Jerusalem, to Bertha, even to bring Mitzi, to show her. How complicated the possibilities seemed, and in the meantime all he saw were the bottles; in the darkness of the warehouse the alcohol was fermenting. He had to make a decision; Mitzi's moderate tone demanded it.

"When was Bertha entrusted to me?" The question arose from some dark depth. "Fifteen years ago." The event seemed so near to him, as if it had taken place during his last vacation.

Mitzi did not tell him what to do. She wanted to see what he would do himself. Only once did she say to him in passing, as she always did: "Maybe she's yours; you can tell me, I won't blame you; things like that happened during the war." She had thought it all out beforehand.

Now he had to act, to prove to Bertha if not to himself, to finish once and for all, to get rid of the nuisance. How close he felt at that moment to Mitzi.

He asked for his quarterly vacation. "To take care of something," he said to Frost.

He wore his good suit, and in the evening he came to Mitzi. "Very nice, very nice," said Mitzi, like a merchant who leaves the way open for negotiations, not over-eager but never refusing an offer.

"Aren't you pleased I'm going to finish it?"

"Of course, of course."

For some reason he was reminded of the headmistress of the institution with whom he had negotiated—the long corridor, girls dressed in blue.

"The institutions here in this country are fine," he said.

"Of course."

"Maybe you'll come with me."

"Better not . . ." she said, as if shaking off some unpleasantness.

The next day he got up early. It was a nice day, mild after the first rains. There was an air of simple festivity on this weekday, little traffic. He thought he would get there quickly by taxi, but meanwhile he was attracted by the shop windows. He never came empty-handed, and he was angry with himself for leaving her so little cash.

First he bought her a short winter coat, then a woolen blouse. In the next shop he bought shoes; the colors matched, colors that he liked. Then he was drawn to the central shops. A sudden fit of spending took hold of him. He ended up with two large packages. In the taxi he started a conversation with a man, telling him that he worked for Frost, and the man in the blue suit said that he also knew Frost.

Suddenly he felt the cool mountain air in his shirt.

"On vacation?" asked the man.

"Have to arrange something," said Max.

It wasn't clear to him what he would do. The certainty started to fall apart. The chill wrapped itself around his neck. He was exposed to the cutting air. He just wanted the journey to go on, to take as long as possible.

"Aren't you afraid of catching cold?" asked the man.

Jerusalem was as beautiful as on the day he had first arrived with Bertha. Lights glittered in the city. For some reason he was slow in his movements. It turned out that the man who had traveled with him was still standing next to him. "I've come to arrange something," apologized Max. They parted.

His head was empty of all thoughts. He wasn't sure for what he had come. His feet drew him to the slope. He caught a glimpse of Bertha's head. Simple indifference was written on her face. She was sitting outside, knitting.

"Bertha," he said. It was the biggest word that he could cut out of his heart; it seemed that only once had he called her that way, once at a Gentile woman's in Zivorka, after the big hunt when he was forced to leave her. It was the same head with the same tangled hair. A small, warm body that needed nothing, that was beyond patience, beyond any change that might come. It asked for nothing except to be left here, among these skeins of wool, to sit and knit thus, like a spider, like a bee; you couldn't call it stupidity, idiocy, or any similar names called to mind by that strangeness. It was something different, something that a man like Max couldn't give a name to, but could feel.

"Max!" she said. Not a muscle moved in her face.

"I came early this time." He too was unable to utter another word.

He got down on his knees. "This coat," he said, starting to take apart the package, "this coat will suit you. It's warm; at this time of the year you have to be careful."

Bertha put down the knitting needles without saying a word. Supreme indifference froze her face. Now he had no doubt she knew everything. But he could not detect any signs of anger in her. She was a princess, a devil, a gypsy, something that could not be contained in any human measure. She was not a girl to whom he could say "I couldn't, I was forced, I never loved Mitzi, it was only a blind incident." But again he repeated: "Bertha"—as if trying to suggest everything in this one word.

He tried to explain to her in the vocabulary that he had carried with him all these years, that had ripened within him.

"Max!" said Bertha, as if cutting short his confession. A deep flush suffused her face.

At that moment, he could not guess how near the solution was. Sometimes catastrophe wears festive garb.

Bertha wanted to put on her new clothes and go to town. She had matured during these months, or perhaps she had just acquired some of the gestures of a woman. She was different.

"Let's go!" she said. This was a new tone that was unfamiliar to him.

They passed by the institution. In the corridor there was confusion. Girls in blue were running around and the headmistress appeared in the entrance. It was an old Arab house that was disproportionately tall. No one noticed them.

Again he didn't know how he had got here; Bertha's cheeks were burning, and they were already in the center of town. The traffic was very heavy. Max suddenly realized why he had come and he said, "You must understand, Bertha, you're already grown up; one must marry, set up a household. You too, you too!"

Bertha turned her head and looked at him.

He wanted to say something else, but the noise in the street prevented it. Afterward, when they came to the quiet side streets, to Ibn Gabirol Street and Rambam Boulevard, it was too quiet for them to speak.

Their walk continued for some time. It was as solemn as a ceremony, as a farewell, as a simple never-to-be-forgotten occasion. You are not in control of yourself, other powers dominate you, lead you as in a procession. Oaths are broken, but another oath, greater than all, takes their place. Your eyes glisten with tears. The lights begin to dance.

Now he was already in the realm of mystery.

A smile lit up Bertha's face, and there was something sharp in her eyes like an inanimate object unexpectedly changing its form. Darkness rose up from the streets, and above them was light. Among the trees there were dark shadows.

When they returned home, her face was very flushed—a fire burned in her. Her eyes were open, but you could see nothing in them. Toward morning she began to shiver.

In the morning, the ambulance came.

She was as light and small as on the day when he had received her; the years had added no weight. He asked permission to go along with her.

The casualty ward in the hospital was full, but they made room for her. A man wheeled her carefully through the corridor on a low bed, as if trying to smooth her passage, as if he did not want to break the silence.

They told him that he must leave. The gate closed behind him.

At that moment he could remember nothing. His eyes saw, his heart fumbled, the tips of his fingers were tingling. Inside the cavity of his skull, something floated as in a heavy fluid.

"Now, my load is lighter," he said naïvely, failing to understand the situation.

The cars crept slowly down the slope, the traffic was heavy, everything flowed as through blocked pipes. He remembered nothing. The sky was clear without a trace of cloud, like glass that had been well polished in order to see through to its depths. Each object was unique: the traffic signs, the posters, and the two people coming toward him.

"Can't I remember anything at all? My memory is gone."

The landscape was bathed in bright sunshine, as if it wanted to exhibit every detail to him slightly more enlarged than usual and brought closer to the eye.

"But I must remember," he said to himself. "Forgetting won't release me."

There was no connection between one thought and another. It was as if they had frozen in one of his arteries. His body was working properly, and you could hear the gentle pulse within it.

The neighborhood began to empty as if it wanted to hide the traffic from him, to illustrate the paralysis of the inanimate landscape.

"I must choose a starting point; from now on I will try to reconstruct. One detail will bring another in its wake, and in this way I can reconstruct all the events to myself."

Nothing came to him, not a single detail that would lead him on or connect anything. His eyes saw, and he could make out everything, still enlarged, as it had seemed to him before. But he couldn't remember a thing.

If some sort of guilt erupted within him, it would make him feel easier. But no feeling of this sort existed in him at that moment. Everything was just more enlarged than usual, everything seemed so close that it made him dizzy.

He turned toward the slope, trying to thaw the solidity, and suddenly he began to feel a current of warmth in his knees. He was still in the grounds of the hospital; a bluish light flickered at the windows, something like the light in Frost's warehouses.

He felt lighter in weight; only something outside him made his walk heavy. Thus he walked around and around the hospital, unable to tear himself away from the circle.

Slowly, like a sharp stimulus, memory started ebbing back, around the thin tubes of his temples. He clutched his head, afraid that it would burst.

A slight chill met him at the entrance to the yard, and he drew his short coat closer around his body. There was a warm light in the streets. Low pinkish clouds stretched across the skies. The copper-colored rooftops glistened in the light. The street was long and exposed; one could see the remarkably straight rows of trees and the white, almost transparent, traffic signs. Then the redness descended, intertwining itself with the roads, and Max tried to submerge his eyes in it.

The street gradually filled with rich colors. The shadows, dumb and cautious, passed across. Dark circles whirled at its end. When he turned his head back, he saw the thick redness strangled by damp powerful arms.

The street emptied and you could see how the mist was being absorbed by the tree trunks.

His vacation permit was in his pocket.

A pain, a kind of stimulus, stabbed him in the ankles, pricking his toes. He remembered that from here he used to leave for work, a long journey that always began with an attack of nausea.

Now, he was already in the realm of forms. Reality, as it were, shed its skin; all he felt was a kind of familiarity, as if he were being drawn—he did not know toward what; to the blue color, to the trees or to the stray dog that chanced to be there. He did not see Bertha. She had become something that could no longer be called Bertha.

He entered the hospital. The nurse told him that the girl had amazed the ward. That was all she said, and the other nurses said nothing.

He became a regular visitor there; the attendants soon recognized him, and let him in as if he belonged there. Most of the day he would sit on the bench, looking at the tiled walls. If they had let him remain at night, he would have stayed. The dream became full of ceremonies. Sometimes she was handed over to him and sometimes a delegation came to claim her from him; sometimes it was in a forest and sometimes in Frost's warehouse.

Was it Bertha, or only a vision? Again details rose up, denying it. The shoes, the beads, the knitting needles, the blue wool—was this Bertha?

Again you went out to search for her the way you searched for her in the forest, the way you searched for yourself in the street. You just found details; you couldn't see her, just as you couldn't see yourself.

The nurse came out again. She kept her distance as if he were a stranger; she didn't trust him. Nurses trailed behind her.

The doctor came over to him, ready to start a conversation.

"Yours?" asked the doctor.

"Mine," he said.

The next day they didn't let him enter. The walls grew higher and the gate was locked. A blue light twinkled in the windows, that familiar blue, the color of a bruise.

Silence descended; it touched his body, slithered through the hair on his head, and was still.

Opposite, there were girls dressed in blue on the pavement, near the side entrance to the institution.

The evening light rested on his shoulders.

Suddenly he saw that Bertha's clothes lay in his hands. He didn't dare to open them—or perhaps these were no longer his hands, but iron rings . . .

Translated by T. ZANDBANK

TWILIGHT

Shulamith Hareven

L ast night I spent a year in the city where I was born. I had long known the password for getting there: Dante's line, "I am the way to the city of sorrow." In a clear voice I said, *"Per me si va nella città dolente,"* and time split open and I was there. In that one night's year I met a man, married, became pregnant, and gave birth to a murky child who grew fast, all without light.

The city of my birth was very dark, extinguished, because the sun had left it and gone away a long, long time ago, and people in the street walked swiftly through the gloom, warming hands and lighting up faces with candles or matches. Here and there someone moved about with an oil lamp. The streets were wide, as I remembered them, but many windows were boarded up, the planks hammered in crosswise. Other windows were stuffed with rags and old newspapers against the cold. As there was no light, not a single tree was left in the streets, only black fenced-in staves. Not one plant showed on windowsills.

I saw no one I recognized at first, yet everyone seemed very familiar, smiling faintly. They never went so far as to break into laughter. They already knew they would live without sun from now and forever more. There was an air of humility and resignation about them. They were as kind to each other as they could be. Two acquaintances meeting in the street would warm one another's hands with a shy smile.

They wore the clothes I remembered from childhood: You could always tell a man's calling by his dress. Policemen wore policemen's uniforms, of course; the judge went about as a judge, alighting from his carriage in wig and gown; the chimney sweep was invariably in his work clothes, and so was the coachman, and so was the Count. The children were dressed as children: sailor collars and lace, and the girls with knees frozen in dresses of stiff scalloped taffeta. Many wore school uniforms: dark blue or brown, high-school badges embroidered on their caps. Everyone knew where he belonged.

No one had died in the city of my birth since the sun had gone beyond recall, and no one had had new garments made. Their uniform-like clothes were not quite tattered yet, not by any means; but they reminded one of the costumes of a theater wardrobe worn over and over for many performances; somewhat graying at the seams, somewhat fraying at the cuffs, stale smells buried in each fold. And yet, such clean people, clean as smoke.

I seemed to require no sleep or food in the city of my birth, but only speech. Now I have slept, I told myself, now I have eaten, and it would be as though I had slept and eaten and could go on. And on and on I went, through the dark streets, only some of which I remembered, and some of which were ruined and not repaired but closed.

One night I drove to the opera in a carriage. The horse defecated as it went, but the odor of the dung did not reach me. I realized all of a sudden there were no smells in this city. The coachman wore an old battered top hat, and when I paid my fare he raised his hat in greeting and cracked his whip in a special way, an expert crack in the air. He knew me for a visitor, but he did not know that I came from the land of the sun. Perhaps he did not know about that land at all, though it was so near, right beyond the wall, only a password between the twilight and it. Most people do not know.

At the opera I met the man I married that night, that year. They were singing Mozart on stage, and the audience was so pleased, so responsive, that at times it seemed audience and singers might be interchangeable. I myself, I imagine, could have gone up there and joined the singer in *"Voi che sapete."* There was a festive mood about it all, an air of goodwill, bravo, bravo, rows of women's hats bobbing joyously.—How can one live without Mozart?

The man sitting by my side at the opera leaned over and said, "We must leave at the intermission, quickly, because the opera will be surrounded by soldiers after the performance and this whole audience taken away to freight trains."

I consented, though wondering how come all these people knew it and none escaped. In the intermission the man took my hand and we left quickly by a side door. Trucks with bored soldiers were already posted in the square, the soldiers preparing to get off and surround the building. Their sergeants, papers in hand, were checking the order of deployment. A young soldier was whistling *"Voi che sapete"* and said to his fellow, "How can one live without Mozart?"

In the dark light, the no-light, I asked the man holding my hand without my feeling its touch how come people weren't escaping, and he said, "Why, this whole thing repeats itself each night."

He drew me over to a door, narrow as a servants' entrance, and beyond it a slippery, winding staircase, mounting to a roof. The roof was very peculiar: We were standing at the altitude of an airplane's flight, perhaps twelve thousand feet, perhaps more, very high. Yet I could see every single detail in the opera square below.

The floodlights of the soldiers' trucks came on suddenly, tearing the darkness, glaring and terrible, and with this evil light came the wails, the shouts and curses. Now everything happened fast. The people in their festive clothes piled up on the trucks, and there was no more telling them apart, batch after driven batch. Only the soldiers stood out clearly, because they had light, harsh and frightful, and because they were shouting so.

"Operation Caldron," said the man by my side. "Every night it repeats itself. Every night they are driven in trucks like that to the trains and do not return. Next evening they are back, going to the opera, and it all starts over again. The only difference is that the people are a little less alive each time. They fade, like pictures in an album. But the process is so slow it is barely noticeable."

"And you—don't they take you in Operation Caldron?" I asked.

"No," he said, "I'm already . . ." and stopped with a wave of the hand. Then he added, "You don't have to go either. Of course, if you want to . . ."

The moment he said that I was seized by a whirlwind. I wanted, wanted mortally to leap from this tall roof into the dark courtyard now filled with shouting soldiers, go out to the opera square. Together with all the children. Together with all the neighbors, whom now I suddenly recognized one by one, Mrs. Paula and Mr.

Arkin and his wife, and Moshe of the haberdashery who used to give me pictures of angels and cherubs to stick in my copybooks, and Bolek the druggist's son. They were all being herded onto the trucks here before my eyes, fearful and apprehensive, the soldiers shouting over their heads. And I wished to leap and be with them. To be taken.

"I did not leap, either," said the man, very sad, as though confessing a sin. The whirlwind began to abate. I held on to the parapet and breathed hard. A fierce desire had come and gone and left me reeling.

One by one the trucks moved off with a terrible jarring noise. In the square lay a child's ballet slipper, a gilt-knobbed walking stick, and an ostrich feather from the hat of a lady in the opera audience. Then they *are* somewhat diminished each night, I thought to myself, and my anxiety found no relief. The emptiness that remained in the square had left my body drained to the core.

"Tomorrow it will all happen again," said the man by my side. Grief was everywhere. It was all over.

"Could we get married?" I asked, like someone asking permission to take a vacant chair in a café. And he nodded and said, "We could, yes."

We did not know where we should live. All that night we wandered through the streets, as there was no telling day from night except for a shade of difference in the depth of darkness; everything was shrouded in the same no-light of the extinguished city. That night we also crossed a park, which since the sun had gone had long ceased being a park; many marble statues were strewn over the ground now, statues of people, some of them smashed. One small statue was very like my grandfather. I wanted to take it away with me, but I had no place to put it. Once or twice I also saw a white marble statue of a horse, its thigh wrenched off, and something like frozen blood on the marble. There had not been so many statues in my childhood days, not just in the park but all over town. They had apparently turned this into a dump, maybe for all the world. The presence of the kind people from the streets was missing here, and we returned to the city that never slept, that always had men and women walking about, huddled against the cold—till we got to a smoky alehouse. A few people, their breath misty in the cold air, their spirits high, were crowded in the doorway but did not go in.

The man with me briefly considered entering the place, then as quickly dismissed the idea. There was a space behind the alehouse, a kind of small courtyard paved with concrete, and in it a tiny shed that I took for an outhouse. He opened its door and we went in; but there was no end to the shed, and its far side had another door, behind which lay, suddenly, a vast deserted residence. It had heavy, very rich furniture, a sideboard and carpets and enormous armchairs, and crystal chandeliers thick with dust and cobwebs. I had always known that this house existed behind some wall or other, and that one day I would inherit it. Generations of my forefathers must have lived here, they and their wives, my grandmothers in their handsome kerchiefs. I went in, unamazed. The furniture was too large and unwieldy, and we decided we would use only one of the rooms, a plain and all but empty one with a kind of stove on the floor to be stoked with paper or wood. The man crouched and lit a fire, the heat of which I did not feel, and his shadow fell across me. I accepted what was to be. He blew on the fire a little, and when it was going somehow he checked the window locks, then stood before me and said, "The wedding took place this afternoon."

I knew these words to be our wedding rites and I was very still, the way one is on solemn occasions. This will be my life from now on, I told myself, in a city without light, perhaps never once leaving this apartment, never entering its large chambers, just this one room, and perhaps one day the soldiers will come for me too, take me to the trucks, the trains, along with all of them, with all of them, with all of them. I shall say to all the children: Wait for me. I shall say: I am coming with you, of course I am coming with you.

All at once the room filled with people, women in shawls, neighbors. They came beaming, bearing gifts, cases, cartons. They all stood squeezed in the doorway, in the room, filling it, joyously offering their blessings in identical words: "The wedding took place this afternoon," they said and kissed me, "The wedding took place this afternoon." The room overflowed with people and with parcels. I opened one, and it held all the toys I had lost as a child and never found. The neighbor who had brought them stood over me, smiling, angelic, and repeated excitedly, "The wedding took place this afternoon." She knew that her present was apt.

Afterward the neighbor women left, their thin voices, fluttery with a small, birdlike gladness, trailing down the staircase, and all the parcels remained: cases and cartons and beribboned boxes. I saw no need to shift them, though they hardly left us space to move about the room.

"This is where we shall live," I told the man in the room with me, and he nodded his head in assent.

So a year went by. We lived like lizards, in crevices, among the empty cases in the room. I do not remember anyone buying food, but every day I crossed the long corridor, past the large, imposing, unheated and unlived-in rooms, to cook something in a kitchen that was like a large cave. Once we even went on an outing. Behind our apartment, not on the alehouse side but on the other, lay a desert stretching for many miles, and beyond the desert, in the distant haze, a range of mountain peaks, very far away. We stood at the edge of the house, a few dozen others with us, and looked at those faraway hills.

"Where is that?" I asked the people with us. They grinned good-naturedly and would not tell me, as though I should have known. One of them said, "Los Angeles," but that was a joke. I went in, back to our room, took off my shoes, my feet weary as after a long walk.

Now and then we would hear shouts from one of the nearby houses: The soldiers come for the kill. They never got to us. We would lie numb, waiting for the night's Operation Caldron to end, the leaden silence to return, the hollow grief.

Toward the end of the year I gave birth. The child tore away from me at one stroke; and I remembered dimly that once, long ago, in my other life, I had loved a man very much, and it was just this way I had felt when he tore away from my body: as though a part of me had suddenly been separated for all time. Then I wept many tears.

The child stood up and walked within a day or two. Next he began talking to me, demanding something, in an incoherent speech I failed to understand; he grew angry and I knew he would not stay with me long. One day he left and did not return. When the man came home he removed his coat wordlessly and we both knew: The child had run off to the opera square. And it had been impossible to prevent.

The days went by, day running into night without any real difference between them. Sometimes kind-hearted neighbors called. Once one of them came with scraps of material, a dressmaker's leftovers; we spent a whole morning sewing children's frocks, except that at the end of the day we had to unravel them all.

One day I knew that time had come full circle: My year in the city without light was over and I was to go back. I said to the man with me, "I'm going."

He nodded. He did not offer to come with me. I would have to fall asleep in order to wake up in the other country anyway, and he could not accompany me into sleep. I think we never slept once in all that year, neither he nor I. Our eyelids were always open, day and night.

I lay down on my bed, which only now turned out to have wheels like a hospital bed, and the man I was with set it going with one hard shove along the corridor, which turned into a steep incline, and the bed rolled into the kitchen. The kitchen, where all that year I had gone to cook, had changed: It had been set up as an operating room. I was not surprised. I lay there waiting, unafraid. All the instruments were apparently ready; only the big lamp above me was still unlit. A stern-faced surgeon in a green coat and cap bent over me, examined me at a glance, and said, "Turn on the light."

The big lamp blazed over my head, and I fell into a heavy sleep, and woke up in my other house.

It was morning. A great sun shone straight into my eyes. Ailanthus branches gently swayed on the veranda, drawing curtains of light whisper-soft across my face. A rich smell of coffee hung in the air, but as yet I could not take deep breaths of it. My soul did not return to me at once.

Through the door came the murmur of my husband's and children's voices, speaking softly so as not to wake me. I cherished them, but could not understand them from within yet, as though they were a translation that had come off well. I lay still, waiting for my soul to flow full in me again, and I knew it was all over and completed: I would no more go back to the city of my birth, to the lightless city. Dante's verse dimmed, faded, returned to the pages of the book, a line like any other: its power exhausted. In a day or two I might even be able to read it without a pang. And sleep too, I told myself wonderingly, be able really to sleep. My past was commuted. From now on I would find nothing there but the stones of Jerusalem, and plants growing with mighty vigor, and a vast light.

I got up to make breakfast, my heart beating hard.

Translated by MIRIAM ARAD

WEGER

Yossel Birstein

Sitting on a fallen log, I caught glimpses of Weger swimming in the gray river. The river was wide, with its banks overgrown with shrub, and a little farther on there was a stretch of burnt bushland. I called out to him, but he didn't seem to hear. So I went closer and called again. Weger wouldn't come out. He merely raised his head in midstream and shook it, just like that time when he was angry and refused to talk to me. Though we had remained friends and were soldiers in the same army camp in Australia during World War II, we no longer shared a tent. Weger moved in with Papadimitrio the Macedonian and with Michailovitch, who had once declared during meal time that no one could equal a Yugoslav and, leaping onto the table, had overturned Weger's dish. Weger warned him not to do it again, but the Yugoslav paid no attention to him. When Weger asked him what it was only a Yugoslav could do, Michailovitch replied, "Swim in the river all day long." Later, in their tent, Weger asked him about it again; they talked the matter over, and both men began going to the river regularly to prepare themselves for the contest. One day Michailovitch went to the river by himself and failed to return. They found his clothes near the river bank. Weber, however, continued preparing himself for the bet.

"What for, Weger?" I asked.

"I promised," he replied.

I recalled how another promise he had once made had landed him in Dachau. He'd promised to write a letter about a lie in Hitler's *Mein Kampf*. That was before the war, after he had been dismissed from the Stuttgart high school and had gone to work for a farmer in a village. He'd seen the farmer reading Hitler's book and saw fit to point out that on such and such a page there was a lie. The farmer goaded him into writing a letter about it, and Weger had done so.

"Only one lie was printed there?" I wondered when he told me of it.

"I promised," Weger smiled.

After Dachau Weger had come to Australia, where he worked off and on as a farm hand. During the war he was drafted and sent with other aliens to a military labor camp, where the soldiers were put to work loading and unloading trains at a nearby inland railway terminus. It was during the shunting of a train of frozen mutton that I had met Weger for the first time. He was sitting on a gasoline drum holding a book close to his face. It was late at night. One train had moved out and, waiting for the next to come in, Weger had sat down under the green station lamp to read. I approached from behind to take a look at what he was reading. Like most of us, Weger wore a sack that peaked above the head and covered the shoulders to protect him against the moisture and chill of the frozen carcasses. He glanced up at me, then continued reading. I leaned forward and, pointing to the lines, said, "Schopenhauer." Weger nodded. When I remarked that I was a pessimist myself, he turned slightly toward me with the look of one who had just raised his face from a page of the Talmud.

"Yes, I'm a pessimist," I repeated, at which Weger shook his head vigorously.

Meanwhile, another train of frozen mutton was shunted in, and by the time we finished work and walked home it was dawning. The camp lay several miles from the station, and the way to it led through paddocks and bush country. Half-burnt trees and desiccated bones of sheep and cattle were scattered along the road. Weger came up beside me, and after walking for a while in silence he asked if there were room for another cot in my tent. Only much later did he tell me the reason: Before turning in he liked nibbling at a bar of chocolate while reading Schopenhauer, but where he lived now his tentmates wouldn't let him do it in peace.

Weger didn't stay in our tent for long, either. We talked too much in Yiddish, and that reminded him of German, which he was trying hard to forget. Even Schopenhauer he read in English. In the end he moved in with Papadimitrio, a man who rarely spoke.

When Papadimitrio the Macedonian was drafted he had hung his head onto his chest. He had left a wife and kids behind in Greece, but now that there was a war on he couldn't get a discharge. Despite threats of imprisonment, his head remained bowed as though he were perpetually gazing down at his boots. On account of his bowed head Papadimitrio wasn't sent out to work with us loading and unloading trains but was given a stick with a nail at the end and ordered to collect the scraps of paper littering the camp. He was very tall, with shoulders towering above most of the other men. Once, while impaling scraps of paper on his stick, Papadimitrio caught sight of Weger, walked up, bent over him, and sniffed his shoulder.

"Like a dog," Weger remarked afterward in our tent.

That had been their first encounter. Several days later, when meat and marmalade were being served, Weger, who loved marmalade but wouldn't ask for a second helping, noticed Papadimitrio shoving his marmalade aside without intending to eat it. As if by tacit assent, Weger transferred his portion of meat onto Papadimitrio's mess kit and helped himself to his marmalade. Soon afterward, Weger moved into his tent.

In the evenings while Weger sat on his cot reading by the light of a lamp and several candles on a box nearby, Papadimitrio would sit opposite on his own cot, elbows on knees, face in hands, and eyes fixed on Weger. The reading of books was a thing unknown to him, and no one he knew read them.

"Doesn't he ever say anything?" I asked Weger.

Once, Papadimitrio had actually spoken to Weger about his scheme to abscond or, failing that, to take a job on a freighter straight after the war and sail home. He had even suggested that Weger join him, each returning to his own home. When Weger told him that he had no place to return to the Macedonian couldn't grasp it. Where you come from, that's where home is and where you return to, Papadimitrio had insisted. But Weger meant to hire himself out to a farmer in some distant village just for his keep and a small wage, as long as he had no worries and enough time to read and to play the piano.

"Live in loneliness like that Macedonian, Papadimitrio?" I asked.

Weger shrugged and said that Papadimitrio had a wife and family somewhere, so he was lonesome. He, Weber, wasn't, since he had no one to long for any more. In Dachau he'd been homesick for his sister and her small daughter, who at the time were still alive. Weger himself had been sure that he'd perish in Dachau, and many signs had reinforced this foreboding. He had stopped using words like "death" and "end," and cut out others denoting "darkness" and "night" until he gave up talking altogether, apprehensive of any sign auguring death. He'd imagine himself already dead, mourned over by his sister and his little niece. Now, however, he had no one left to long for, and wherever he happened to be, there he was and didn't have to be anywhere else.

After watching Weger for a long time, Papadimitrio got himself a small black-bound prayer book with a cross embossed on its covers. Whenever Weger sat down to read in the evening he, too, would place some lighted candles on a box beside his own cot and begin chanting in his native tongue prayers whose words and tune kept recurring endlessly.

Most of his free time Weger still spent swimming in the river. That day he had gone there on a Sunday morning after a shave and a haircut, and I had followed him a little later to keep an eye on him.

Michailovitch's body was found entangled in the weeds a week or so after he had disappeared. Those who had brought him in said that he was unrecognizable. Michailovitch! The rowdy Yugoslav and braggart! The very first day on entering the camp he had boasted that there was nothing to equal Yugoslav blood. It was then that the Greeks had put forward Papadimitrio to defend their honor. They had been standing near the kitchen during mess parade and the Yugoslav, catching sight of one of the cooks with a frying pan in his hand, suggested that they have a slamming match with frying pans to see who'd hold out the longest. No sooner said than done. Another frying pan was fetched from the kitchen. Both the Yugoslav and the Macedonian threw off their caps and began banging each other over the head. It wasn't a wild brawling, nor the flinging of one man upon the other, but the dealing of a whack and waiting for a whack.

Greeks and Yugoslavs split into two camps while all the other soldiers—Jews from various countries, Italians, Germans—joined in the fracas with whistling and shouting. Michailovitch was a merry fellow who loved causing a commotion. He relished being the center of attention, and from time to time while dealing a blow or receiving one he'd burst into laughter. Papadimitrio, on the other hand, dealt his blows without a sound, even morosely, his drooping lower lip smiling like that of a horse. His head remained bowed, enabling the smaller though sturdier Michailovitch to reach it easily with his frying pan.

The contest continued into the dark. But the soldiers, who were by now creating a big racket, kept shoving and jostling and wouldn't let them remain stationary. At first the Yugoslav and the Macedonian allowed themselves to be pushed, but soon they moved voluntarily—a step and a whack. Soldiers carrying burning branches lit the way out onto the main road, past paddocks and bush, and a little beyond it to the small township. It became obvious that, whacking along, they'd soon be entering the town. No one could stop the Yugoslav or the Macedonian now; certainly not the enthusiastic soldiers surrounding them. It had been attempted, first by the officers, then by the captain himself, but he quickly left off. He knew by then what he was up against, remembering the incident with the old rifles, a truckload of which had been delivered into the camp, some time ago, for rifle practice. The captain had requested them to enhance his own prestige and prove that he was a commander not of simple laborers but of soldiers ready for combat. He had to wait a long time for the consignment, and when the truck drove into the camp he was radiant. But the rifles remained in the camp for only one day. Word spread quickly, and soldiers began prowling about the locked storehouse where the rifles had been stacked. They gathered in small groups, arms akimbo or hands shoved deep into pants pockets, sizing up the strength of the wooden doors with secretive glances and flicks of the tongue, making sounds incomprehensible to the commander and officers. That same night, while the soldiers were asleep, the commander himself together with his officers loaded the rifles back onto the trucks and dispatched them out of the camp. Since then, no more weapons had been brought in.

The Yugoslav and the Macedonian kept up their contest—a stride and a whack. A group of soldiers, returning from work, stepped aside to make way for the rowdy procession of torchbearers accompanying the contestants amid yelling and bellowing. Then Weger turned up, walking on his own as usual, not from work but from the township, where he'd lately struck up a friendship with an old Australian who owned a piano and let him use it. Instead of stepping aside, Weger walked straight into the path of the duelists and would have gone on had the soldiers at the back not barred his way. It was the Macedonian's turn to deal a blow. He raised the frying pan—but stopped short, seeing Weger beside him in the light of the burning branches, and, instead of returning the blow, let his frying pan drop from his hand. The Yugoslav too, stayed his hand. Then, hurling his own pan like a plate into the night, he thrust Weger aside and swore to eternal friendship between Yugoslavs and Greeks; and in acknowledgment of Papadimitrio's persistence and staying power he was going to move in with Papadimitrio that very night.

Weger wasn't at all keen on sharing his tent with the Yugoslav as well, for living with Papadimitrio was like living on his own. On passing their tent in the evenings I could tell by their shadows on the canvas walls how they were sitting, each on his cot, and could hear Papadimitrio repeat his endless chant in low, somber tones. Papadimitrio and his stick were a familiar sight in the kitchen, where he occasionally procured a can of marmalade for Weger who, in the absence of chocolate, would take licks of marmalade from a teaspoon and read Schopenhauer before dropping off to sleep.

Most evenings Michailovitch got tipsy and liked a lively atmosphere around him. He had pinned up cover girls on his part of the tent and, as a token of friendship, a full-length poster on the slanting roof above Papadimitrio's cot. He had another one just like it, which he meant to pin up above Weger's in such a way that when Weger lay on his cot he'd have the whole length of the girl before him.

But Weger wouldn't have any of it, which surprised Michailovitch. He went up and tickled him. Weger wasn't amused. Michailovitch was, and roared with laughter, his drunken eyes gleaming as he twirled his handsome whiskers.

"Look at her! Look at her!" he shouted, pointing at the girl stretched out across the wall.

Weger didn't respond. But when, on entering their tent later that evening, I pointed at the girl on the poster, Weger remarked in German, *"Nun ja, die Gretchen Frage."*

Above his own cot he had pinned the photograph of a man.

"Otto Weininger," Weger explained—a young man who had written a philosophical work that had brought him fame. He had also been a woman-hater and, at the age of twenty-three, had put a bullet through his brains on the steps of the Beethoven Auditorium. Weger had cut the photo out of a book and pinned it up to shake off the Yugoslav and his assertion that the wall was too bare and needed decorating. Otto Weininger succeeded, at least around Weger's cot, in dislodging the Yugoslav's pinup girls.

Papadimitrio no longer looked into his prayer book but lay stretched out on his cot to gaze up at the girl on the poster above him. In the evenings the Yugoslav was away boozing or playing cards in the mess hut till late into the night. Papadimitrio rarely went there himself for, like Weger, he felt uncomfortable among people.

"I'm still running away from my past," Weger told me, "and the furthest spot is beside that Macedonian."

One day, however, the Macedonian tried to make Weger line up with us Jews in the camp. It was during Hanukkah, when a Jewish army chaplain had come to preach to the soldiers. On a Sunday morning when the men weren't working, we Jews had gathered in the mess hut and the rabbi, a tall graying man in the uniform of a high-ranking officer, got up on a bench, lit the candelabrum, and started his sermon.

"When I kindle the candles . . ." he intoned and began talking of the times when the Jews had lived in Palestine, of Antiochus the persecutor, and of the wars between Jews and Greeks.

Not only the Jewish soldiers had been in the mess hut at the time but also Greeks and others sitting at the farther end of the hall playing cards. They would hardly have paid any attention had the rabbi not begun raising his voice as he warmed up to his sermon, talking of the heroic deeds of the ancient Jews and of their constant struggle with the enemies of the Jewish God. He was quite oblivious to the hints given him by us to keep his voice down, for others at the back of the hall had begun taking notice and, here and there, a Greek looking up from his cards was sniffing the air and listening in. Someone whistled, another answered. Suddenly, a Greek with long sideburns flung down his cards, vaulted onto the table, and called for all pure-blooded Greeks to come over to his side. A commotion ensued as tables and benches were thrust aside and turned over. Amid a babble of Greek the word *Kanadesos* was bandied about—the nickname given to the Jews by the Greeks in the camp, just as we Jews, among ourselves, had labeled the Greeks *Gimmelech*. For several years the Greeks had been living in the same camp with us Jews quite unaware that we'd once been enemies and had even waged wars against each other. Now, on hearing the words of the rabbi, the Greeks were stirred and left the mess hut *en masse*. We Jews also filed out and took up positions on the parade ground opposite them, getting ready for a brawl.

When Papadimitrio, lying on his cot in the tent, heard the call for pure Greek blood, he got up and went, stick in hand, to take his place among his compatriots. Weger had also left the tent to find out what was going on, but he stood aside. Papadimitrio, observing Weger standing by himself, stepped out of his group and walked up to him. He took Weger by the arm, led him toward the Jewish camp, and went back to his Greeks, but on turning around he saw Weger standing apart once more. Again Papadimitrio walked up to him with lowered head and stick in hand.

"Beat the *Kanadesos!*" someone from the Greek side called out, not knowing that Papadimitrio and Weger shared a tent and were friends.

"Beat the *Kanadesos!*" they shouted, to encourage Papadimitrio.

But the Macedonian just stood there in silence, his head bowed low over Weger as one in mourning.

Then Michailovitch, astride a horse, galloped in among us. He often hired one in the township and rode it about the camp. When he saw the men standing in two separate groups he galloped in among them, assuming them to have made way for him. Pulling at the reins so that the horse reared, he proclaimed in a loud voice that his name was no longer Michailovitch, since Michailovitch the erstwhile leader of the Yugoslav nation had turned traitor; from now on he was to be called by his new name—Tito.

Next day, returning from work, Weger brought back with him the skull of an ox that he had picked up on the road. I was walking beside him carrying it part of the way. Weger thought it might come in handy for the lessons he meant to give Papadimitrio on the origin of man. For, straight after the incident with Michailovitch and his horse, which had diverted the excitement of the opposing groups onto the Yugoslav, Weger had sat down in their tent to explain to the Macedonian why he had stood apart, and why Papadimitrio ought not to have pushed him into the Jewish camp.

"Why ever not?" I asked.

"That's what had also puzzled Papadimitrio," Weger said, handing me the skull so he could wipe his glasses. We were stripped to the waist, for it was still very hot in the afternoon sun. There was a fence along one side of the road, and a little beyond it stretched the railway lines. The ground was pulverized earth, and a suffocating heat rose from it. Putting his glasses back on, Weger observed that living by oneself was a kind of luxury and as far as he was concerned he could live like that to the end of his days. He found it unbearable standing in line for food, shoving and being shoved against backs and shoulders. After the war, he assured me, he was going to live on a farm somewhere far away.

But several years after the war, Weger had come to Israel and turned up at the kibbutz where I had settled some time before.

One day about lunch time, as I was leaving the sheep pen where I was working then, I caught sight of Weger, apparently waiting for me. He was dressed in khaki as he had been in our army days, though a considerable time had passed since then. He stood with one knee slightly bent in shyness, smiling uncertainly, either on account of his short-sightedness or because he had refused to make up after a quarrel we'd had at one time and wasn't sure now how I'd receive him.

I took him to the dining hall for a meal, after which he informed me of his intention to stay on the kibbutz. The next day, as I went with him to collect his belongings, he admitted that he had already looked over several other kibbutzim but had found the food here most to his liking, particularly our barley soup, which reminded him of his home and childhood. When we reached his place it was too late to return, so I stayed the night. He turned his own narrow iron bed over to me and bedded down on the floor beside it. The gray blankets on the bed called to mind our years together in the army, and at the foot of the bed stood the kit bag, with his name and number still faintly discernible. A small photograph hung on the wall, and at closer scrutiny I recognized Otto Weininger. It occurred to me that, were I to peek under his bed, I'd discover there the skull of the ox Weger had brought home that day in order to teach Papadimitrio the origin of man.

The skull had been discovered one day under Weger's cot by the commander of our camp during one of his inspection tours. Like most of us, Weger was away at work, and only Papadimitrio was in the tent at the time. He was no longer collecting scraps of paper at the end of a stick but was repairing torn tents instead. He had by then taken a dislike to the skull and, when asked who it belonged to, readily explained that it was Private Weger's property. The commander remembered Weger on account of the incident with the piano in the mess hut, the one Weger often used to play on. One Sunday, happening to listen in, the commander asked him what he was playing. Then, shrugging the reply off with a paternal pat on his back, advised him to "leave Bach and all the other Mozarts alone" and strike up a tune the soldiers liked. Leaping onto the table, he clapped for silence and announced his plan for amusement in the camp: Girls from the township would be invited to dances and Private Weger would provide the music. Taken aback, Weger shook his head in violent protest. Still smiling, though vexed that a subordinate dared to contradict him in front of all the soldiers, the commander shot out a finger, nodding to Weger in support of his proposal. But Weger shook his head back at him, and for a moment both their heads moved in opposite directions in defiance of each other. Weger outshook the commander. When a number of soldiers backed the captain up with noisy interjections, Weger shook his head to all of them. He never touched the piano in the mess hut again. Unable to live down such a rebuff, the commander took every opportunity to settle accounts with him. Now, pouncing upon the skull, he had it chucked onto the garbage heap and gave orders that if Weger wished to see the skull of an ox he was to come and see him. And Weger did. He came to him straight from work, un-washed and all.

Seated on Weger's narrow bed I reminded him of all that, and Weger, on the makeshift bed on the floor, replied that what he'd been missing above all since arriving in Israel was a piano. He told me that he couldn't even afford to rent one now, with the little he earned planting trees and clearing stones for the Forest Commission. One day, however, while working in a kibbutz in front of the dining hall he caught sight of a piano within and had entered, pulled up a chair, and sat down to play. It was after dinner, and only those cleaning the tables were present. An elderly man went up to him and proposed that he stay on and become a member, for then he could play the piano to his heart's content. Such a thing hadn't occurred to him, and he'd almost been ready to accept the proposal. But the piano was broken—a veritable ruin—and the food was tasteless. However, taken with the idea, he'd begun making the rounds of kibbutzim in the vicinity to sample both food and pianos. He often found a piano, but then the food was poor, or if he liked the food, there was no piano. Until he came to my kibbutz.

Even before looking me up in the sheep shed he'd already set eyes on a grand piano on the stage of the communal hall. And after tasting the soup, which reminded him of home and childhood, he had resolved to settle in my kibbutz. He'd also struck up an acquaintance that same afternoon with the man in charge of the hall, a widower from Austria who played the fiddle, and in the evening members strolling through the kibbutz might have caught strains of music wafting through the open windows of the hall. At supper time Weger looked fresh, if somewhat flushed. He regretted not having looked me up earlier. Had he known of it he'd have joined my kibbutz long ago.

Early the next morning, when the air was still cool and moist, we set out for the kibbutz with all of Weger's belongings stuffed inside his kit bag and a small suitcase. The Arab house where Weger had lived stood at the far end of a field. The path leading from it to the road was a sandy track flanked by tall eucalyptus trees, beyond which green pasture and wasteland extended to isolated houses on both sides. Weger remarked that during the summer, when all was dried up, it reminded him of the Australian landscape where the army camp had been. We reminisced about the small country town, the stifling summer heat, the dusty road to the railway station, the skull of the ox he had picked up and which, on hearing the approach of a group of soldiers on their way to work, he had covered with his shirt so as not to attract their attention. The soldiers, marching in step, had now and then joined in the refrain of a song one of them was singing:

. . . *Yossel Shoite,*
Du geyst veren a soldat bei di Roite. *

Waiting for them to pass out of sight and hearing, Weger said that he bore people no malice but avoided being part of any crowd.

*". . . Yossel you fool,
You're going to be a soldier with the Reds."
[from the Yiddish.]

I reminded him of the slamming match between the Yugoslav and the Macedonian and how, instead of stepping aside, he had walked straight into the crush around them. Transferring the skull to his other arm he recalled that it had been a very dark night and that, on hearing the racket, he had thought that the soldiers had set fire to a tree, a popular pastime of theirs. But the fire had moved, advancing in his direction, and for a moment it had seemed as if they were leading someone to the stake, as in earlier times. Weger never finished what he was saying, because at that moment a herd of stampeding bulls and heifers had come charging at us. I leaped across the fence and shouted to Weger to do likewise, but he walked on, straight into the thudding herd. When the animals had passed and the cloud of dust had settled, he was standing a small distance from where I'd left him, still holding the skull under his arm though the shirt that had covered it was gone, swept along by the runaway herd and lying not far off, trampled into the dust. Weger handed me the skull so he could wipe his glasses again, and on the way to the camp he told me of an incident that had happened to him during his university days. He'd been walking to one of the lecture halls situated in a narrow lane in the ancient cobblestoned town when a gang of fellow students armed with sticks were advancing toward him. It had become popular by then to smash shop windows and beat up Jews. Owing to his shortsightedness he'd seen them only when they were almost upon him and there was no escape. All the gates and doors were shut in the early hours of the afternoon, when people took their naps. So he had simply walked on and passed through their midst.

Soon after Michailovitch drowned and Papadimitrio had been sent out of the camp, Weger had the tent all to himself. Even before sharing quarters with the Macedonian and the Yugoslav he had already cut himself off from all those he'd befriended during his first days in the army, resenting their stinginess and constant accounting for the bars of chocolate or slices of oranges one owed the other. Things had been altogether different with Papadimitrio and Michailovitch. Papadimitrio never turned down the proferred bar of chocolate, which he munched while humming his endless chant, and

Michailovitch couldn't care less about his belongings, which were usually scattered all over the tent. When he returned from his frequent visits to the township his pockets would bulge with bottles of beer for Weger and Papadimitrio, and after a lucky bout of gambling in the mess hut till late into the night he often brought back with him hot frankfurters or hamburgers purchased from the cooks there. Awakened by their savory smell Weger and Papadimitrio would sit up and, without a word, start munching in the dark, drowsily listening to Michailovitch going on endlessly in his own corner about how they never played cards, never got drunk, never had any fun, but lived lives as dull as dishwater. Weger had once given him a flashlight so he wouldn't stumble over things and cause a racket at night, waking everybody up. But Michailovitch, who misplaced the flashlight each evening, never ceased marveling at discovering it the next morning. Occasionally, after winning at cards, he'd treat his tentmates to drinks in the township pub or bring back with him juicy cuts of steak, which Papadimitrio would grill for them in the kitchen. Michailovitch never returned from a furlough empty-handed, and furloughs he got more than others, for even the officers were scared of him. Once, after all leaves were suspended indefinitely, the Yugoslav went to the captain, opened the fly of his pants, and showed him his penis. He came away with a leave pass for two weeks. That time he returned with a water bag so there'd always be cold water in the tent even during the hottest hours, and had hung it above the entrance right by Papadimitrio's cot, where there was a perpetual breeze. It happened to coincide with the time Weger had brought home the skull of the ox and had begun instructing Papadimitrio on the origin of man.

"Man comes from the monkey," Weger had taught Papadimitrio.

Weger was sitting on his cot with the skull, lit up by several candles stuck into its cavities, on a box beside him. Papadimitrio, stretched out on his back, kept moving his eyes from the pinup girl above him to the dripping water bag, watching the drops take shape, wax full, and gleam before plopping onto the blanket of his cot, where a dark blotch was forming gradually.

"People come from monkeys?" he asked, watching a new drop evolve.

His schemes for sailing home hadn't materialized, and with the extension of the war no more news reached him from his family in Greece. Every now and then he'd draw a photo of his wife and two kids from his breast pocket and look at it, humming his endless tune.

"Man comes from the monkey," Weger repeated, while Papadimitrio's finger traced another drop from the water bag to his blanket.

"Men, you say, come from monkeys?" he asked again, fixing his eyes upon the pinup girl on the poster above him.

Michailovitch entered and, on hearing what they were talking about, burst into laughter. Weger once again had amused him, and he swore that he'd tell the joke to everyone the next day. Let them all have a good laugh. Papadimitrio pointed a finger at the water bag, then at the growing blotch on his bed, and gestured to the Yugoslav to remove the bag. But Michailovitch took no notice. He stood twirling his blond whiskers, and when he laughed his square white teeth glittered.

The following morning Papadimitrio asked Weger if he still meant what he'd said the previous evening and pleaded with him not to repeat it. The Yugoslav would drum it all over the camp and make a laughing stock of him—the last thing he, Papadimitrio, wanted to see. "After all," he argued, "you're a learned man."

But Weger wouldn't budge.

This exchange had taken place in the morning before Weger left for work. When he returned in the evening, he found Papadimitrio lying on the cot, his eyes following each falling drop. The blotch on his bed had spread and soaked through to the under-blankets. When Michailovitch came in, Papadimitrio again pointed to the bag, but quite unconcerned, Michailovitch went out almost immediately to gamble at cards in the mess hut.

"Macedonians also come from monkeys?" Papadimitrio asked Weger.

"Everybody does," Weger replied.

That evening Papadimitrio asked no more questions, nor was he heard to hum. He just lay on his cot, his hand occasionally groping for the moist patch beneath him.

Next day Papadimitrio stepped up very close to Weger and laughed into his face.

"The Yugoslav is right! You're simply putting me on, aren't you!"

Weger shook his head. Then Papadimitrio stopped laughing and begged him not to do such a thing to him. They'd been friends for so long and he respected Weger. Let him admit that it wasn't true.

"But it is!" Weger insisted.

"They all laughed in the kitchen when the Yugoslav told them about it," Papadimitrio said, warning Weger that they might come to blows over it. But Weger stuck to his guns. Then, leaning forward, Papadimitrio asked, "And Jesus? What about Jesus?"

"Jesus, too."

Alone in the tent the following night, Papadimitrio suddenly sat up on his cot. Its blankets were by now thoroughly soaked. He picked up his stick, stepped outside into the dark, and made for the mess hut. The glow of lamps shining through canvas here and there guided his steps, though he'd also have found his way there blind-folded.

He entered the mess hut, stick tucked under his arm. It was noisy within, and the air was smoke-filled. He looked about him and walked up to where a soldier in a baker's cap was frying frankfurters to be sold later on. Bending over the frying pans Papadimitrio took a deep breath, his drooping lower lip smiling down at them. Passing several tables he paused momentarily beside a soldier sketching the contours of Jesus onto a black cross. The soldier somewhat resembled Weger—high forehead, long nose, and blue eyes behind thick lenses. Smiling up at Jesus, Papadimitrio hitched his stick more firmly under his arm and went on. He came to a table crowded with baccarat players and slowly scanned face after face. He heard music and caught sight of the Yugoslav sitting with four other soldiers playing poker. Next to him, on the floor, his feet tucked under him, a small Greek was playing a mandolin. The Yugoslav liked listening to music while gambling and had the Greek sitting at his feet strumming away on the instrument. Papadimitrio planted himself behind the Yugoslav who, smiling up at him and gesturing with a finger to his mouth to keep mum, took a pound note, spat on one side of it, and slapped it onto the forehead of the little Greek. The latter, feeling the note on his forehead, broke with added gusto into the very tune Papadimitrio was always humming to himself. Drawing the stick out from under his arm Papadimitrio brought it down with both hands onto the Yugoslav's head, replaced it under his arm, and strode out of the mess hut with his own head raised high.

The Yugoslav, crumpling very slowly, was still smiling as he lay blood-spattered on the ground. Later, one of his fellow gamblers told us that he'd just then held a winning hand. The Yugoslav was taken to the hospital, where he remained for three months, whereas Papadimitrio was deprived of his stick. Now that his head was uplifted, he was given a new occupation—to walk about the camp and mend torn tents.

The kibbutz lay several miles from the bus stop, and while waiting for a passing vehicle to take us up we surveyed the hills overlooking the valley, the orchards touching those hills in the distance, and the vineyard bordering the roadside where we stood. The vineyard, sloping gently down to a wadi dried up with the summer, extended to the other side, where it rose with the same gentle slope, ending beside a small forest of eucalyptus trees. The two slopes resembled the wings of a bird in flight. A man plowing near the wadi was guiding horse and plow between the rows of vines and was slowly advancing toward us.

"It's your friend, the widower from Austria," I told Weger. "Only remember to speak English with him, for he's in love with that language."

Weger's head almost shook with his protest. Still back in Australia he had been at odds with both the English language and the British Empire. That's why he had never taken on Australian citizenship. After his discharge he'd been offered a post at the university provided he became a naturalized citizen. But by the time he was called upon to swear his oath of fealty to the British Crown he'd already decided to throw in his lot with the Jewish State and saw fit to tell the official that he disapproved of British policy in Palestine. He was no longer required to take the oath and also forfeited the university post. That's when he had turned to the Zionist Organization to learn Hebrew with the aim of going to Israel. He knew little about Zionism, and, when the secretary inquired which party he wished to join, Weger, assuming that she was joking, had answered in the same vein: "The Christian Zionist Party." The girl had given him a second, sidelong look, and afterward he was called into another room, questioned tactfully, and given a long list to choose his party from.

The widower from Austria was coming toward us, his head bobbing in unison with that of his horse. Both man and animal glistened with perspiration.

"A real pioneer!" Weger murmured.

The other waved his hand in recognition. He pulled up his horse and stepped out of the rows of vines, striding toward us. Weger grasped the extended hand.

"Ah, our Australian!" he said admiringly. He was eager to know if Weger had seen Queen Elizabeth during her recent visit to Australia.

"Weger keeps away from women," I said, recalling how he used to back out of the cinema just before the end of a film to avoid having to look at the Queen appearing on the screen during the playing of the anthem. That was when he had been disqualified for Australian citizenship while waging his lone battle against British policy in Palestine. One day he also heard the British anthem being played at a function of the party he had joined. That was something he hadn't bargained for! Taking a look at his membership card and discovering that this party advocated a Jewish State within the British Commonwealth, he had immediately cancelled his membership. Though he'd been told that his card was an old one and that their policy had changed, Weger remained suspicious and joined a party that had always fought for a Jewish State without partners.

Weger began working in the kitchen, washing innumerable dishes, and later on took charge of the huge boiler that supplied steam to both kitchen and laundry. He had turned down a teaching job, giving his poor Hebrew as the pretext. For here in Israel he all but forgot the little Hebrew he'd acquired already, and could scarcely put even the two words *"yesh kitor"* together to announce to the women in the kitchen that there was steam. By the time he reached the kitchen window he'd often forget how to say it.

Weger made friends with the widower from Austria, who occasionally accompanied him on his violin. The latter had free access to the auditorium, and they frequently played together. He had given Weger a key of his own to the hall, and Weger could be heard playing the piano there till late into the night or in the early mornings when he didn't have to go to work. The widower had introduced Weger to another Anglophile friend of his, a spinster from Canada who, he had confided to him, had been in love with a ship's captain, though he'd never been able to figure out if the captain had left her or had drowned at sea. She had come to Israel and joined the kibbutz, living here like a nun in a cloister. The widower and the nun conversed only in English and called England the "British Isles." During one of her visits there she wrote letters to him addressed in the old English style, using the title *Esquire*. The letters were full of descriptions of the palaces she had seen and the names of royalty she had rubbed shoulders with at garden parties. They showed Weger an album into which they had pasted pictures of the Queen at her coronation and of all the members of the royal family. In the winter the nun's room was warmer than Weger's, for, being an old-timer, she had a better room and a proper heater; her chairs were softer and her shelves were full of English books. Whenever Weger and the widower dropped in, she'd serve them tea brewed the English way.

Their friendship had lasted until the day the widower had asked Weger to play a waltz and Weger had refused indignantly. Play Strauss after Beethoven and Brahms! Disregarding the remark, the widower had struck up a waltz, nodding to Weger to join in. But Weger sat at the piano in frozen silence. The widower started the waltz all over again, not to tease Weger but rather to urge him on, seeing no harm in it at all. Infuriated, Weger said that, had he known such a thing were possible, he'd never have played with him in the first place. If so, the widower retorted, he could damn well play the piano somewhere else, and a day or so later he changed the lock to the hall.

Blue with rage and trembling all over, Weger came to see me. He wasn't going to take it lying down, he said, and wanted me to help him force the lock. I did my best to talk Weger out of getting into a fight with the widower, who had been in charge of the hall for years. But Weger wouldn't listen to me and dashed outside. Later that evening he was back, asking me to spend the night with him, for he was scared to remain by himself. On our way to his room he told me that he had tried forcing the lock, and the widower, passing by just then, had looked on, grinning broadly. Walking alongside me Weger kept up a one-sided wrangle, demanding to know why the widower had changed the lock and why he wouldn't let him use the hall. Weren't hall and piano the property of the entire kibbutz?

Afterward, in his room while sharing a snack with me, he calmed down a little. He lived in a kind of cellar and now, as once before, he turned his narrow bed over to me, bedding down on the floor beside it. Several boxes served as bookshelves, and a large packing case without a lid as a wardrobe. The photo of Otto Weininger hung on the wall, properly framed now. Years ago in the tent it had only been pinned to the canvas, like the pictures Michailovitch had cut out of magazines, though after he had been taken to the hospital his pinups, being tattered, had peeled off one by one. Only the water bag, completely dried up, had remained in its place. Papadimitrio had taken once more to chanting his monotonous prayers in front of the opened prayer book while Weger was occupied with reading. Now that his head was upright he could be seen walking about the camp during the day equipped with shears, a long needle, and a ball of string, and wherever a tent was in need of repair he'd dismantle it, mend it, and pitch it again. In the evenings he'd munch the chocolate Weger offered him or together with him lick spoonfuls of the marmalade he had procured from the kitchen. He'd stop chanting now and then and, as he used to in the beginning, would sit opposite Weger and stare at him reading his book.

One such evening Michailovitch had turned up again. He looked different now, a mere shadow of his former self. He had entered quietly and, smiling sheepishly, had sat down on his cot. His face was lean without the whiskers, and although his teeth were still strong and square, they shone forth as from an alien mouth. He no longer called himself Michailovitch or Tito, but went by his real name—Yanovitch.

The Yugoslav and the Macedonian became good pals and were constantly seen in each other's company. Michailovitch neither gambled nor drank now but kept trailing Papadimitrio like an obedient son. He even helped him repair torn tents. In the evenings the two would sit together in the mess hut beside the little oven where frankfurters were being fried and sold, both smiling down at the frying pan that sizzled and spurted with oil. Occasionally, Papadimitrio would draw from his pocket the photograph of his wife and kids and show it to Michailovitch, who'd ask him for their names and ages in a voice that was both gentle and meek.

Late one afternoon we returned from work to find almost all our tents overturned and slashed to pieces. We heard from Michailovitch that soon after everyone had gone and the camp was virtually deserted, Papadimitrio had begun tearing down the tents and slashing away at them. He'd even asked him, Michailovitch, to help him with the job. Accustomed to seeing Papadimitrio with his shears dismantling tents and pitching them again, the few men left in the camp had paid no heed to what he was doing, and by the time they realized what he was up to, almost all the tents were ruined and Papadimitrio had vanished into the bush. He was caught several days later and dispatched to a mental hospital.

Now that the Yugoslav was by himself, he let his whiskers grow again and, when they were long enough to be twirled as before, he leaped onto the table in the mess hut to announce that he was Tito once more and that no one could equal a Yugoslav. That was when he had upset Weger's plate and both had agreed to test their endurance in the river.

It was still dark when Weger rose from his bed on the floor, but by the time he returned and roused me, it was broad daylight. He stood near me unable to utter a word, but later on I learned that he'd gotten into a fight with the widower from Austria. Awakening in the dead of night, the thought of the widower not letting him go back to sleep, Weger had gone to meet him on his way to work to have it out with him, to ask him why he had changed the lock and denied him access to the piano. But the widower, seeing Weger beside him, was so startled at the sudden confrontation that he jerked his head aside as if in anticipation of a blow. At that, Weger's hand had reached out instinctively and landed the very blow that the other had prematurely wanted to ward off.

Weger was called to account before the Arbitration Committee and told to apologize, but he couldn't bring himself to do it. He was in the doldrums about it for quite a while. It was then that he decided to accept the German reparation money, after all. He'd buy his own piano and a prefabricated hut to put it in, and would no longer have to rely on the widower's favors. But that idea had to be ruled out, for he'd be required to hand his money over to the kibbutz, after which all the members would decide how it was to be spent; and acquiring a second piano seemed unlikely.

"But it's my money!" Weger argued when I tried explaining to him that owning money ran counter to the principles of the kibbutz. If so, he said, he'd go to Germany, purchase the piano and the prefab himself, and return with both to the kibbutz.

With that in mind, Weger left his kit bag and belongings with me and the suitcase full of books with the nun. She and I were waiting for him to come back, and whenever we ran into each other Weger was our common topic. The nun was tall and slim and may once have been pretty. She'd question me about Weger's past, and I would tell her of our years spent together in the army, about Michailovitch the Yugoslav and Papadimitrio the Macedonian. She was intrigued by what had brought Weger to Israel. I then told her about a visit he had paid Papadimitrio at the mental hospital where he had remained after the war. Weger might not otherwise have recognized him, but he caught sight of him sitting on a bench in that characteristic pose of his and had sat down beside him. He talked to him about old times, but Papadimitrio didn't respond. Then, sharing the silence with him, Weger seemed to hear him say again, "Where you come from, that's where home is." And after he left Papadimitrio the words began to haunt him. He had just finished reading a book by Martin Buber about God and Hasidism, and only long afterward did he tell me how Papadimitrio and Martin Buber, merging in his mind, had brought him to Israel.

Meanwhile no word came from Weger.

"He'll return," I told the nun. "I'm sure he will."

But all that came was a postcard addressed to her, which she waved in her hand as she saw me coming toward her. In widely spaced handwriting Weger informed us that he was lodging with an elderly couple he had known in former times, that he had bought a piano and was meanwhile earning his keep by giving private lessons in English.

"He'd never have left if it hadn't been for that piano," the nun remarked, recalling how Weger had shaken with rage and his thin lips had turned blue. I then told her of another incident back in our army days that had caused a similar rage in him. Soon after moving into our tent, his countrymen had organized a New Year's Eve party, asking everyone to chip in with a shilling, but Weger had given only half a shilling; and when he turned up and was shown to his seat he saw half a banana, half an orange, and half a glass of wine set out for him. He had stormed into our tent, shaking all over and blue with rage, and all that night he tossed about on his cot, unable to calm down.

At that moment the widower from Austria joined us, interrupting our chat. The nun took her leave and, as I was watching her receding form, another scene from those days flashed in my mind.

The sun was already setting by the time Weger stumbled up the sloping bank after having swum in the river all day long. He was running toward the place where he had left his clothes but collapsed before he got there, curling up on the grass like a baby. When I reached him he was blue all over and shivering as though he had been seized by a spasm. I talked to him and he responded only with a smile through his chattering teeth. I fetched his clothes, covered him with them, and sat down on the grass beside him, waiting until he stopped shivering altogether.

Translated by MARGARET BIRSTEIN

KLEIN

Yitzhak Ben-Mordechai

For a long time, perhaps too long, Ida Klein lived alone, without a husband. The upheaval of the war scattered them about like dust blown by the wind, and nobody knew what to do. Nobody knew whether to run away or wait for better times, nobody knew whether to believe in the insistent whisper of the rumors. The tide of events was swifter and stronger than they were, buffeting even the strongest and most confident between terror and hope, action and apathy.

And so it came about that the vigorous, red-cheeked Klein, robust in body and spirit, who had recently married and built his wife a solid stone house—this same Klein rose early one morning, kissed his warm, still drowsy wife, and set out on horseback for his stables. He did not return at noon—but this was no cause for concern, since he sometimes liked lunching with the grooms.

In the evening Ida stood at the window waiting for the tall figure on horseback, for the moment when the rider would recognize his waiting wife and wave his hand in greeting. With all her body she waited for Klein, feeling the hot blood throbbing in her thighs, coursing through her veins and stirring up a strange storm in her body, quickening and shortening her breath. Day and night, with a gradually dwindling shame, she would eagerly await his warm, solid body, the tempests it would stir up in her body, the galloping rides to the peak of happiness. All these new sensations filled her with astonishment and delight, and now she stood looking impatiently at the people passing by until it grew dark.

When night fell, anxiety began seeping into her heart. As she put on her warm clothes she kept imagining that she heard the horse's hoofs clattering on the cobblestones. But the road remained empty, black and mysterious, and in the windows of the houses lights flickered and shone. For a moment she stood outside without moving, and then she went to wait in the house of her uncle Gantz, the wine merchant. She listened to his soothing words, to the giggling of his daughters, and saw the exchange of meaningful looks between her uncle and his wife. The over-sweet tea did nothing to dispel the chill that had seized hold of her, and when he harnessed the horses to his cart and wrapped himself in his cape she sat beside him silently, huddled up in her coat, with her hands in her sleeves and the wind whipping her face. They drove on and on, down the long, empty road, until they reached the stables. As they rode Gantz smoked one cigarette after another, and the burning tips looked like red spots on his face.

The warm smell of the horses rose in her nostrils, and she heard the barking of the dogs. Gantz banged on the cabin door, taking no notice of the barking dogs. The grunts of Lashek the watchman mingled with the squeaking of the hinges and the locks, and Ida heard Gantz speaking in the rural dialect; she heard the hostility in the watchman's voice. According to him, he knew nothing. The master had been there in the afternoon, he had seen him with his own eyes. And later on, gentlemen from the city had been there. Buying or selling, no doubt. He didn't know what they wanted.

"And Klein?"

"He was here. In the afternoon, he even bawled out one of the stable boys. You can ask the boy. He's not a liar. And then he left."

"When?"

"Later on, in the afternoon. Toward evening."

"Was it already dark?"

"No, before dark. The master left before dark."

"Where did he go?"

"He just rode off. The same as always."

"Did he go home?"

"Where else? The master doesn't do business at night! Everybody goes home at night. The only one who doesn't go home is me, the night watchman."

"Did you see what direction Klein took?"

"No, I didn't. I didn't see anything."

The dogs were leashed to his forearm. Their barking split Ida's ears. Gantz scratched the back of his neck and blew his nose. The chill penetrated her bones, and she smelled Lashek's sour breath and saw the white stubble on his face. As if from a great distance she heard Gantz' uncertain voice saying, "Come along, Ida, let's go home."

In Gantz' house his wife turned one of her daughters out of her bed and put Ida to bed between the warm sheets. Whispers reached her from the corner where Gantz lay with his wife, but she couldn't make out the words. In her sleep she heard the crack of a whip and the galloping of horses' hoofs, and in the morning she woke early to the sound of Gantz' moist coughing. She heard Gantz' shoes squeaking and his nose being blown. Then the door creaked: Gantz had gone to sell his wine. Silently she rose and dressed herself, and silently she slipped out and went home. There she took up her post by the window and saw the sun breaking out of the distant horizon and smelled the good, fresh smell of the dawn. All day long she went on standing by the window, as if she had been nailed to the spot, and the next day too. After a month, when all hope of seeing Klein riding up on his horse was lost, Ida sold the flourishing stables, deposited the money in a bank in the big city, and wondered what she should do next.

During all this time she never stopped hearing the thud of horses' hoofs galloping in the distance, and in her mind's eye she saw Klein riding at their head, bending low over his tall horse. His figure was like a silhouette and his face, for some reason, began to blur in her memory. The horses galloped without stopping, round and round in wide circles, shattering clods of earth as they galloped. And even when Klein galloped toward her, he never seemed to come any closer. Sometimes he was no more than a tiny dot on the landscape, disappearing into the distance.

Perhaps this was why Ida would sometimes take the bundle of photographs out of their paper parcel in the chest and contemplate them with a certain stirring of emotion. In the pictures Klein looked alive; his face was clear, but as soon as she tied them up again and put them away his face vanished from her memory and all that remained was the silhouette galloping toward her and never coming any closer.

In financial matters she was advised by Gantz. He urged her to withdraw her money from the bank and transfer it to another, safer country. Because in their country, he said, there was no knowing what the morrow would bring. Rumors and all kinds of stories were rife, and they reached her ears too. She took his advice, and soon afterward he told her that now she too must leave for another country. War was about to break out and terrible times lay ahead. She must come with them, to Palestine.

Ida had no idea why war was about to break out, but Gantz' words echoed the feeling in the air. The months sped swiftly by and from her window she saw the seasons change, summer turning into autumn. Klein had disappeared without a trace; nobody knew anything, nobody had seen, nobody had heard. And all she had left was his galloping silhouette.

One day she went with Gantz to the big city, to a tall building with a flag flying from its roof. She signed many papers, and so did Gantz. He took various officials aside and held whispered consultations with them, a worried look on his smiling face. For the next few weeks she saw the evident signs of strain on his face, but at last he announced triumphantly that the passports had arrived, everything had been satisfactorily arranged. And now all that remained was for them to buy their tickets and set sail as soon as possible for the warm shores of Palestine.

2

On the train on their way to the port Ida imagined that she heard horses galloping behind them. She was squeezed into a narrow compartment with the entire Gantz family, but even the chattering of the daughters, all dressed up like young ladies, and the incessant clattering of the wheels could not dull the sound of the horses' hoofs. She looked out of the window and saw the flat earth, the fields and the villages gliding by. All the way to their destination Klein followed her, and when they reached the port and climbed onto the deck of the ship she felt his eyes on her body, watching her from afar.

The next day, as the ship set sail, she searched the crowd on the docks with her eyes, but she recognized no one. Opposite her was a solid mass of people, warehouses, quays, jetties—and the farther away she sailed the smaller they grew, disappearing into the waves. Now there was a vast ocean separating her from Klein, and she knew that the horses could not cross the water, and Klein would be able to follow her no further.

Suddenly she felt a great pain growing in her chest and her breasts —her arms and her hands gripping the railing. The damp air clouded her mind, and she said to Gantz, who was standing next to her, that she felt nauseous. Gantz' wife placed a damp handkerchief on her forehead and Gantz said that it was only a symptom of seasickness and nothing to worry about. Even seasoned sailors succumbed to this peculiar affliction; it was nothing serious and would soon pass. Gantz' elder daughter, Dina, felt giddy too, and the two of them lay on their bunks in the narrow cabin, one bunk on top of the other, opposite Gantz's wife groaning in her sleep with rheumatic pains.

In Palestine, underneath the boldly shining sun, Ida knew that Klein was lost to her forever. She no longer saw his galloping silhouette or heard the distant echo of beating hoofs, and as the months slipped past, Klein was transformed into a frozen figure resting in the dark depths of her memory. The horses, too, vanished as if they had never been. Every now and then longings stirred in her for the happy nights, for the joys and delights Klein had created in her body—but these, too, became less and less frequent. To her distress she lost the bundle of photographs, perhaps on the journey, and thus she remembered only the postures and poses: she sitting with her arms folded and Klein standing behind her, proud and erect; Klein wearing a high-crowned hat, leaning on the barred iron gate; Klein on horseback in a cavalry officer's uniform, tall and noble. Sometimes she tried to remember his face—and she could not do so. At first she wondered about this, but in the course of time she stopped wondering and she stopped trying.

3

At the beginning they stayed in a hotel, and Gantz ran all over town until he found somewhere for them to live. It was a three-room apartment, close to the commercial center. Gantz and his family took up two of the rooms, and the third was given to Ida. Although she tried at first to find a place of her own, Gantz was adamant. They were in a new, strange country, he warned her, and she had to be careful. A woman alone led men's thoughts astray, and there were a lot of Arabs around, too. And especially in the case of a woman like her, young and beautiful, as she herself knew very well. Surely one tragedy was enough for her.

Ida acquiesced, without understanding why a woman alone should lead men's thoughts astray, or what made the Arabs different from anyone else. She became more involved in the affairs of the Gantz family, and as time passed she found herself growing increasingly close to Gantz' daughter Dina. The latter had suddenly matured—her body had rounded out—and in the early hours of the evening, when the fading light was soft and dim in the room, she would come to chat and gossip about their acquaintances in the town. The gossip was entertaining and innocent enough, but things didn't stop there.

Dina, like her father, was discreet. In the beginning the conversation touched delicately on Klein, his habits, his stables, his skill as a rider. Ida would drag up all kinds of details from the depths of her memory and tell them to Dina as if she were repeating things she had read in a novel. As the hour grew later and the dusk deeper Dina's eyes would begin to glitter and her questions grew more intimate—inquisitive, insistent questions, prying into the details of Ida's relations with Klein. Dina would ask her questions with a kind of shrewdness, sly and innocent at the same time. And although Ida was well aware of what Dina was after, she felt a strange, new pleasure rising in her as she answered the questions. The darkness in the room seemed to her like a gathering fog, with only Dina's eyes gleaming in it, like two bright embers. In a dreaming voice she would describe how Klein would take her in his arms, undress her, garment by garment, and slide his hands over her body, from head to foot, cupping her flesh in his hands and trampling it like a horse. Dina demanded more and more, and Ida hid nothing from her.

Afterward, at supper time, the fog would fade away and she would sit and listen, rather bored, to Gantz discussing the state of his affairs, the people of the town, and his many plans. Recently Gantz had opened a liquor store with facilities for drinking on the premises, a kind of tavern, and with his native business acumen he soon succeeded in attracting customers. Ida had passed the place on a number of occasions and had seen people sitting on high chairs, leaning their elbows on a long, high table. Topics of conversation at the tavern ranged far and wide, embracing the war raging in Europe and the comings and goings of the people of the town. Over supper Gantz would tell them about his day, and Ida, in her boredom, would be sorry that her hours of intimacy with Dina were over.

These evening hours, with the memories of her pleasures and the awakening ghost of Klein, were like stolen hours of happiness. The memories came thick and fast, rising one after the other into her thoughts. In whispered words she would tell Dina all the things that Klein had done to her and all the things that she had done to him. It was like a conspiracy between her and Dina, and between the two of them and Klein. From time to time Dina would peep around the edge of the door to see if anyone was listening.

After supper Ida would return to her room and read her books. She borrowed the books from the local library, hesitantly at first and then with increasing enthusiasm. The books told of love and disappointment, and all kinds of fascinating adventures, and she read them with an avid curiosity. Here and there, when she walked down the street, she noticed men staring at her, but none of them attracted her. For some reason she had no wish to meet people or make friends with them. She spent a lot of time in her room with Dina or with her thick library books.

But Dina was fast becoming a woman in her own right, and even Hedva, Gantz' younger daughter, had begun to develop curves. In the outside world the war expanded and spread from country to country. Ida began to work in a women's underwear factory, where she sewed pink brassieres of various sizes. Dina was already quite the young lady, and every now and then, from her window, Ida would catch sight of young men escorting her. The nightly visits to her room became less frequent, and it seemed that Dina no longer needed her stories. Ida's money was still in the foreign bank, where she could not touch it because of the war. But when the war was over, Gantz told her, she would be rich. The interest alone, he said, would be enough for her to live on.

At Dina's wedding Gantz wore a dark suit and a top hat. The guests sang and danced and got drunk on the lavish supply of wine. Although the war was raging fiercely on all sides, there was a strange gaiety in the town, which was reflected in the eyes of the people. Klein was swallowed up in the recesses of time, together with the memory of her nocturnal joys, and Dina already had stories of her own to tell.

4

The months passed and turned into years, and still the nations fought. At supper time Gantz told them that the whole of Europe lay in ruins, Berlin and London were on fire, Paris was occupied, and in the deserts too the opposing armies had begun to fight. At the factory Ida heard stories about men and women, widows and refugees. A short woman who threaded elastic through blue panties bemoaned the fate of her sister, stranded here in town with her two children while her husband rotted somewhere at the ends of the earth, and who knew if she would ever see him again. People, so they said, were being massacred like flies, and even those who managed to escape were broken vessels. Ida heard the stories and the rumors, and sometimes she remembered Klein. Now Klein was no more than a name to her, and their one year of marriage seemed remote and forgotten.

Once, toward evening, when she was sitting in her room and trying to read the novel in her hand in the dim light of dusk, Gantz came and sat down opposite her. He lowered his eyes and stared at his shoes. There were signs of emotion on his face, and while she was still wondering why he had come to her room she heard his moist voice speaking. There's news, he said, evidence, about Klein. A witness had seen Klein in captivity, being taken to the concentration camps, the camps nobody came back from. There was a witness who had seen everything.

Ida looked at him without understanding why he was so excited. She herself knew very well that Klein was gone, that there was no hope of ever seeing him again. Gantz fell silent for a moment and said that from now on everything would be different. His voice was eager. With the help of the one witness they would find others; he would take care of it himself. Ida asked what they needed more witnesses for and Gantz laughed impatiently. Didn't she understand, he said, that now she would no longer be an *aguna,* a woman whose husband was missing; she would be able to marry again, there were witnesses to his death. The war would soon be over, the defeat of the wicked was imminent, he knew it, and the right man would come along. She would have plenty of money, money that belonged to her by right. From now on she was the legal inheritor. Everything would be different, she was still young, not yet thirty years old.

At supper she chewed her food without tasting it. Hedva looked at her curiously. Ever since Dina had left home there was a kind of emptiness around the table, for Hedva took after her mother, quiet and watchful. Ida did not tell Gantz that she had no desire to marry again—never mind what happened—and allowed him to make his plans.

And just as he had said, the war came to an end—although it made no difference to Ida. People went about their business as before, and their faces showed no change. In the underwear factory she heard terrible tales of the atrocities perpetrated in Europe, about the camps, about starvation and death. The numbers cited sounded impossible, but Gantz was adamant: It was all true, every word.

After the war was over, people who had survived the hell in Europe began to appear: pale, emaciated, cowed, speaking foreign languages. The Gantz family and Ida had already mastered the mysteries of the Hebrew language, and Gantz even peppered his speech with a few common phrases and words in Arabic. In the factory Ida saw one of the survivors, in strange clothes, and listened to her terrible stories. And sometimes she wondered if Klein, too, had met his death in such cruel circumstances.

After some time had passed, Gantz told her that he had found another witness. The witness had seen Klein in a remote camp somewhere on the northern borders of Russia. And he had no doubt whatsoever that Klein was dead: It was the cursed railway line that had killed the prisoners in the thousands, working in the terrible cold from dawn to dusk; none had survived. Ida bowed her head—not because of Klein, but because of Gantz' scheming. And now, said Gantz, there's nothing to it—two witnesses are enough. As for her, she didn't have to do a thing. He would take care of everything. Wasn't he her uncle, wasn't he like her own father? And besides, now she would come into her money. The war was over, international trade had begun again. She was a rich woman.

And thus, on the authority of three rabbis, Ida became a widow. God willing, said one of the rabbis, God willing, she would live to raise a family in Israel, a great *mitzvah*. She took the signed document and put it away in a drawer. What difference does it make, she said to herself.

But Gantz thought otherwise. Now that she was a free woman, she should start going out in company. She had wasted enough time sitting at home reading rubbishy novels. Dina was already married and Hedva too, God willing, would soon be a married woman. Surely she didn't want to stay single all her life? Gantz urged her to throw away her old clothes and buy new ones, to go to the parties and celebrations that were held in town from time to time. At these parties she wore her new clothes and met friendly, cheerful men. She was often invited to dance, she sometimes laughed at the men's jokes and witticisms, but whenever one of them asked her to go out with him alone she would become evasive and would refuse.

Months went by and Dina gave birth to her first son, and soon afterward Hedva married too. And now, said Gantz, now only Ida was left at home. And if she was unable to find a husband for herself, he would do it for her. There was no need for her to upset herself —he wasn't going to put pressure on her or force her into anything. Everything would work out for the best; all she had to do was put her trust in him.

And thus Anshel began coming to visit.

5

At first, as if by chance, Gantz mentioned that an old friend of his was coming, a friend he hadn't seen for years. Ida herself knew what the war had done to people's lives, and now, suddenly, by sheer chance, they had come face to face in the street. It was fate. Who would have hoped to find Anshel among the living, and here in Tel Aviv of all places? Of course he had asked him to come and visit them at home, eat and talk with them, see familiar faces. He was coming the very next day, in the evening. And if Anshel came a little early, Gantz urged Ida to keep him company until he got home from work.

The next day, in the afternoon, Ida sat by the window and looked at the people walking past. With a certain indifference she thought of this Anshel who was about to disturb her routine. At this time of day she liked reading her love stories, so full of adventure and romance. The stories were all about the relations between men and women, and no matter how deep the despair they always ended in great happiness. In the most moving parts she could not hold back the tears that gathered in her eyes. Whenever she came to the end of one of her books she would be so sorry at having to part from the heroes that she would sometimes read the same book over again two or even three times, concentrating on the most stirring and exciting parts.

Through the window she saw a tall man, and when he stopped opposite the house she saw his face. A moment later she heard the doorbell ring and then she heard voices. Gantz' wife greeted the guest, since Gantz himself had not yet come home from the tavern. And then there was a knock at Ida's door. She opened the door and Gantz' wife, giggling in embarrassment, asked if she would mind keeping the visitor company in her room until her husband arrived. Ida saw the innocence in his face and a new sensation stirred inside her. Hesitantly Anshel entered her room. Gantz' wife disappeared on some pretext, and silence fell. And then Anshel smiled.

That evening Gantz came home late. The whole thing seemed to have been prearranged by Gantz and his wife, but Ida could see on Anshel's face that he knew nothing about it. Gantz' wife served tea and cake and stole glances at Ida. Anshel spoke quietly, in a soft voice, and radiated a kind of tranquillity that enveloped her and filled the whole room. Gradually evening fell and Ida suddenly heard her own voice telling him about the books and their heroes, about the factory and the war that was now over.

At supper Gantz put on a jovial air and asked Anshel when he was going to ask Ida to go out with him to a café or the theater. And thus the next day the two of them found themselves sitting on the terrace of a café overlooking the sea next to a band playing sentimental tunes. Anshel told her about his desire to work in the garment industry, since that was his trade. In Europe he had been the owner of a textile factory. He had a little money of his own, and he would be able to borrow some too. Gantz, for example, would be sure to lend him something.

At that moment Ida remembered her own money, lying uselessly in the foreign bank. When she told Anshel that she too would be able to lend him some money, perhaps even a considerable amount, the memory of Klein, his warm, firm body, suddenly flashed through her mind. In the presence of Anshel she felt a kind of calm relaxation—a sensation whose like she had never known before, neither in her life with Klein nor afterward. With Klein she had known stormy feelings, her own burning body, her abandonment to his wild, galloping passion. Anshel thanked her and said that perhaps there would be no need for him to take her money. Then they danced. And his hands brushed her arms and back.

Anshel was different, of that she had no doubt. With Anshel she strolled down the streets in the evenings or on Saturday morning and talked. It seemed that she was unloading things that had been bottled up in her for years. The words poured out of her mouth as Anshel listened with a kindly expression on his face. Again and again she contemplated the innocence that made his face beautiful and she wondered when he would come into her body. A tense expectation was already stirring in her limbs, mingling with the memory of distant sensations coming back to life. And on Saturday evenings, when they danced on the terrace overlooking the sea, borne on the current of the music, she longed for him to clasp her ardently to his body, like the passionate men in her books, like Klein.

6

Shortly after the war, whose echoes alone had reached them, the country began to seethe. At first the signs were insignificant and unregarded, and then they grew more violent and turned into a long, drawn-out struggle. Every day the newspapers reported additional incidents: People were arrested and imprisoned, army camps were attacked, one whole wing of a big hotel was blown up with everyone in it, and from time to time the town was placed under curfew. The cafés along the promenade emptied of their occupants, and even the strains of the music sounded dulled.

In the factory Ida heard about the terrorists ruthlessly fighting the British. Anshel seemed indifferent to all this, but Gantz followed events with great interest. When Anshel came to dinner with them Gantz would discuss the latest news with him. Anshel spoke little and allowed Gantz to expound his opinions at length and analyze trends in detail. Ida too knew that the British had to be expelled from the country, but nevertheless, recalling their politeness and civility, she thought it should be done differently.

The tide of events moved swiftly. In the factory the women spoke excitedly of important decisions about to be made, about the declaration of an independent state. Passions grew more and more inflamed and in the end another war broke out—this time it was here, and not far away in Europe—and Gantz held forth about the Egyptian invasion and the bloody battles. After a while Anshel too was conscripted into the army, although Ida doubted his ability to contribute much to the war effort. In the evenings she would go to visit him, standing next to the fence of the training camp on the outskirts of Tel Aviv.

Anshel's textile works were deserted. Only a few months before he had bought the machinery, and just when things were beginning to run smoothly the war broke out. There was fighting now in all parts of the country and Anshel was sent to the southern front, as a gunner in the ranks. In the factory Ida heard about what was happening at the front, about the victories and the defeats, and more than once she found herself, to her surprise, worrying about Anshel. When he came home on short leaves he would sit silently and allow Gantz to analyze the progress of the war without interruption.

In his letters Anshel wrote to her about the war. Most of what he wrote she already knew, for in the novels she read wars broke out too, and men wrote letters from the front to their sweethearts. She answered him in long letters describing life in the town, the food shortages, the sorrow and the hope. His letters arrived irregularly; sometimes they came in batches, one after the other, and sometimes they were delayed for various reasons. And then, in one of his letters, Anshel departed from his usual custom: At the end of a rather confused and embarrassed confession he wrote that he wanted to marry her—and for a moment Ida wondered if she were reading a passage in one of her novels.

For a few days she put off writing. Then, hesitantly, she wrote that they would have to wait until the end of the war, and then, she imagined there would be nothing to prevent their getting married. At the bottom of the page, next to her signature, she wondered whether to add something of a more intimate and personal nature, the kind of thing the heroines in the novels would have written. Later on, in the evening, she took up a book and began to read, and between the pages and the lines she wondered if she really loved Anshel.

When the war did not come to an end, Ida decided to leave her work at the underwear factory. With Gantz' help she managed to find two workers and to revive Anshel's silent textile machines. Gantz helped her to sell the products too and at supper, after some discussion of the events of the day, he liked to sit and make plans for her wedding reception. Ida did not know how he had found out, and when she asked him a self-satisfied expression spread over his face. He had a way of knowing things of this nature—he had known about Dina's marriage before it was announced too, and also Hedva's. He understood human nature. And he knew too that after every war, weddings multiplied like grains of sand on the seashore.

The war went on for another few months. It ended in unquestioned victory and the town began to return to normal. The sandbags were removed from the entrances to buildings, the sticky tape was peeled from the windowpanes, the bands began to play again in the cafés along the promenade. A ruddy-faced Anshel came back from the army, Dina and Hedva's husbands came home too, and all was ready for Anshel and Ida's wedding. Gantz hired a small hall and made arrangements for catering on a lavish scale. He insisted on meeting all the expenses from his own pocket, saying it was a great joy to him to give Ida away in marriage.

And one warm evening with a hint of summer in the air the guests gathered. Most of them were friends of Gantz, and only a few had been invited by Ida and Anshel. Ida invited a few of the women who had worked with her in the underwear factory, and Anshel invited an old uncle and aunt who wept copiously throughout the ceremony. Feeling a little faint, Ida listened to the rabbi's speech about the releasing of women whose husbands were missing and their entry into matrimony in the independent state of Israel. In his soft voice Anshel repeated the marriage vows, and to the sound of applause he lifted his foot high in the air and smashed the glass with his shoe. Gantz beamed with happiness, mingled with the guests and plied them with food and drink, conducted the three-piece band, and danced with his two embarrassed daughters. When the hour grew late Dina pressed Ida's hand fervently and gave her a moist kiss. Gantz' wife clasped her to her bosom in silence and Gantz himself stood between her and Anshel and announced that his last daughter had now been married off, and that he was looking forward to more grandchildren. He had done all that could be expected of him; nobody could have expected more.

Ida was now Anshel's lawful wedded wife, and that same night she already knew that she would remain unsatisfied.

7

For the first few days she was frantic. She tried to hide her disappointment and told Anshel that she did not feel well. Before they got into bed she would try not to look at his thin white body, his emaciated limbs. And when he entered her she could feel his quick, shallow breathing on her face. A spasm of lust would seize him and for a moment his body would sway above her, light as a feather, so careful not to hurt her that she scarcely felt his touch. And afterward, when he lay panting on his back, she would wonder why she felt nothing at all, neither pleasure nor passion.

And then, one night, she found herself thinking about Klein. Anshel was already asleep, a quiet, soundless sleep, and in the dim light of the night lamp she saw his peaceful face, his chest moving up and down as he breathed. Before this, while Anshel was crouching over her, Klein had floated into her thoughts and become inextricably interwoven in them. A kind of grief, new and strange, welled out of his image and penetrated her, invading the depths of her body.

She nearly cried. Her eyes stung, and she felt the dammed-up tears swelling behind them. Klein's face loomed before her, every line and feature clear, as if it had been waiting all these years for the moment when it would have to emerge from the depths. The sorrow lay between them, hurting her body, and when she looked at Anshel she felt sorry for him also. In his face, too, she saw a certain melancholy, hidden deep within the refining and concealing innocence. Beneath Klein's glittering eyes her body grew weaker and weaker until it sank into a deep sleep and she felt the bed plunging with her into the depths of the earth. In the morning she couldn't open her eyes. Anshel brought her a cup of tea and said that she had better stay in bed; she seemed to have a fever.

For about a week she lay hallucinating, hardly opening her eyes, hearing sounds dimly. Anshel sent for a doctor and Gantz brought another, and the pair of them plied her with medicines. Sweat poured from her body, wetting the sheets. Sometimes, in her delirium, Anshel took on Klein's features, and she wanted to raise her hand and touch his face to see if he really was Klein. Once more the horses galloped in the distance, the erect figure at their head as tiny as a dot. She waited for him to approach her, lift her onto his horse, and bear her far away to the flat blue plains on the horizon. In the airy light blue she rode with him and the wind washed her face. Mournfully she lifted a limp hand and touched Anshel's arm.

For a week she lay burning in waves of heat, which bathed her in rivers of sweat, or shivering with violent chills. Afterward the fever receded, leaving her weak, exhausted, and indifferent to everything around her. And when she rose to her feet Anshel's anxious eyes gave her a guilty conscience, and she felt a dull emptiness spreading inside her. Anshel's thin body no longer troubled her, and when he lay on top of her at night she let him have his satisfaction while she waited for the sudden spasm that would bring his activity to an abrupt end and leave him limp and sleepy. She had once read about something similar in one of her romances, but there—unlike real life—the woman had left her husband and eloped with her lover for the isles of happiness. She knew very well that she would never be capable of acting in this way—she would not run away and she would not say anything to Anshel. His kindly smile tortured her, and she repeated to herself over and over again that she would never do anything to hurt him.

8

Her life now proceeded calmly enough; seemingly, she and Anshel were a loving couple. She began pretending, and as the months passed she grew accustomed to the mask of happiness covering her face. From time to time Gantz and his wife came to have tea with them or to sample Ida's cooking. Jovially, Gantz would congratulate Anshel on the prize that had fallen to his lot. You didn't find women like Ida in the marketplace, no sir—and but for him Anshel would have remained a bachelor to this very day, alone in the world as a dog. Now he had a wife like Ida. And who did he have to thank for it? Gantz' wife sipped her tea and looked at Ida in silence.

Recently Gantz had expanded his business, despite the worsening economic conditions, the rationing and the austerity. But Gantz wasn't the kind of man to lose heart—and he began a black market trade in edible goods: sausages, chocolate, canned meat. He supplied Ida too with all kinds of delicacies, and when Anshel offered him money he refused it with a sweeping gesture. He didn't need money. It was a grandson he wanted, not money.

But the grandson did not arrive. Month followed month—a whole year had passed since her marriage to Anshel—and Ida's belly remained flat and empty. She was not concerned, since she had no wish to become pregnant. The idea of having Anshel's children filled her with revulsion mixed with an obscure fear, and when she imagined them she immediately thought of children resembling their father: helpless, lamb-like creatures.

But Gantz did not despair. Although Anshel said nothing and made no demands, Gantz kept urging them, coaxing, encouraging, tempting. And once he even sent his wife to speak to Ida, woman to woman.

Ida looked at the skinny little woman sitting silently opposite her. It was morning, when the sun came into the house and flooded it with light. Ida knew why she had come and what she wanted to say. At first she spoke about Dina's and Hedva's children, the great joy they had brought into their parents' homes, and then she fell silent. Ida could not understand what great joy there was in taking care of screaming children. From time to time, in Dina's house, she would smell the stench of urine and see the mess—and to Gantz' wife she said that she did not know why she had not become pregnant. Her periods were regular, as always, and Anshel had intercourse with her regularly.

Gantz urged them to see a doctor, and in the end they gave in to his pressure. The tests showed that the fault was with Anshel, and that it could, perhaps, be corrected with time and a course of treatment. Ida saw the lines of sadness on Anshel's face, and she knew that it was on her account, that he was sorry for depriving her of the joys of motherhood. She knew that she had to keep silent, silent forever.

From now on there was a new dimension to her life: the sorrow that Anshel felt on her account. This weighed on her conscience and increased the guilt she felt toward him. She should have told him the truth, from the beginning, and now she had let it go too late. It was all her fault. She would have to keep on pretending, pretending to be happy in her love for him. And he, in his innocence, had even told her that if the medical treatment failed he would not stop her from finding someone else. He did not want her to remain in her emptiness for the rest of her life.

She listened to him with astonishment, a confused, embarrassed, and anguished smile on her face. If she could have, she would have cried, and gone on crying for days on end. How could she have let things go so far, made such a fool of him in his innocence, entangled him in such a web of lies?

Perhaps this was why she pressed him to devote himself to the improvement and expansion of the textile workshop. Despite the rationing he obtained a large order for a considerable amount of underwear, commissioned by the army for its draftees. If the goods were satisfactory, he was told, there was every chance that he would receive additional orders.

She encouraged him to acquire the latest textile machinery. Later, with Gantz' help, he borrowed money and transferred the workshop to new premises, outside the town. And the workshop was now transformed, on Gantz' advice, into a textile plant. It was at this stage that Ida suggested withdrawing her money from the bank at last, and Gantz agreed with her. But Anshel refused, with an obstinacy uncharacteristic of him. Gantz tried to persuade him that Klein no longer existed—the money was Ida's, lawfully hers, why shouldn't she use it? But Anshel was adamant in his refusal, and Ida, with a sudden cunning, distracted Gantz' attention.

The textile plant kept up with the orders. The inspectors praised the quality of the products and brought Anshel more orders and more profits. Before long he had paid back all his debts to the bank, and Ida saw their wealth accumulating. Anshel bought himself a car and learned to drive, and Ida followed suit. She drove about the town, looking at the shop windows and telling herself that she could buy whatever took her fancy.

Gantz found them a spacious new apartment in a northern suburb that was just beginning to develop. The apartment was full of light and overlooked a flourishing avenue of trees. When Ida climbed the broad staircase she saw walls covered with pale marble and big windows.

Some time after this, Anshel built a new wing onto his plant. He paid regular visits to the hospital for his medical treatment, and the chances of a cure improved. Soon, he told Ida, soon everything would be all right. She would become pregnant and give birth to children before it was too late. They were no longer young. She kissed him on the cheek and wondered if she still did not want to bear his children.

In the mornings she would wake up late, long after Anshel had left for work. With a certain languor she would lie in bed, listening to the music on the radio, letting thoughts drift through her head, half awake and half asleep. Afterward she would get up, choose her clothes, and do the housework. There wasn't much to do, for Anshel had insisted on employing a maid to help her. Sometimes, when she had the use of the car, she would drive to the center of town, wander through the busy streets and buy anything that caught her eye in the shop windows. Sometimes she would sit for hours in a café, gazing at the passersby. And when she stayed at home she would lie back in an armchair, and when the sun burst through the window she would let its rays enter her body and warm it.

In her leisure hours she went on reading novels. The plots were all more or less the same, the subject matter love, hope, and despair, but she went on reading them devotedly and was sorry every time she came to the end. She was very curious to know what happened afterward, after all the misunderstandings were over and everything ended happily. For she now knew that happy endings were impossible and that the way the novels ended misled the people who read them.

9

One winter evening Ida and Anshel were sitting at their table and eating their evening meal. Lately Anshel had been coming home late; there was so much work at the plant, and he had taken to eating his main meal in the evening. When they had finished eating, Anshel would look at the newspaper while she washed the dishes in the kitchen. There was a knock at the door and Gantz came in, his face full of excitement. He inquired after their health, asked how business was going, and told a story about Dina's baby son. Ida served tea in patterned china cups, and while they were drinking Anshel spoke about the plant. Recently they had added an extra shift, and new problems connected with it were cropping up every day. He had the army commission in his pocket, but nevertheless he was thinking of slowing the pace of production. Money wasn't everything; he was satisfied with what he was making already. Ida saw that Gantz was in a turmoil and that his thoughts were elsewhere as Anshel continued talking about the plant.

After a while Anshel fell silent. Gantz sat tapping the empty teacup with his fingernails. He coughed and cleared his throat. Well, he said, hesitatingly, he hadn't just dropped in for a visit, not this time. He had heard something this morning, something they had no reason to fear but they should nevertheless know about. He himself didn't believe it, since it was impossible—out of the question, in fact. "What is it?" asked Anshel curiously, and Gantz succumbed to a prolonged fit of coughing.

Ida saw Anshel's curiosity; she saw Gantz blowing his nose, burying his face in the depths of his handkerchief. When he raised his head she saw the embarrassment on his face. He had heard a rumor that morning, he said slowly and carefully, quite groundless he was sure, like most rumors. But in any case, someone had told him about a group of new immigrants who had just arrived in the country, after all kinds of vicissitudes, and among them, according to his informant—among them was Klein. Or someone very like him. That was what the man had said. But they knew for themselves how many mistakes were made, and how people spread all kinds of stories that had no basis in fact. He himself didn't believe it. Two witnesses had sworn that Klein was dead. Dead men do not come back to life. So they have nothing to worry about. He was quite sure the man couldn't be Klein, but he thought they should know about it nevertheless. There was really nothing to worry about. If he, Gantz, had allowed himself to get into a state over every rumor he heard, he would have gone mad long ago. That's what it was like working in a tavern—people got a little drink into them and said whatever came into their heads. A faint resemblance immediately became the basis for the wildest gossip, and people were prepared to swear solemn oaths on the purest nonsense. Here Gantz coughed again, and Ida sat and watched him recover, look about him, and say that it was getting late, he was tired, and he had to go home to bed. At the door he said again that they had nothing to worry about, he knew the man who had told the story, and you couldn't rely on a word he said—a drunk with his head full of fantasies, and what was more, he had never even known Klein properly.

When he had gone Ida sat opposite Anshel and for the first time in her life his face was inscrutable to her. Gantz' news was incredible. As far as she was concerned, she had no doubt at all that the man was not Klein. Klein was dead, had been dead for years. If he had been alive, he would have found her long ago. He wouldn't have waited for so many years. He would have escaped from the camps and galloped to meet her, over plains and mountains, through fire and water. Of this she had no doubt.

Anshel sat in silence. She began speaking to him soothingly, saying that he must not believe it. She, who had been his wife, knew that Klein was dead. Beyond the shadow of a doubt. In these matters there was nothing like a woman's intuition. Without a doubt, she told him, without a doubt. He mustn't worry or think stupid thoughts. He knew as well as she did that she would soon be pregnant and they would both laugh at this groundless rumor. She stroked his hair and urged him gently to go to bed. He was tired and tense; sleep was the best thing for him. In the morning he would get up and forget the whole thing. She herself had forgotten it already, he must believe her. She did not take such nonsense seriously for a moment.

After Anshel had gone to sleep, Ida stayed up reading about the trials and tribulations of a young girl who had risen to fame and fortune from the gutter. When she finished the book, in the early hours of the morning, she wondered if the height of success had brought happiness. Afterward she mulled over Gantz' news. She had felt no excitement on hearing it, since she was convinced that the man was not Klein, and she was not one to be fooled. Klein had died many years ago and he could not possibly come back to life again. Even in novels there were no ghosts.

The next day Ida slept until noon. She rose lazily, put on a pretty dress, and went out to stroll in the streets of the town. It was a fine winter day and the sun warmed her body.

10

For the first few days Anshel seemed distracted and upset, preoccupied and silent. Ida did her best to calm his fears. One evening they went to the theater to see a light comedy, and the next day she felt a sudden desire to dance and dragged him off to a brightly lit dance hall. "Look, it's just like old times," she said to him, "it's as if we were becoming acquainted all over again." A few days later Gantz told them that the man had come back to the tavern and confessed that he was no longer sure that the person was Klein. He was not sure at all. Perhaps his imagination had been playing tricks on him. Hadn't he told them himself that the man was not to be trusted?

And when two whole weeks had gone by without anything happening, Ida saw Anshel relax. He started talking to her about the plant again, and resumed his medical treatment. She urged him to take a short vacation, and they went to bask in the warmth of Tiberias. Tiberias was a popular winter resort, and the town was full of vacationers and tourists. They stayed at a small pension and enjoyed bathing in the hot springs, sailing on the lake, and eating the fresh grilled fish. She surprised him with all kinds of little gifts and saw his grateful smile.

A new feeling toward Anshel had come into her heart: Ever since Gantz had come to them with that silly rumor she had stopped doubting her desire to become pregnant and have his children. Now she was quite sure that the day would come, and soon, when her belly would begin to swell, and that the birth of the child would bring an absolute change with it. Her days would no longer slip by in boredom and inactivity. And she would bring the baby up, right from the start, to be strong and daring. She would not let him be weak and flabby. He would be her child and she would bring him up as she wished; she would take no advice from anyone.

When they returned from their vacation Ida went to see Anshel's doctor, determined to find out the truth. She questioned him closely about Anshel's condition and the progress of the treatment and urged him to do everything possible to bring it to a speedy conclusion. The doctor told her that the treatment was proceeding to his satisfaction, and that it would not be long now, not long at all. They would have to wait for about three months, no more. During these three months the glands would begin to function normally and after that there would be no more obstacles, he promised her. And they would be fruitful and multiply, he was sure. He knew they were no longer young, but there was still nothing to prevent them from having a dozen children, if they wished. She was strong and healthy. She could go home and relax; everything would be all right.

That same evening she told Anshel what the doctor had said. The news of her initiative brought a look of surprise to his face, soon giving way to a kindly smile. Eagerly Ida started chattering to him about babies and children, about the different names they could choose and about all the things they would have to buy when the baby was born. She seemed unable to stop the spate of words; there was so much that she wanted to say. One thing led to another, until she saw the lines of tiredness on Anshel's face. After he had fallen asleep she took up a novel, as usual, but this time she did not succeed in concentrating on other people's lives. Between the lines she thought of her pregnancy and the adventure of the birth in store for her.

In the morning she rose early and rushed into town. For hours she walked around the shops examining baby furniture, baby clothes, and all the other things a baby needed. Here and there she asked about prices and quality. And on the following days, too, she thought incessantly about the coming birth.

Thus the days went by. In the textile plant the second shift went into high gear and Gantz began making plans for a third shift too, trying to sow the seeds of the idea in Anshel's mind. Ida continued getting up at noon, but now she knew that it was only temporary. When the day came she would have to get up early, to take care of her baby son. At night she still read novels, but she knew that they too would soon have to be set aside for a while.

And one morning, in the middle of winter when the gray skies leaked onto the ground, Ida stood at the window looking at the wet, deserted street. Passersby were few and far between, bundled up in heavy coats, hiding underneath their umbrellas. In the cars the windshield wipers flicked back and forth. After a while she turned away from the window and sat down to mend a skirt whose hem had come undone. Then she made herself a cup of tea and drank it in slow sips. When the doorbell rang she knew it was the man from the laundry.

She called to him to wait a minute and quickly buttoned up her gown. She thought pityingly about the people obliged to go out in the rain and cold, stretched out her hand to straighten an embroidered cloth that had slipped from its place, and when she opened the door she saw that the man standing there was not the man from the laundry. She asked him what he wanted and for a second she wondered at his silence, but only for a second. The man called her by her name and in his voice she heard the echo of galloping horses' hoofs.

11

And after he had gone, too, she heard the sound of galloping. The horses' hoofs shook the earth and made it sway, and she had to walk slowly away from the door, clinging to the wall for support so as not to fall. Falteringly she reached the sofa and felt her body drop, felt the coarse weave sinking under her. Her limbs seemed to be dissolving, and all that remained were the galloping hoofs filling the earth with their thundering. The herd of horses came racing toward her from the broad blue plains, with Klein's chestnut horse at their head, skimming over the surface of the ground.

When Ida awoke the sounds had grown softer, but they had not disappeared. In the distance the galloping continued to echo. She rose and went to the window. Her legs were weak, as if the strength had been drained from her body. Her body was damp and sticky, and in the deserted street the rain continued to pour down. A grayish light filled the room. She looked at her watch and abstractly calculated the time until Anshel's return. She had to prepare his meal properly, so that he would not be suspicious, so that he would not sense anything wrong. She washed her face in cold water and brushed her hair, and then she went into the kitchen and put a pot on the stove.

Anshel came home, and the horses began to neigh as they ran. She served the food lackadaisically, and sat down opposite him, forcing herself to eat so that he would not notice anything. After the meal Anshel read the newspaper and she vomited her food out into the toilet bowl. The neighing of the horses rose to the sky. Only at night, when she was in her bed, did the galloping stop and the horses fall to grazing in the distant dust. Their noses nuzzled the earth and a great calm descended on her.

Until Anshel fell asleep she lay staring at the black lines of print on the page before her. When he was asleep she put the book down and lay with her eyes open. Anshel lay on his side, his head slightly lowered. The horses lay on the ground with their legs stretched out before them, and their breath rose hotly from their nostrils.

The next morning she awoke at dawn. Through a slit in her eyelids she saw Anshel rise, careful not to disturb her, get dressed and put on his shoes. She heard him in the kitchen. The horses stood up, rubbing against each other as if for warmth, their nostrils quivering, and then the door closed quietly and they began to run.

She got out of bed and dressed herself in warm winter clothes. In the kitchen she boiled water and drank strong coffee. The weakness left her and gave way to a feeling of suspense, impelling her to pace from window to window, from room to room. The horses galloped toward her, racing past villages and fields. The sun broke out of the clouds and entered her body.

An hour later Klein arrived. The years had furrowed his face and given it a more determined expression. She felt her blood flowing faster, her thighs growing hot. The horses began to neigh. It seemed to her that her body was coming alive and she wanted to neigh with them, to bring the walls of the house down with her neighing and sweep everything inside them away. Klein's hand held her warm arm.

The horses were waiting below, stamping their feet impatiently. Klein lifted her onto his horse and the street seemed dwarfed. The horses took off and started galloping toward the open spaces, trampling the asphalt streets, looking for a way out. She felt her body clinging to the body of the horse, rising and falling with it in an increasingly rapid rhythm. Klein's breath was on her neck. The sun shone more strongly, dispelling the rain clouds. A yellow light flooded the earth. Every now and then one of the horses neighed, and Klein calmed it with a clicking of his tongue. His burning hands clasped her waist.

The horses galloped faster and faster. Clods of earth flew from their feet. Ida crouched down and clasped the horse's neck. Klein bent over her, covering her body with his and urging his horse on. On and on and on. The blue mountains grew sharper and clearer. A warm wind whipped her face and tossed the horses' manes. She felt as if she were floating and knew that she was finally about to conquer the peaks of happiness.

Translated by DALYA BILU

LA PROMENADE

Michal Govrin

"For the time being we can rest here," said Moniek Heller when they reached the bench at the edge of the beach. "It's nice here, opposite the sea." And the soft sound of the Polish words in his mouth was accompanied by an interrogative lilt.

"Fine, fine." Lusia Taft nodded, the little smile on her face below him expressing partly submission, partly uncertainty, and partly an effort to convey thanks.

"We can wait here for the others to arrive," said Moniek, hastily pulling a large handkerchief from the pocket of his light-colored suit and sweeping it over the bench before indicating to Lusia, with a ceremonious flourish, that she could sit down.

He smoothed his pants and sat, straightened his slender back, crossed his legs, and placed his hands one on top of the other on his right knee. Then he raised his chin and surveyed the broad beach, which was covered with mist and bedecked with a string of little flags at the water's edge, dancing in the breeze in the distance.

Lusia carefully straightened the skirt of the suit she had had specially made for the voyage and sat down on the light green bench. A woman has to try to look her best, and she set her bulky purse down neatly, next to the knees peeping out of her skirt.

"A beautiful day," said Moniek, and he went on looking at the ocean lying motionless at the bottom of the slope, as if it had been put to sleep by the mist that had shrouded the seaside resort all day long.

"Yes, a beautiful day," confirmed Lusia.

And they sat for a moment without talking, gazing in front of them at the sea. The white sand came all the way up to the bench, penetrating the little holes in the weave of Moniek's leather shoes and sticking to the heels of Lusia's broad shoes. Moniek straightened his hands neatly on his right knee, and Lusia held her full body a little more erect than was necessary.

"Really, everything is beautiful here," she suddenly announced, shifting in her place. "I don't know how to thank . . ."

"No need, really, no need." Moniek Heller drummed with the

fingers of his right hand, and the signet ring on his finger glittered.

"The beach is so big," continued Lusia, a shade dramatically, turning her head from the glitter of the ring to the glint of the water at the edge of the beach. "After so many years a person forgets."

"Yes, yes," replied Moniek, and after a while he added, "I'm here every weekend regularly from April to June, twelve years already. In the summer I go for the cure to Montecatini, and last winter I tried the baths at the Dead Sea. It was nice there. No question about it." He shook his head slightly from side to side and then added, "And we met there too. That was also nice."

They both smiled, as was only fitting at such a moment. Moniek patted Lusia's right hand lightly with his left hand, after which he replaced it on his knee.

"Very nice what they've done there. Every convenience," Moniek recommenced.

"Yes, yes, very grand," replied Lusia in an animated tone, taking care to keep her purse upright.

"No question about it, they've done great things there in Israel!" summed up Moniek.

"No question about it," replied Lusia.

And neither of them had anything to add, especially since the country in question appeared no more real at the moment than the tiny figures of the bathers moving like dots at the edge of the water.

"I didn't ask yet how things are at the shop," said Moniek, and his fingers resumed their drumming.

"June isn't the best time of the year for wool," replied Lusia, "but as long as the shop stays open I'm not complaining."

"That's right," agreed Moniek.

"A person needs a break every now and then. After a while you get tired—you know how it is. It isn't easy with all that tension all the time," said Lusia, and her heavy voice stood in the air for a moment around the light green bench at the edge of the shore.

Behind them rose the cliffs with their grand summer houses, preserving a nostalgic *fin-de-siècle* royalty in their ornate façades. And on the beach the white planks of the walkway led right down to the changing booths at the edge of the sea.

"No, it isn't easy," repeated Lusia after a moment.

"It isn't easy," said Moniek too, and after a while he asked, "It's not too hot for you . . ." He almost said "Mrs. Taft," but thought the better of it and concluded on a more familiar note, "Lusia?"

"No, it's very nice here," replied Lusia, and she went on to ask the question that was expected of her, "And how are things at the shop?"

"Could be worse," said Moniek. "We're busy with the new autumn models already. Plenty of worries, as usual, but for the time being, not bad at all."

He raised the hand adorned with the signet ring, tugged at the knot in his fine woolen tie, and straightened his crossed knee. Then he replaced his hand, and finally he let his knee fall back into its former position too.

"And why not?" he went on. "The children are fixed up. And ever since Rouzia died I try to do whatever the doctors say."

And after a short pause, during which he made a number of little pecking motions with his sharp chin, he said, "And now we can begin again together, no?"

And only the drumming of the fingers of his right hand on his left went on moving the signet ring up and down.

"Yes. There's quite a lot in common," said Lusia.

"*Nu,* like we already said, wool and ladies' wear go together quite well," said Moniek with a laugh, uncrossing and recrossing his thin legs.

Lusia laughed too, and then there was another silence, which was not even oppressive, so peaceful was the expanse of sand receding into the water. For a moment Lusia lifted her orthopedic shoes out of the sand, and then she sank them back again.

"Good afternoon to Mr. Heller and Mrs.—"

"Taft!" cried Moniek, making haste to rise to his feet and turning to face the roly-poly person approaching them along the esplanade at a pattering kind of run. His full face, almost completely hidden behind his sunglasses, beamed all the way up to the crown of his bald head, and his whole appearance proclaimed that he was on vacation: from the perforated white shoes teetering rapidly to and fro to the open mesh of the shirt flapping around his thighs and the white hairs peeping through it on the broad expanse of his sunburnt chest.

"Sitting on the beach, eh?" he called as he approached. "Just the two of you!" And a burst of heavy laughter rocked his body.

"The lady is from Israel. From Tel Aviv," said Moniek when the laughter of the holiday-maker had somewhat subsided.

And Lusia turned herself around with the erectness appropriate to the occasion and put out her hand: "Pleased to meet you."

"Hirshel Feingold!" Moniek hurriedly announced.

The latter skipped from his place and lowered himself rapidly over his round belly to Lusia's hand. "The pleasure is mine entirely, mine entirely," he said, and he went on, smacking his lips admiringly, "So, she's from Israel? Very nice, very nice!"

"This is Hirshel Feingold, who I already told you about," said Moniek, as if for Lusia's ears but loudly enough to let him know that his name had already been mentioned between them.

"Oho! What did you tell her already?" cried Hirshel in mock alarm, and although he made a sign with his hand as if there were no need for them to tell, it was evident from his smile that he was waiting eagerly to hear.

"Nu," Moniek shrugged his shoulders in mock resignation. "I told Mrs. Taft a little about your business interests on an international scale, your branches in Hamburg, New York, London, South Africa—nu, the whole list, more or less. Also how right after the war, still in the D.P. camp, you already began making money in real estate."

"You shouldn't talk about it!" exclaimed Hirshel Feingold, swinging himself around the bench, and before Moniek had time to finish saying politely, "Sit down with us, Hirshel," Hirshel was already sitting and wiping the sweat from his brow with a pudgy hand. And leaning forward stiffly over his paunch he went on in the same breath, "They didn't open La Promenade yet? It's already after five! Everybody should be here in a minute. Henrietta's arriving in a minute too. I went out first. I couldn't stand it shut up in those four walls any more. When we come here I always say: 'You have to get the most out of the sea air, and not stay shut up in your room!' "

And after breathing in a noseful of the air, he turned to Lusia Taft and said, "So, the lady has come to us for a little rest?"

Lusia was embarrassed, and Moniek began to mutter, "No, the lady . . ."

But Hirshel Feingold went on without waiting for a reply, "Nice, nice, very nice. And I'm just leaving next week for my hotel in Natanya! You know the Hotel Repose there? Not bad, eh? I put it up in '62. *Nu*, I've got in Eilat and Nahariya too. We have to support the state, no? Not a bad living. But plenty of problems, as usual in Israel. *Nu*, so how can you do business with Jews already?" And he burst into laughter, which wobbled his shoulders, convulsed his belly and legs, and in the end set his hands shaking too, at first opposite each other and then clapping one against the other. Moniek too hurried, if a little late, to join in the laughter, and Lusia nodded her head after them.

"Henrietta! So you got out at last!"

Hirshel reared his head and waved his chubby hand at a tall woman in a narrow-skirted suit, who was limping toward them along the esplanade. Even from a distance it was evident that it was an effort for her to put one foot in front of the next, and it was clear that in spite of Hirshel's explanations they had set out from the hotel together.

"Come on, come on, meet some new people!" Hirshel went on calling out toward her, without rising from his seat.

Lusia watched with pursed lips as the woman approached, and then she stood up and held out her hand. "Lusia Taft. Maiden name Mandelstein."

"Pleased to meet you. Henrietta Feingold," replied the woman, and her handshake drooped.

Moniek rose and bowed. "Hello, Mrs. Feingold."

And the haggard woman limped around the bench, passing close to her husband's back in order to sit down in the empty place beside him. But before she got there Hirshel cried, "I saw Arlette riding on the beach!"

And turning quickly back to Lusia and Moniek as if he were addressing an audience, he said, "Our daughter's fantastic! She knows how to live!"

"Arlette's riding?!" cried Henrietta, and sat up in alarm.

Hirshel dismissed her cry with a downward flap of his hand and was about to turn back to his audience when the sound of a shutter being rolled up was heard, and immediately afterward iron chairs being banged down on the terrace: At last the La Promenade café had opened its doors for the afternoon session which, more than anything else in the seaside town, was taken as supreme proof of the fineness of the weather.

Hirshel Feingold leaped to his feet and said, "Over to La Promenade, everyone!"

And he hurried off to make sure to get their regular corner on the terrace. Right behind him, Henrietta lifted her body from the bench and limped after him with an expression of concentration on her face.

Lusia Taft and Moniek Heller remained sitting where they were a moment longer, but Hirshel Feingold was already urging them on from the café terrace: "Moniek, Mrs. Taft. What's the matter? What are you waiting for?"

He himself was busy dragging the round iron tables together and waving chairs about in his short arms.

"Coming! Coming!" called Moniek Heller in reply, and he went on sitting on the bench with Lusia Taft, facing the white sand and the little fleet of sailing boats whose solid bellies were cut out like blue silhouettes in the mist. In the end he bent over Lusia and offered her his arm.

In the meantime Hirshel Feingold had completed his arrangements in the corner. The chairs stood untidily around the tables, as if at the end of a party. In the corner, next to the canvas partition that marked the boundary of the café premises, Henrietta sat erect, preoccupied, and silent. And as if to fill the vacuum left by her silence, Hirshel sent cries of encouragement toward Moniek and Lusia, who were coming up from the beach with heavy steps, and waved both hands at two couples who were approaching along the esplanade. "Over here! Over here!"

Among the other people strolling up and down the esplanade, bordered on one side by the café facades and on the other by the expanse of sand stretching into the mist and the sea, there could be no mistaking the destination of the two couples who were making for the corner of the weekend regulars at the La Promenade café. The deliberate tread, the way in which the ladies gripped their purses as if they were traveling bags, the embarrassment with which the man at the right buried his hand in the pocket of his loose-fitting suit, or the determined air of recreation surrounding the checkered cap set jauntily upon the head of the man at the left. The latter approached arm in arm with his yellow-haired wife, the bright pink of whose costume matched her husband's vacation air. Next to them, the couple at the right appeared somewhat ill at ease.

"I see we have new visitors today!" Hirshel Feingold declared happily.

And the owner of the checkered cap hastily dropped his wife's arm and pushed the new couple forward as he announced: "Mr. and Mrs. Harari from Ramat-Gan."

"Mrs. Taft from Tel Aviv." Hirshel promptly took his turn as sponsor.

And in the hubbub of greetings and handshakes filling the café terrace with Polish sounds, Moniek bent over to explain to Lusia, indicating the man in the checkered cap and the woman in the pink suit, "The Honigers, from Paris. In synthetic underwear. A first-class business."

Hirshel Feingold made impatient gestures with his hands. "Sit down, sit down!" he cried. "Why are you standing?" And he pointed at the circle of chairs standing chaotically around the tables.

Mr. Honiger gallantly pushed the chair closest to him toward Mrs. Harari, whose gray hair was gathered into a bun behind her

head. Mr. Harari drew in his legs and folded himself into the chair
next to his wife. Mrs. Honiger sat down beside him like a genial
pink chaperone. Last to be seated were Moniek Heller and Lusia
Taft, and Lusia turned her chair carefully around so that she could
see the sea from where she sat. Only Henrietta did not get up while
all this was going on; she remained in her place next to the canvas
partition in the corner. Mr. Honiger jumped quickly to his feet again
and held out his hand to Henrietta over the tables. And Hirshel
Feingold called out to the assembled company, *"Nu,* what's everybody drinking?" He beckoned the waiter with a proprietary air.

The waiter, who was apparently well acquainted with the weekend regulars, folded his hands across the white napkin over his arm
and waited while Hirshel counted off the orders one by one:

"Tea, coffee, lemonade," and in the end he turned to Henrietta,
who said, "I'll have tea with lemon," as if she were committing
herself to a fateful decision.

Hirshel sent the waiter off, and all agog at the new audience he
turned toward them and made a number of unclear, agitated motions
with his hands. In the end he burst into a long laugh of contentment.
When he had finally calmed down, and all the others too had
finished signaling their participation in the mirth, Hirshel wiped the
moisture from his forehead and said, *"Nu,* not bad here in Europe,
eh?"

Marek Harari nodded his dark, pointed head and lowered it with
a smile. "Not bad at all."

"Good, good," continued Hirshel, without paying any attention.
"Good, all this reminds me of the joke . . ."

But Gusta Harari, who felt the need to add something to her
husband's words, leaned over to Henrietta and said, full-throatedly,
while Hirshel was still telling his joke, "We only came because of
the Honigers. They insisted we should come here to them for a rest
on our way home."

And when Henrietta made no response Gusta continued, turning
to Lusia and smiling at her confidingly, "Otherwise how could we
possibly have afforded it?"

Hirshel burst out laughing, and his laughter was echoed by Mr. Honiger and Moniek Heller. Marek too stretched his face, but his eyes remained sunken. And Henrietta, who had almost disappeared behind her husband's gleefully agitated limbs, dismissed the joke with a pursing of her lips and shifted slightly in her chair.

The waiter arrived with a nickel-plated tray loaded with jugs of tea and coffee and tall glasses of lemonade. He put the orders down in front of the people seated around the table according to their instructions. Hirshel placed his thick hand on the bill and closed his fist around it.

"It's on me!" he cried.

Mr. Honiger and Moniek Heller attempted to protest. Hirshel Feingold waved both his hands in the air and proclaimed again and again, "No arguments! It's on me!"

They all smiled in enjoyment and stirred their drinks. The mist on the beach thickened and brightened, almost hiding the glitter of the sea from the eyes of the people sitting on the café terrace. A number of vacationers strolling along the esplanade turned their heads curiously at the sound of the hubbub.

Mr. Harari lowered the china cup from his mouth to the saucer and said, "The espresso is really very good here."

"The lemonade, too." Mrs. Harari followed suit.

Hirshel gave the little cup of coffee engulfed between his hands an energetic stir and said, with the self-satisfied air of a man who has just brought a business deal to a successful conclusion, "Yes, yes, not bad. Not bad at all."

And Henrietta, bending her whole height over the table, squeezed the lemon in her glass with tiny movements, making innumerable clinking noises with her spoon against the side of the china cup.

Mr. Honiger took advantage of the pause in Hirshel's stream of words and began, "A government auditing committee came to my factory—five Jews, can you imagine?"

"I'd rather not . . ." began Moniek Heller, wrinkling his forehead slightly, but Hirshel replaced his little cup on its saucer with a bang, slapped them both down on the table, and burst tempestuously into the conversation. "Ten days ago when I flew . . ."

"And what was your maiden name, may I ask, Mrs. Taft?" Mrs. Honiger turned with a gold-framed smile to Lusia Taft.

"Mandelstein," replied Lusia, and she leaned over the table. "Lusia Mandelstein."

"Mandelstein?" repeated Mrs. Honiger, thrusting her pink-clad bosom toward her. "And where are you from, Mrs. Taft?"

"Tarnów," replied Lusia. "And you, Mrs. Honiger?"

"Chrzanów," answered Mrs. Honiger.

"My late husband had family from there," said Lusia.

"What was the name?" asked Mrs. Honiger.

"Romek Taft," replied Lusia.

And Mrs. Honiger nodded her head. "We were in Israel until '55, and then we moved to Paris."

"Yes, yes." Lusia too nodded understandingly.

Hirshel's laughter drew to an end like a roll of thunder receding into the distance, and rubbing his fat hands in satisfaction he turned his attention to the newcomers.

"So what brings Mr. and Mrs. Harari to us at La Promenade?" He flung this out of the corner of his mouth at Henrietta, who was still squeezing the lemon against the side of her cup. "They're from Ramat-Gan. Having a little vacation in Europe, eh?" He answered himself, and he was already turning to Moniek Heller, about to begin a new subject, when Mrs. Honiger said suddenly, "Tell them! Tell them!"—and her pink earrings swayed excitedly on the lobes of her ears.

Hirshel turned to face her with an air of pleasurable anticipation, and cried, "What, not for a vacation? So you came to get rich at our casino, eh? We have to beware of our Israelis—one of these days they'll break the bank!" He waved a fat finger at them.

"It's not important, Hella," said Mr. Harari to Mrs. Honiger. "Really, it's not important."

"What's the matter? It's nothing to be ashamed of! You can tell them," Staszek Honiger joined in from the other side of the table.

"We're in a free country here!" And he tried to laugh in order to make his encouragement more emphatic.

Marek Harari lowered the long head sticking out of his suit, and the skin of his neck tightened. He shrugged his shoulders and said in a reflective tone, "What difference does it make? We were in Munich." And again he concluded with a weary shrug of his shoulders. "Now we're on our way home."

"Really, there's nothing to be ashamed of!" cried Hirshel gleefully. "The mark's a strong currency, and in business you do whatever's necessary. It's nothing to be ashamed of!" And his last words were swallowed up in loud laughter, which tossed both his hands about and ended in a rapid, triumphant *glissando*.

Moniek laughed loyally with him, and Lusia smiled too. But Mr. Honiger persisted in his explanation nevertheless. "No, they . . ."

"We gave testimony in Munich," said Marek Harari, and he concluded with a limp, downward flap of his hand, "You know what it's like."

"We came on Monday," continued Gusta Harari, "and finished on Thursday. On the way back the Honigers offered us a rest in their villa by the sea."

"On Thursday it was all over, and we went to Paris," said Mr. Harari again.

"Who was the case against?" Moniek Heller asked quickly, in an apologetic tone.

"Heineke," said Marek Harari, and he shook his pointed head.

"Heineke?" asked Lusia Taft.

"What?" asked Moniek.

"No, I thought . . ." said Lusia.

"He wasn't there!" exclaimed Gusta Harari bitterly.

"Who wasn't there?" asked Moniek Heller uncompehendingly.

The Honigers, who were already acquainted with the facts, shook their heads in an aggrieved way. Gusta Harari clutched her purse, although it was already firmly ensconced in her lap, and said as if she were reciting, "When we arrived they told us that he was sick and couldn't stand up to the strain of the trial. We waited in the hotel for two days without going out. They told us to be ready to testify the moment he recovered. On Thursday they said they didn't know when he would recover. They took us to the court, and they wrote our testimony down in the protocol. They said that in the meantime they were collecting background information. Then they let us go, and it was over. Fela and Abel Gutt were with us too. From Holon. You know them maybe? Also from Bochnia. They went back on Thursday. We're going back tomorrow. It's over," concluded Gusta Harari, and after a moment she suddenly burst out with a fury ill-suited to the pleasantness of her gray bun, "What good did it do anyone? Tell me—what?"

"Don't say so, Gusta," said Marek Harari rebukingly, as if continuing an old argument.

"Yes, I know." Gusta took a firmer grip on her purse, and her face woke momentarily from its darkness. "It's important, but who to?"

"What are you saying, Gusta?" asked Mr. Honiger in a soothing but perfunctory tone. "What are you saying?"

"The Germans? They dragged us all the way there to tell us that he was sick," continued Gusta Harari obstinately. "Our children, perhaps? Better they shouldn't know. And anyway, they don't care. They're too busy with other things."

Marek Harari nodded his head, as if he knew all about it and was resigned to the situation.

"Yes, yes," said Lusia Taft to herself.

"Gusta, really, you shouldn't upset yourself." Mrs. Honiger threw all the weight of her genial presence into the calming efforts. "It's enough!"

Hirshel Feingold drummed his short fingers restlessly on the tabletop and burst out laughing. "They wrote about my painting collection in the papers! You know what they said? The condition for a good investment in art is ignorance!"

"We've never spoken about it to Arlette!" Henrietta Feingold's voice cut through her husband's laughter. "Never!" She jabbed her head forward for a moment and then relapsed into her stiff-backed silence.

"Yes." Mr. Honiger quickly confirmed, without knowing exactly what, as long as it put an end to the embarrassment. "Yes, today it's something else again; you can't go on forever living . . . with . . ." And since he didn't know how to go on, he fell silent.

Moniek Heller said, crossing his legs more firmly, "We deserve a little peace and quiet too, don't we?" And he smiled carefully at Lusia. But she did not notice his declaration, because at that moment she was absorbed in the movements of the tiny figures on the edge of the beach.

Mr. Harari put his lemonade glass down next to the flask of water standing on the table. His glass was dry, and the water flask was empty. He shifted slightly in his chair and drew in his neck again, as if he were trying to fold himself up inside his loose suit.

Mr. Honiger straightened his checkered cap and directed a polite and perfunctory "Hmm" toward Hirshel Feingold.

In the end Moniek Heller said, "I think we'll go to eat now. What do you say, Mrs. Taft?"

Lusia looked back from the beach and replied, "Yes, yes."

"Excuse us," said Moniek, and when he stood up he too saw the figures gleaming in the dense light of the sun hanging low in the yellowish mist.

Lusia carefully straightened the skirt of her costume and patted her hair into place with a heavy hand. She bent down and shook the hands of the people sitting around the table, and when she parted from the Hararis she said, "If we don't see each other again, have a nice trip."

Hirshel, who stood up in order to supervise their departure, made haste to intervene. "You'll see each other, you'll see each other," and he concluded with a patronizing laugh: "We don't say goodbye so quickly over here."

Moniek stretched over Henrietta's hand. "Mrs. Feingold." And he escorted Lusia out of the café terrace.

No sooner had they taken a few steps away than they heard

Hirshel turning to the people left sitting around the tables: "What's the matter? Why shouldn't Moniek marry Mrs. Taft from Tel Aviv? Maybe he should better start running after young girls at his age?"

"Not so loud, Mr. Feingold." Mr. Honiger tried to silence him.

"What's the matter? What's the matter? It's nothing to be ashamed of," Hirshel went on obstinately shouting.

Lusia Taft turned her head away from the esplanade for a moment and saw the Hararis sitting between Mr. and Mrs. Honiger on the terrace of La Promenade, shrinking a little between the checkered cap and the bright pink suit.

They walked up the esplanade, climbing steeply above the bluff. Lusia Taft tugged at her jacket, which tended to crease at the back. With one folded arm she clasped her purse to her body, and with the other she beat time heavily as they walked, as full of concentration as if they had just set out on a long-distance march. Moniek Heller walked beside her with long steps. His head nodded to itself, and his fingers rubbed incessantly together as if he were rolling something between them.

"What time is it?" asked Lusia.

"After seven," replied Moniek.

"I've lost the sense of time." Lusia lifted her head. "I'm not used to such long evenings any more."

"Yes, yes," said Moniek, and he contemplated the sea, which had grown somewhat darker and bluer. His fingers went on rubbing against each other, and the signet ring shone as it traveled back and forth. He nodded his head and seemed about to say something to Lusia. But he merely smiled distractedly, and she smiled mechanically back. Her swollen feet, supported by the buckles of her orthopedic shoes, clattered and dragged alternately on the esplanade.

At the top of the bluff they passed a stone balcony jutting out from the heights of the esplanade like a platform suspended in midair. A black iron mast pointed at the shifting clouds above it. They passed it without stopping.

"That's the Wind Rose observatory," said Moniek, and he

laughed a little, as if to apologize for the fact that they had walked all the way up the hill without exchanging a word.

"Yes," replied Lusia, as they started down the hill toward the row of restaurants.

The sea air was dense and briny, and the foreign voices spread over the esplanade. She tightened her grip on her purse and looked at the people sitting on the restaurant balconies, at the festive little flags, and at the slender women walking in front of them along the esplanade on their high, pointed heels. Then she looked at Moniek Heller walking by her side, his head lowered to the pavement.

"We'll eat out tonight, eh?" said Moniek in the end. "We're on leave from the hotel, we only took half-board." And he creased his lips in an effort to laugh.

"Nu, gefilte fish they won't give us, but we'll try to make do with the French cuisine." He went on, stressing the words "make do" and tightening his tie in order to affirm his membership in the world of the seaside resort.

But the restaurants were full, and the tables outside on the pavements were all occupied too. The diners sat crowded together nibbling at shellfish piled in white heaps, and it was evident from the satisfaction with which the waiters turned Moniek and Lusia away that business was prospering this weekend at the beginning of summer.

"Here!" Moniek pointed at an empty restaurant, where the tables were all set for dinner, and signaled Lusia to go in in front of him. The waiter who hurried out to meet them shrugged his shoulders and said unwillingly, "We're waiting for an organized group, but if you like we can set one more table for you outside." He pointed to a table for two standing at the edge of the terrace, close to the glass wall of the restaurant.

"That's quite satisfactory," said Moniek, and cleared a way for Lusia between the tables. He brought up the rear and helped her pull up an iron chair and slide it beneath her, as she straightened the skirt of her costume. Then he pulled up the chair on the other side of the table and sat down.

Lusia sat up straight in order to announce that it was a very nice restaurant. She hesitated for a moment, and decided in the end against hanging her purse on the back of the chair. She placed it on her knees and clasped it to her bosom.

"Do you think we'll see the Hararis again?" she asked.

"Why?" asked Moniek.

"I want to give them a letter for Israel. For the children, you know," said Lusia.

"Don't worry about it." Moniek dismissed the subject with a smile, picked up the menu that was standing on the table, and presented it ceremoniously to Lusia. "I'll translate for you," he announced, emphasizing the importance of the occasion.

"Yes, yes." Lusia opened the folded cardboard menu. "Because if something happens they won't know where to get in touch," she said, and stared at the list of names in the unfamiliar language.

"Don't worry, really. We're here now. There's a beautiful view, and also . . ." But Moniek did not finish the sentence.

"Yes, beautiful!" Lusia quickly agreed, turning down the corner of the menu.

Moniek took his eyeglasses out of his jacket pocket and put them on. The thin lines of the gold frame gave him a scholarly air, arousing speculation as to what he might have become if he hadn't gone into ladies' wear. For a moment he concentrated on trying to find the exact Polish equivalent for the names of the dishes on the menu, while Lusia bent stiffly forward, all attention. In the end she said, "Really, it's all so expensive. The meal, the trip . . ."

Moniek interrupted her with a complacent air. "*Nu,* please. There's no need . . ." And he beckoned to the waiter.

Lusia folded the menu and replaced it carefully on its stand, just as it had been before.

The waiter wrote down the order, removed the two menus, and rapidly poured water into their glasses. Moniek smiled in satisfaction at the efficient service, and glanced at Lusia like a wealthy man showing off his possessions. Lusia took a slice of bread and pinched off a piece between her fingers. She filled her mouth and chewed slowly.

Moniek smiled and said, *"Nu,* it's not easy to find the right woman."

"What?" Lusia stopped chewing.

Moniek rested his hands on the table, but quickly drew back when the waiter arrived and deposited their orders before them on the table.

"Bon appétit!" he said to Lusia Taft, as if they were in the habit of exchanging such civilities. He poured a little wine into his glass, tasted it, and then poured for Lusia.

"Good, the wine is good." He smacked his lips like a connoisseur.

Lusia stuck her fork into the steak and began cutting it slowly across.

"We can still begin again!" said Moniek.

"Yes," replied Lusia. She put the meat into her mouth, praising it as she did so. "The meat is very good."

"Yes, it's good," said Moniek, stretching his legs under the table, and he addressed himself to the plate in front of him.

They sat chewing, on either side of the table, sipped their wine, and resumed their chewing.

"Nothing like this in Israel, eh?" said Moniek, scraping the meat from the bone. He straightened his woolen tie and continued, "Everything is so tense there. A hard life. Here at least a person can live in peace. Afford to take a break in a seaside resort from time to time."

The waiter stopped a number of people who were about to sit down on the terrace of the restaurant.

"Inside if you wish. Outside all the tables are booked!" he said as they tried to argue with him, pointing in an aggrieved way at Moniek Heller and Lusia Taft.

When their dessert was placed before them the sun had already set, and the bluish light of the long evening had enveloped the terrace. The esplanade was full of weekend vacationers, and their light clothes were also covered with the blue dust.

They had already placed their spoons next to their glass dishes, and Lusia had opened her purse and removed her lipstick in order to freshen the makeup that had smeared on her lips, when a large tourist bus drew up in the street in front of the restaurant. It maneuvered heavily until in the end it parked right outside the terrace, completely hiding the fishing harbor on the other side of the esplanade and the play of light and evening on the clouds.

The waiter hurried to the entrance of the terrace in order to welcome the people descending from the bus two by two and talking loudly to each other in German. At their head marched a short, plump man who seemed to be the tour organizer. The waiter ran behind the tourists and showed them to their places. The organizer made jokes, and from time to time he slapped the shoulders of the seated tourists. And in the space of a few minutes the terrace was packed full of couples sitting in crowded rows. And all alone in the corner, as in a tiny enclave, stood the table of Moniek and Lusia.

The manager of the restaurant came out. He was wearing a black suit and a bow tie in honor of the occasion. He too received a friendly slap on the back from the organizer, and then he hurried off behind the waiter to collect the orders from the diners and to see that everything was to their satisfaction. The waiter deposited bottles of beer and wine along the tables, which was greeted with cheers and an outbreak of loud chattering.

Moniek screwed up his napkin and wiped his mouth with it several times. The waiter banged their glasses of tea down in front of them and hurried off with his tray to serve the German tourists.

"Comment-ça-va?" The man sitting closest to their table at the end of the row of diners turned his face toward them with a broad smile.

His words attracted the attention of the people next to him to the couple sitting on the terrace, and they all turned smiling faces toward Moniek and Lusia.

"Non parler français." A second man, wearing a brown-checked suit, joined in the conversation, laughing with the full weight of his body.

The wives of the two speakers stared at Lusia with the respect due to a native of the place. One of them, whose hair hung like a fair ball around her head, pointed to her lips in order to indicate that she did not speak the language, accompanying this gesture with a low laugh.

The first man, who apparently knew a greater number of words, went on. *"Nous bataillons ici, comprenez, bataillons, Krieg."* He pointed to the people sitting around the tables and, broadening his smile and shaking his head from side to side in an exaggerated way as if he were telling a story to children, he continued, *"Maintenant ici. Visite. Visite. Avec Frau. Comprenez?"* he asked, and burst into friendly laughter.

And as if waiting for a signal to join in, the man in the three-piece brown suit and the two women also laughed, nodding their heads at Moniek and Lusia.

The waiter returned and unloaded his tray.

When Moniek picked up the bill lying on the table, the Germans were already tackling their first courses. Moniek placed some bank notes on the saucer with the bill and rapidly counted out the coins for the waiter's tip. He stood up. Lusia stood up too, and gathered her bulky purse to her bosom.

The man with the square chin turned toward them, smiling through his chewing, and said, *"Au revoir madame, au revoir Monsieur!"* He waved his hand at them.

The two women also turned their heads, and the man in the brown suit quickly wiped the grease off his lips with his napkin before calling out in a broken accent, *"Au rouvour! Au rouvour!"*

Moniek and Lusia squeezed their way to the exit along the space left between the outer wall of the restaurant and the chairs of the diners. Moniek went first and Lusia, treading heavily in his wake, had difficulty finding a place to plant her orthopedic shoes. Sounds of satisfaction and chewing filled the terrace. Laughter accompanied the raising of beer and wine glasses and the jokes and anecdotes. The people seated next to the wall of the restaurant turned their heads to look after them with expressions of enjoyment at the food and the cheerfulness of the occasion.

They walked away along the esplanade, and the German voices from the restaurant terrace were gradually swallowed up in the noises of the evening. The restaurants were still full, and the empty shells of the white shellfish stood in piles. A troop of youngsters in black leather jackets and tight boots passed them. Moniek and Lusia made their way through the people standing next to the brightly lit show windows, and when they approached the Municipal Casino they saw women in evening dresses and fluffy fur capes stepping out of black limousines and disappearing up the marble staircase like huge moths, leaving a train of darkness behind them.

As they reclimbed the bluff opposite the observatory Lusia glanced at Moniek and saw that he was looking down at the pavement. They walked without saying a word. Lusia's heels clattered in the intervals between his steps, and she clutched her bulky purse tightly to her bosom still, as if she were leaning on it for support as she walked.

The darkness spread toward the street lamps, and down below, on the beach next to the water, the twilight trembled. Lusia shifted her purse from hand to hand and drew the lapels of her jacket together to arrest a sudden, chilly breeze.

"Did the doctor send you to have tests?" she asked.

"Yes," grunted Moniek.

"What were the results?" continued Lusia.

"He said there was nothing to worry about in the meantime. But still, I should start taking things a bit easy. Get used to the idea that things aren't what they used to be."

"But he was optimistic, no?" persisted Lusia.

"Yes, I think so," answered Moniek, as they passed the balcony of the dark observatory.

After a second Lusia said, "That's encouraging."

The lamp on the post rising from the observatory was unlit, and the balcony with its shell-shaped stone balustrade hung over the sea like the shadow of an obsolete grandeur.

"I don't know what kind of world we're living in!" Moniek suddenly burst out, and his sharp chin trembled. "How they can come here without being ashamed, I don't understand!"

"Don't think about it," said Lusia, almost to herself.

"There are some things I just don't understand," continued Moniek, striking his head passionately with the palm of his hand. "I just don't understand!"

"Romek also used to say that people should learn from the past. He was a man with values," said Lusia. "But how long can you go on thinking about the same thing?"

"The cheek of it!" continued Moniek, and his voice grew tired.

"Really, Moniek, you shouldn't upset yourself," said Lusia, and there was a certain tenderness in the way that she beat time with her free hand.

"Yes," said Moniek, and he tugged distractedly at the hem of his jacket.

They descended the esplanade from the top of the bluff and the observatory, and Moniek's steps resumed their subdued tapping between Lusia's heavy strides.

"Yes, there are still a few good years in front of us," he said.

"Yes," said Lusia, and nodded her head.

When they turned their backs on the light that was still clinging to the sea, Lusia continued, "Whatever happens, I'm getting some repairs done in my apartment. The marble on the sink top in the kitchen, and the balcony blinds."

"Whatever happens," Moniek repeated after her.

They walked along the spacious street of the seaside resort. The ornamental trees planted between the street lamps on the avenue swayed in the evening breeze coming from the sea.

"Remind me to take a sleeping pill when we get to the hotel," said Moniek.

"All right," said Lusia.

When they were approaching the hotel, in the light of the elegant display windows, Moniek Heller turned his head and stole a quick glance at the woman who was walking beside him with a heavy tread.

The next morning Moniek knocked on Lusia's door, as arranged.

"Mrs. Taft. Lusia." He bent over the door in the passage.

"Yes, yes," answered Lusia, who was already awake in her bed.

"Sorry I have to hurry you up," continued Moniek behind the door, "but Hirshel Feingold called and invited us to a celebration. I didn't understand exactly of what."

"I'll be ready in a minute," replied Lusia, and she sat up in bed among the big pillows and the sheets, which were still starched although she had already slept in them for two nights. The big room was dim, and underneath the high ceiling strange smells drifted. The night had left a murky residue in her. She supported herself on both elbows and descended slowly from the high bed. She pulled the curtains apart and pushed the balcony shutter open. On the sunlit wallpaper countless shepherds and shepherdesses with their flocks rested under pale blue trees. They climbed to the ceiling and disappeared behind the big wardrobe.

She went into the bathroom and rummaged in her old toilet bag in order to take out the toilet articles that for some reason she hesitated to leave displayed in the place intended for them, on the glass shelf glittering underneath the mirror. She turned her back— for years now she had avoided looking at herself naked in the mirror —and mechanically finished fastening her corset and pulling on her orthopedic stockings. Then she turned around, and with a few vehement strokes she painted the vivid color over the slit of her lips. When she had finished powdering her forehead and cheeks she threw her things back into the toilet bag and straightened her crushed coiffure.

When she had finished dressing she sat down for a moment on the corner of the high bed ready to leave, with her bulky purse already in position on her knees. For a moment she ruminated on the Sabbath day here, which stretched on into the Sunday after it, and then she immediately bent stiffly over her purse, with her short legs dangling, and made sure that she had not forgotten to put in her compact. And while her hand was busy delving into the bag, she also made sure that she had her medicines. She stood up, wondering apprehensively whether she had creased her skirt, and straightened the bedspread, whose design of sailing ships affirmed the holiday atmosphere. From the balcony window she saw the two trees in the hotel garden. She crossed her hands under her bosom around the strap of her purse, and went out of the room.

When they had finished eating breakfast Lusia took the lipstick out of her purse again, and roughly repaired the drawing around her lips. Moniek crumpled the napkin and placed it on the table. He rose from his chair and approached Lusia to offer her his arm. A heavy smell of perfume rose from her body. He was wearing his brown silk tie today, and it shined smoothly and darkly between the lapels of his jacket.

When they stepped outside he was troubled by the pressure on his chest, which had grown worse since the chestnuts had come into blossom. This morning too the sky was covered with a mist, and the air was not yet really warm. Only a few bathers had ventured onto the white beach, and the little flags strung between the lifeguard stands waved limply. They hastened down the wooden walkway on the beach in the direction of La Promenade. Moniek leaned over to tuck his hand in Lusia's arm, together with the strap of her purse. Lusia patted her hair, and every time she put her heels down on the wooden planks the noise of their dragging dissipated the air of uncertainty that accompanied her deliberate tread.

At the other end of the wooden walk Hirshel Feingold, who had come out to meet them, was already waving his hands at them, like a bright, capering dot on the open beach. He covered the distance between them at a scampering run, and the coconut trees emblazoned on his shirt this morning swayed violently from side to side.

"They wrote about it in the newspaper!" he shouted, spreading a big sheet of paper out in front of them.

When he reached them he grabbed Moniek by the arm, pumping it up and down in his agitation. "I took the Hararis to the casino last night, to let them have a look. But with Hirshel there's no such thing as just watching. I started playing with a hundred, and ended up by breaking the bank! They shut the casino down when I won!"

He burst into expansive laughter, and hit the rustling paper with the back of his hand. "Take a look!"

Lusia and Moniek bent over the newspaper and saw a dark picture of Hirshel embracing two uniformed croupiers against the background of the roulette table, his round face beaming.

Still laughing, Hirshel snatched the paper away, disappearing for a moment behind the sheet spread between his two hands and emerging again with a gleeful face after he folded it. Once again he grabbed Moniek's arm and started pulling him behind him.

"First we'll have champagne at La Promenade," he announced, "and after that lunch at the Excelsior. Hirshel never misses a chance for a celebration!" And he was off again, running in front of them with his low shoulders swaying from side to side, and with them the coconut trees on his shirt.

On the terrace of La Promenade Henrietta stood tensely, twisting and untwisting the strap of her purse. Next to her stood a man in a striped suit and a brown hat. Moniek presented him to Mrs. Taft. "Allow me to introduce—Lusia Taft, Mr. Tzuker."

"Pleased to meet you," said Lusia with her polite smile, and she shook hands with Henrietta, placing one foot in front of the other in order to indicate that as far as she was concerned the walk was over.

"He was with us in the same DP camp," whispered Moniek into Lusia's ear. "Also in ladies' wear. He never comes before Saturday night—can't afford to shut his business down earlier."

Lusia nodded her head understandingly and went on smiling at the owner of the brown hat.

"Arlette hasn't arrived yet!" Henrietta burst out.

"But Mrs. Feingold," said Mr. Tzuker soothingly, obviously for the umpteenth time, "You know what the youngsters are like today. Really, there's nothing to worry about."

But Henrietta was not appeased, and she went on wringing the strap of her purse with small, rapid movements.

Hirshel clapped his hands from the table. "Mrs. Taft, Mr. Tzuker, Moniek! We're all waiting for you!" and he signaled to the waiter, who hurried to uncork the bottles of champagne standing on the table.

They sat down in their usual places, except that this morning Mr. Tzuker seated himself helpfully between Lusia and Henrietta. Hirshel rose to his feet and poured the frothing liquid into the glasses with a flourish.

Marek Harari choked a little and coughed. Gusta Harari hurried to pat him on the back. Marek's sallow face flushed like an elongated copper dish. When his coughing had subsided he raised his face apologetically and smiled at Hirshel Feingold, who was already refilling the glasses. Hella Honiger laughed, and her broad bosom looked more authoritative than ever inside its pink jacket. Mr. Honiger nonchalantly emptied his second glass of champagne, and Lusia whispered confidingly to Moniek, "I'm not used to drinking so much."

"A little celebration never did anyone any harm," replied Moniek, clinking his glass ceremoniously against hers.

"Us too! Us too!" Staszek Honiger called out from the other side of the table, stretching across to clink his brimming glass against Mrs. Taft's and half rising to his feet as he said, "Really, you should only be . . ." But he sat down again without finishing his sentence. "They haven't said anything official yet, so maybe it's better not to be in too much of a hurry," he muttered to himself, and in order to cover up his over-hasty gesture he addressed the rest of his toast to Henrietta: "They should only be happy, the young ones!" And he gulped down the rest of his champagne, holding his jaunty checkered cap in place with the back of his hand.

Hella Honiger chipped in quickly, "Yes, the young ones should only be happy!"

Mrs. Harari too raised her glass in a burst of emotion and announced, "They shouldn't suffer; they should live in peace! That's the most important thing. In peace and quiet!"

"Drink up! Drink up! Don't be lazy!" urged Hirshel Feingold, lifting another bottle from the tray, which was already covered with a puddle of champagne, and impatiently filling the glasses. "You should have seen the people in the casino last night; they were fit to burst!" he said, pouring the champagne onto the table without paying any attention to what he was doing. He added, shaking with laughter, "I think they won't let me into the casino again! Ha ha!"

Marek Harari leaned toward Mr. Honiger and said something to him. Gusta Harari nodded quickly in agreement. Mr. Honiger agreed too, and hastened to say, "We have to start moving already. The Hararis have to be at the railway station."

"Yes, yes," said Marek Harari, jumping up from his place. Gusta rose immediately after him and stood beside him, ready to go.

Hella Honiger said, summing up with an official air, "It was a pleasure!"

Lusia Taft made haste to rise after them. "I'll give you my telephone number. If you could get in touch . . ."

"Out of the question! You're not going like this!" Hirshel cried, clapping his hands for the waiter. "We're all going to see our Israelis off. *Nu, nu!*" He urged Mr. Tzuker on, signaling him to support Henrietta, fumbled with his wallet, and rapidly placed the bills in the waiter's hand.

Lusia Taft finished writing the telephone number down on a piece of paper and bumped into a chair as she hurried around the table to Gusta Harari. The waiter folded the bills into the pocket of his coat, highly satisfied with the generous tip he had received, to judge by the number of times he bobbed his head at the celebrants as they withdrew. Moniek smoothed his brown silk tie and waited for Lusia Taft.

Henrietta Feingold rose to her feet and announced, "I'm not going. I'm waiting here for Arlette!"

"But Mrs. Feingold, really, there's nothing to worry about." Mr. Tzuker, who depended on the good will of Hirshel Feingold for his living, immediately renewed his coaxing. "Nothing has happened!"

Hirshel bustled the company out between the tables and ran on ahead of them up the esplanade, his hands churning at his sides. After him Mr. Tzuker hurried to give his arm to Henrietta, who rose obediently to follow her husband, and it was evident that he was torn between his desire to run loyally side by side with Hirshel Feingold and his duty to keep up with the limping pace of Henrietta, who kept her head back in the effort to locate Arlette.

Mrs. Honiger, a cordial guide, sailed beside the embarrassed, slightly charred figure of Marek Harari like a heavy pink ship. Lusia threw her pencil back into the belly of her purse, and Gusta Harari closed her own purse on the envelope with a sharp click. Gusta, in her old traveling costume, hurried after Mr. Honiger, who thrust out his head in order to emphasize the carefree holiday air proclaimed by his checkered cap. And the last to leave were Moniek Heller and Lusia Taft, who brought up the rear of the little procession.

Marek Harari hurried behind the limping Henrietta and the swaying Mr. Tzuker, as if he were taking shelter under the shade of Hella Honiger's bosom. His narrow forehead stretched, giving his whole figure a questioning air. "I hope there won't be any problems," he said.

Mrs. Honiger turned both hands toward him and began encouragingly, "But Marek, everything will be all right. You'll arrive in time. You'll take off in time. And this evening you'll be at home already." Her bosom forged ahead like the vanguard in front of the troops.

"Yes, yes," Mr. Harari submitted.

"It's good that you came for a little rest," said Staszek Honiger behind them to Mrs. Harari, pulling his cap backward and forward on his head.

"Really, there are no words to thank . . ." said Gusta Harari, "It was all such an effort . . ."

"It's good that you came!" Mr. Honiger cut her short. "A wonderful opportunity to see the villa we bought here. *Nu,* so we achieved something in the end. If we'd stayed in Israel, who knows . . ." He looked a little pityingly at Marek Harari, and returned the checkered cap to its proper position on his head.

Marek Harari bowed his head to the pavement, and the skin of his neck tightened. "I don't know how we'll go back to everyday life after all this," he said, and his chin reached out to the sea, distant at the bottom of the bluff. "It won't be easy. No, it won't be easy."

And Mrs. Honiger pursed her lips in disgust and made no more efforts at encouragement.

Lusia was tired of running back and forth, first from the hotel to the café, and now from the café to the restaurant. She tightened her grip on the purse beneath her bosom, dug her heels heavily into the pavement, and made an effort not to lag behind in the climb up the hill. Moniek smiled wryly, perhaps because of the fast pace, which was quickening his breathing, and perhaps as a result of the debate taking place inside him. "It's all coincidence," he announced to Lusia, as if he were making a confession, "why we landed up here instead of somewhere else." He fumbled with his tie, and the square signet ring on his finger wandered to and fro. "In the beginning we wanted to get established, and afterward the children were already used to it."

"Yes, yes." Lusia swung her arms heavily and concentrated on the effort of walking.

"That's the way it is," continued Moniek. "A person doesn't always end up where he wants to." Lusia shrugged her shoulders and tightened her hold on her purse.

"If we start thinking about what we really wanted . . ." said Moniek, and let out a laughing groan. After a moment he made a couple of bobbing movements with his head as a sign of cheerfulness, tucked his hand into Lusia's elbow, and said, "So what? We've still got a few good years in front of us, eh?"

Lusia's broad shoes beat the pavement heavily, and she said, "As long as we've got our health. That's the most important thing." And she shifted her purse to her other hand.

The people strolling along the esplanade turned their heads to gaze after the cavalcade advancing between the calm seaside villas and the bright signs of the delicatessen shops. At the head the coconut trees emblazoned on Hirshel Feingold's shirt waved frantically to and fro. After them dragged the limping Henrietta, with

Mr. Tzuker bursting coaxingly forward. Bringing up the rear in sudden spurts were Hella Honiger's pink bosom, Gusta Harari's little face, and the stubborn figure of Lusia Taft.

When they reached the top of the bluff, next to the balcony of the Wind Rose observatory and the mast sticking out of it, Henrietta suddenly stopped. The people coming up behind almost bumped into her, like the ragged tail of a carnival dragon. "I can't go on!" she said firmly.

Hirshel, several paces ahead, came back at a run and went on jumping from one foot to the other on the spot, as if the sudden halt had not interrupted his running at all.

"I can't run any more!" Henrietta flung at him. Then she pulled her hand from Mr. Tzuker's arm and dragged herself to the stone parapet of the esplanade. She leaned against the parapet and scanned the beach anxiously.

The unexpected halt cast the Hararis into confusion, and they opened feverish consultations with the Honigers about the amount of time left before they had to catch their train.

Moniek and Lusia stood where they were, as if waiting for instructions.

From the other side of the bluff the German tourist group advanced on the observatory, and the echo of their laughter and loud voices rose in the street.

"I think we'll have to go," announced Marek Harari apologetically, pointing to the watch peeping out of his sleeve.

Gusta chimed in like an echo, "Otherwise we'll be late."

On the balcony of the observatory the war veterans crowded. They pushed toward the shell-shaped balustrade in order to examine the old Wind Rose carved into the stone with its arrows and its famous pictures of towns. Peals of laughter accompanied their exultant shouts: "Hong Kong! New York! Berlin! *Ja, ja,* Berlin! *Auch* Düsseldorf!"

Hirshel Feingold skipped across the space between him and the Hararis, and the coconut trees waved in agitation. He shook the Hararis' hands rapidly. *"Bon voyage! Bon voyage!"* he cried, slapping

Marek Harari on the arm. He capered up and down and announced, "I'm going on to tell them to expect us at the restaurant." He waved at the little group with a chubby hand, crying firmly to the Honigers, "This afternoon as usual at La Promenade, eh?" And, turning his head, he charged toward the observatory, where the veteran warriors were at that very moment emerging, accompanied by their wives. Hirshel waved the folded newspaper tucked beneath his arm at them in passing, as if to say, Yes, yes, that's me! And his short, bright figure disappeared into the dense stream of tourists.

Gusta and Marek Harari made haste to take their farewells from Henrietta, and after them the Honigers too took their leave.

"I hope that nothing has happened to Arlette." Henrietta stared distractedly.

"But really, Mrs. Feingold," said Mr. Tzuker rebukingly, in a louder voice than usual, in order to make his words heard above the vociferous conversations eddying around them like a current flowing past some small obstacle in its way.

"Don't forget to call," Lusia Taft thrust forward in the direction of the Hararis.

"The minute we arrive!" said Gusta, smacking her purse as she spoke.

Moniek approached to say goodbye, but he gave way to Mr. Tzuker, who ran up to shake hands, bowing and making his brown hat bob up and down.

"Nu, good." Mr. Harari shook hands with Moniek Heller and Lusia Taft, who was standing next to him.

A moment of confusion ensued as the Hararis got ready to leave but were prevented from doing so by the organized group of German tourists blocking their way.

"Good luck for the future," said Gusta Harari in the meantime, and she and her husband nodded their heads in the direction of Moniek Heller and Lusia Taft.

Hella Honiger crossed the road with a confident air. Staszek hurried after her, calling out to the Hararis to follow them down the road disappearing between the buildings of the little seaside town.

The esplanade emptied of the group of Germans, who started down the bluff in the direction of the row of cafés, and Hirshel had long ago been swallowed up behind the observatory on the other side. Mr. Tzuker was unable to persuade Henrietta to continue the walk to the restaurant, despite all his calming efforts and all the brown noddings of his hat. He left her where she was, collapsing against the stone parapet, and stationed himself a couple of paces away, like a bodyguard. His face was turned half to the esplanade and half to the sea, as if he were announcing a time-out.

Moniek Heller linked his arm in Lusia Taft's and took a few slow steps up the hill with her. Next to the observatory balcony he said, "*Nu,* in the meantime why don't we . . ." and he pointed to the two steps.

"Really, the beach is so big," said Lusia, clattering her shoes on the steps and approaching the balustrade.

"Yes," said Moniek.

Lusia leaned her elbows on the carved stone balustrade, between the miniature etching of the churches in Stockholm and the one of Negroes bathing in the sea in Cape Town. Moniek too rested his hand on the balustrade and called out at random: "Shanghai!"

"Tarnów we won't find here, and Tel Aviv didn't exist when they built the observatory," he said, and laughed.

Lusia contemplated the mist covering the beach and the bay. Moniek fingered his signet ring limply, and after a moment he placed his hand over Lusia's between a picture of Brussels and one of Amsterdam.

"Yes," he said, as if in continuation, "the main thing is that we're here." And without waiting for an answer he added, "That's already a miracle."

Lusia nodded her head mechanically. "Yes, yes."

And she turned her head from the beach to the street. For a moment, she saw the regulars of La Promenade scattering to the four points of the compass—Hirshel Feingold bouncing like a brightly colored ball in the direction of Moscow, where the arrow pointed; the Honigers and the Hararis disappearing into the shadows of the street between the old hotels in the direction of Madagascar; Mr. Tzuker standing guard on the latitude of São Paulo; and Henrietta frozen next to the parapet, her face turning toward some unknown point in the distance, a mask of anxiety.

"We can begin again too. Why not?" said Moniek. The words came out of his mouth at first with animation and in the end with uncertainty.

"Yes, yes." Lusia went on nodding her head, without remembering exactly what it was that she was agreeing to.

Once more Moniek tucked his arm in hers, and they climbed the two steps from the observatory to the esplanade. And they set out again. Moniek Heller lifted his chin. Lusia Taft's heavy shoes clattered. Dutifully she breathed in the healthful air of the seaside town.

Translated by DALYA BILU

THE
TIMES MY
FATHER
DIED

Yehuda Amichai

One Yom Kippur my father stood in front of me in synagogue. I climbed up onto the seat to get a better view of him from the back. His neck is much easier to remember than his face. His neck is always fixed and unchanging; but his face is constantly in motion as he speaks, his mouth gaping like the doorway of a dark house or like a fluttering flag. Butterfly eyes, or eyes like postage stamps affixed to the letter of his face, which is always mailed to faraway places. Or his ears, which are like sails on the sea of his God. Or his face, which was either all red or white like his hair. And the waves on his forehead, which was a little, private beach beside the sea of the world.

It was then that I saw his neck. A deep wrinkle, almost a crack, ran right across it. It was the first time that I saw a deep, sun-scorched wadi, though I was still far away from Israel. Perhaps my father had also started out from just such a wadi. The rains hadn't come yet, and on that Yom Kippur the summer heat lay sweltering on the land where I had not yet been.

Only now do I see his face on the photograph that I keep in my closet. It is the face of a man who has started eating his favorite dish and is disappointed to find its flavor somewhat unsavory. The edges of his mouth, drooping at the corners, attest to this fact, as do the wrinkles on his nose and the mute birds of sadness hovering in the corners of his eyes. I can collect a great deal of evidence from the face—not in order to pass judgment on him but to judge myself.

That Yom Kippur he stood in front of me, so very busy with his grown-up God. He was all white in his "shrouds." The entire world around him was black, like the charred stones left behind after a bonfire. The dancers were gone and the singers were gone, and only the blackened stones had remained. That's how my father, dressed in his white shroud, was left behind. It was the first time I remember my father dying.

When they got to the *aleinu* prayer, my father went down on his knees like all the others and touched the floor with his forehead.

I thought he was drinking with his forehead, that maybe God flowed down there among the legs of the tables. Before he kneeled he spread out his velvet *tallith* bag so as not to get his knees dirty. He didn't worry about dirtying his forehead. Then he was resurrected. He got up without moving his feet, which he kept close together. He got up, and his face changed color a number of times and he was alive again and mine, and I climbed onto the seat to have a look at his neck and the wrinkle in it. He was flesh and blood that was resurrected. Why are living people called flesh and blood? You only see flesh and blood when a man's been crushed, when his body is injured, or when he's dead. When people are alive you see other combinations. You see not flesh and blood, but skin and eyes, a smile and dark hair, hands and a mouth.

I went up to the women's gallery to tell my mother about the resurrection. Up there they had apples filled with spices to keep the women from fainting. I envied the women. I have always wanted to faint but have never been able to—to be wiped off the board, to retreat from everything aimlessly and unresisting. The women were holding the spiced apples in their hands; I was also in their hands, and so was the entire globe. They held me up to the large clock to check the time with me. They looked at me in the light of the fires that were going to burn down the synagogue. From up there in the gallery I saw them stripping the white mantles off the scrolls of the law. They took hold of the shoulder straps and pulled the mantle off, leaving the scroll of the law naked and cold. Then my father came back to life, and in the evening he broke his fast after the *ne'ilah* service. The year was a huge wheel, a wall enclosing days and seasons. An odd game! My sins and my atonements were still folded up, and both of them looked the same. That evening, the moon circled the city like a gleaming white chicken used in the atonement ritual.

My father died many times more, and he still dies from time to time. Sometimes I am there, and sometimes he dies alone. Sometimes his death occurs quite near my table, or when I am working, writing pretty words on the blackboard or looking at the colorful countries on the map. But there are times when I am very far away when he dies, like the way it happened in the First World War. It's a good thing sons don't see their fathers at war. And it's also a good thing that I wasn't in the same war, otherwise we might have killed one another; because he wore the uniform of Kaiser Wilhelm, while I wore the uniform of King George, God having put a gap of twenty-five years between us. I put his medals in the same box where I keep my own World War II decorations, as I had nowhere else to keep them. One of his medals has a lion on it and two swords crossed, as in a duel between two invisible swordsmen. Beasts of prey are prominent on most emblems: lions and eagles and bulls and hawks and all sorts of other ferocious creatures. In the synagogue they have a pair of lions holding up the tablets over the holy ark. Even our own laws, too, can only be protected and upheld by wild animals.

In Germany once, a long time after the war, my father put on a black frock coat and pinned on his decorations; then he donned a shiny top hat and went off to the dedication of a war monument. The names of all the dead were listed in alphabetical order. Where did the monument stand? In the public park near the playground, right next to the swings and sandboxes. I don't remember what the memorial looked like, but it must have had stone soldiers pointing stone rifles under stone flags, and stone mothers weeping stonily. There must also have been all sorts of wild beasts to immortalize the greatness of man and of his generals and emperors.

For four years my father died in the war. He dug a lot of trenches. They told him that sweat saves blood, and that the soldiers' blood saves the sweat of generals, and that the generals' sweat, in turn, saves the manufacturers and kaisers a lot of sweat and blood, and so on all down the line, a regular savings scheme. My father dug a lot of trenches, dug himself a whole lot of graves. He was wounded only once. All the other bullets and shrapnel missed. When he really died, many years later, all the bullets and pellets that had missed him got together and smashed his heart all at once; and that's how he never got out of the last trench, which others had dug for him. He went through a great many battles and was very often among those reported killed in action in the arithmetic of battle or those killed in the statistics of stormed positions. His blood glowed like those buttons you press to put on the electric light in apartment-house hallways, so that death should be able to see and light up his body with his blood. But death never pressed the buttons of his blood and my father didn't really die. God, in Whom he believed, hovered over him like a white, saving parachute, high above the trajectory of the shells. He never involved his God in matters of war, but left Him among the laws of nature and the stars, above him, like a light foam that topped the dark, heavy beverage of his life.

Sometimes, when the war went hard, his body became like a tree that had shed its leaves. Only the branches of nerves remained, while his entire life dropped off like leaves. He sent back a great many letters from out there. At first the letters were infrequent, but during the four years of the war the letters accumulated into packs and bundles, and the packs hardened like stone. This is what happens to letters. At first they flutter in, fleet and white like a dove's wings; and later all the letters get hard like stone. The letters also wandered from storeroom to storeroom, from one chest of drawers to the other, into the closet and on top of the closet, and from there up to the attic and later right under the roof tiles. When my father really died, he leaped in one plunge much higher than his letters on the roof. When the real resurrection of the dead takes place, he will have to undo all those bundles and read his letters aloud. In his lifetime a man gives off a large quantity of sweat, blood, body waste, poetry, and letters.

Once he told us about some French prisoners of war at Verdun who asked him for water in their language *(de l'eau, de l'eau)*, and he gave them all that was left in his water canteen. Since then I have never forgotten their calling out for water. Sometimes they come to me asking for a little water. Perhaps my father told them about me, but I hardly think so, since I wasn't born yet at the time. But in war—which jumbles people and earth together and throws everything into confusion, making people who are standing sit down, and those who are seated lie down, and turning the recumbent into pictures on the wall—in war everything is possible.

Once, just before Hitler came along, my father's former brothers-in-arms invited him to a regimental reunion. They sent him a nice letter on notepaper headed by the regimental emblem: a hunter's cap, antlers, and a couple of crossed rifles. Why did it have such an emblem? It was a hunting regiment with a glorious tradition behind it, a *corps d'élite*. Originally they used to hunt hares and stags; later they went hunting human beings in the war. Not just to hunt them, but actually to kill them. Nor was it to eat them, like one did hares, but simply to kill them and even to mangle their bodies, so that one could see flesh and blood, and not smiles and hair and arms and caresses and other fine combinations.

My father didn't accept the invitation, and this too was death, because they liked him very much and used to call him David. During the war, they used to give him some of their rations on the Day of Atonement so that he might be able to fast. They would gather in the stars for his prayer and maintain moments of silence for his quiet devotions. In return he would keep their spirits up with his faith and with the funny stories he told.

After that he died frequently, a great many times.

He died when they came to arrest him for throwing into the garbage the Nazi pin I had found. The black uniforms came to our door. The black uniforms broke it down. And the boots tramped in. It was terrible for me to see that my father was no longer able to defend our house and withstand the enemy's onslaught. That was childhood's end. How could they just burst into our house like that against Father's wishes!

If I had been bigger then, I would have covered up my father, as Shem did when he walked despondently.*

He died when they stationed bullies outside his shop to keep people from buying there because it was a Jewish shop.

*See Gen. 10:23.

He died when we left Germany to emigrate to Palestine, and all the years that had been died with him. When the train went past the Jewish Old Age Home, which my father had supported, all the old people stood waving their bedsheets from balconies and windows. They were not waving them in surrender but in farewell. There is no difference between surrender and goodbye, for in either case you wave white flags or handkerchiefs or even bedsheets.

He died a great many times, for he was made up of different materials. Sometimes he was like iron, sometimes like white bread, sometimes like antique wood, and all of these must die. There were times when I saw him cloaking his face with his hands so as not to let me see it stripped and bare. There were times when his thoughts overburdened his small body, and he sagged under their load. And there were times when he stood firm and strong like a chain of telephone poles, and his thoughts were wonderful, brilliant, and fleet like the stretched wires. Even the songbirds would then alight and perch on them.

When he really died, God didn't know whether he was really dead. Till then, he always used to rise from the dead, but this time he did not rise. A few weeks before he had had a heart attack. They call it a heart attack, but what attacks what? . . . Does the heart attack the body, or the body the heart? Or does the world attack both?

When I came to see him one day, he was lying next to an iron oxygen bottle; his eyes were like the glass tumblers they crush underfoot at weddings. When I went over to him, I heard the large oxygen bomb hissing. Once an angel stood next to the sickbed, but now there are bombs full of hissing oxygen. Sea divers and airplane pilots are also given oxygen tanks. Where was my father going? Was he going to dive, or go aloft maybe? At all events he was leaving us. He beckoned me over to him. I said, "Don't talk and tire yourself out," and he said, "There's the cat mewing on the neighbor's roof. Maybe it's shut in and wants to get out." I went over to the neighbor's to release the cat. And again all we heard was the hiss of the oxygen. There was a clock fitted onto the oxygen tank to measure the pressure. My father had as much time as the oxygen in the tank. My mother stood at the door. If only she had been able to, she would have stood at his bedside like the oxygen bomb giving him of her life force.

After that, my father slowly began to recover. Every day he regained a little of his color, as if all his colors had fled from his face and dispersed when his heart had been attacked and were now returning, like refugees after an air raid. The oxygen tank was put outside on the balcony. The day he died they gave him a cardiogram. The doctor came and opened up a sort of radio and hooked it up to my father with all kinds of electric wires. When you love a person you don't need such a complicated gadget to examine his heart, but you do when somebody's ill. The needle traced zigzags on a roll of paper, like a seismograph in an earthquake. My father looked like a broadcasting station, completely covered with wires and antennas. That day he transmitted his last broadcast. I heard it.

The doctor said, "We're all right," as if anybody had doubted that he himself was all right too. He then dismantled the apparatus and showed us the zigzags, which he thought were all right.

In the evening I took my wife to see a movie. When the exaggerated faces on the screen had stopped laughing or crying, we went out to the street. My wife bought some flowers from a man who kept them in a bucket, just outside an artists' café. This place was frequented by sad-looking young poets who were forever gazing into the distance; men who sported a variety of battle pins; men who limped because of war injuries, and those who limped because it looked aristocratic; men who brandished moustaches; lovers of war in civilian clothes and peace lovers in uniform; and girls who liked keeping company with all of them. We bought red roses, possibly because we wanted to hasten the color to my father's cheeks.

We went back to sit down by my father's side. My wife put the flowers in a vase, where they breathed more freely. We drew up chairs around the bed and my father started telling us about a man who had arrived in the country after he had jumped off a train and had been hidden by good *goyim*. Tears welled up in my father's eyes as he spoke of the good people who had given shelter to a fugitive. His eyes filled with tears and an odd gurgling sound filled his mouth. His speech stopped all at once, like a film that snaps at the movies or like a radio program when another station suddenly cuts in. What other station could have cut in on my father's broadcast, causing both stations to go dead, his and the one that was making all the interference? His mouth opened wide, as if he still had a host of stories to tell about a lot of good people and his mouth couldn't get them all out at once. I rushed over to him, embraced him, and kissed his cold forehead. Perhaps I had just remembered that his forehead had once touched the ground on Yom Kippur—or did I wish to bring him back to life as Elisha had done? My mother came running in from the bathroom. My wife called the doctor. The doctor came and confirmed what was already a confirmed fact. A good neighbor came in and saw to the arrangements. A rabbi, an acquaintance of my father's, came in and supervised the rites; he had the furniture shifted around and windows opened and shut. He was used to people dying. He placed a lighted candle on the floor, like a lantern near a building that is going up or a road under repair. Then he opened a book and began whispering. The oxygen tank was no longer needed to whisper.

The next day they washed my father at home. They moved the furniture out of the room, poured out streams of water, and wrapped him in rolls of cloth. After he was buried, a whole lot of relatives and acquaintances came visiting. Aunt Shoshana came up from the country, glad to get away from her hundreds of chickens and meet friends she hadn't seen for a long time.

There were many occasions for mourning. We let pass the occasion for the loud, bitter wail of grief. Perhaps it was because he had died in the middle of telling a story, or because all the radio stations had suddenly closed down, or perhaps it was because the heart would have had to open up as wide as a trumpet mouth and it wasn't large enough for that. One could mourn with the shriek of the train that went up to Jerusalem through the oppressive, haunting mountains, or silently, like an unclosed window that silently suffers.

We have only a few facial expressions: sorrow, fear, a smile, and a few others, like the large mannequins in shop windows. Fate manipulates us, as a window dresser fixes his dummies into position, lifting an arm here and turning a head there, and that's the way they remain all through the season. It's the same with us.

I let my beard grow in mourning. At first it was bristly, but later it grew soft. Sometimes, when I lay down, I would hear shots or the rumble of tractors down in one of the valleys, or blasting from the stone quarries. My father was like those quarries; he gave me all his stone and depleted himself. Now that he was dead and I was built up, he remained gaping, void, and deserted, with the forest closing in around him. When I go down to the coastal plain sometimes, I see the stone quarries at the roadside, and they are deserted.

I ordered a tombstone. The evening before I went to order it I saw a girl standing near one of the tombstones, fixing her sandal strap. When she saw me coming she ran away between two tall buildings. I ordered a horizontal tombstone, with a stone pillow as a headpiece. The stonemason, like a tailor, asked me about measurements and seams and lines and materials.

The cemetery lies near the border. In times of crisis the dead are left to themselves, with only a few soldiers turning up from time to time. Next to my father lies a German doctor who doesn't have a tombstone but only a little tin marker. As you look toward the city you can see the Tnuva Dairy tower. Towers don't help us very much any more, but the Tnuva tower is actually a refrigerator. There are also water towers, which have to be high enough to fill all the houses with water. God, Who is very high up, filled my father up to the brim.

I was filled with other things, and not always from high towers. Sometimes the pressure was weak and I was only half filled with dreams and ideas. I was in the cemetery a few days ago. Each grave bears a name and a verse. No one knows where Moses was buried, but we know where he lived and we still know all about his life. Nowadays everything is the other way around. We know only where the burial places are. Where we live is unfixed and unknown. We roam about, we change, we shift. Only the burial place is known.

I, for my part, go my way, developing some of my father's qualities and some of his facial features and traits. I develop some, and discard others.

But, as I have said at the beginning, my father still keeps dying. He comes to me in my dreams and I am afraid for him and say: Take your coat, walk more slowly, don't talk, you mustn't get excited, take a rest from this awful war. I myself can't rest. I must keep going, but not to pray. I place my phylacteries, not on my arm and forehead, but in the drawer, which I never open any more.

Once I was walking along the ancient Appian Way in Rome. I was carrying my father on my shoulders. Suddenly his head sagged and I was afraid he was going to die. I laid him down at the side of the road and put a stone under his head, and went to call a taxi. Once they used to call on God to help; now you call a taxi. I couldn't find one, and I got farther away from my father. Every few steps I would turn around to look at him, then run on toward the stream of traffic. I saw him lying by the roadside; only his head was turned in my direction, following me. I saw him through the ancient arch of San Sebastian. Passersby stopped, bent over him, and then went on. I finally got a taxi, but it was too narrow and looked like a snake. I got another one, and the driver said: "We know him; he's only pretending to be dead." I turned around and saw that my father was still lying by the side of the road, his white face turned to me. But I didn't know if he was still alive. I turned around again and saw him, a very distant object, through the ancient arches of San Sebastian's gate.

Translated by YOSEF SCHACHTER

AFTERWORD

FACING THE NIGHTMARE:
ISRAELI LITERATURE ON THE HOLOCAUST

GERSHON SHAKED

The following passage from Yoram Kaniuk's *Adam Resurrected* is an appropriate phrasing of the relationship of Hebrew literature to the Holocaust:

. . . And what remains, what's left? Wretched, nerve-racked, hopeless sticks. Are they beautiful? I don't know. Beautiful grotesques. Human beings who have been halved, quartered—the Rabinowitzes, the Spiegel family, the English teacher Mrs. Spring, all of us. During the day we may be complaining, yawning, making money, building houses, scrambling around as fast as we can, but at night we are insomniacs in our spacious houses, our modern apartments, our magnificent cars, at night we dream

nightmares and shriek, for Satan has tatooed our forearms with blue numbers. Do you know, my dear Mrs. Seizling, why these cries, these shrieks, are heard in this land in the dead of night? All those numbers screaming and crying because they have no idea of the why or the wherefore or the how or the how long or the when or the whereto of it all? They cry because there is no escape. The insult scorches. The knowledge, the final realization that they were simply raw material in the most advanced factory of Europe, under a sky inhabited by a God in exile, by a Stranger, this information drives us crazy. Such humiliation! So we have turned this country into the largest insane asylum on earth. (Yoram Kaniuk, *Adam Resurrected,* London, 1972, pp. 51–52.)

This passage provides a forceful expression of the quality of the "material" under discussion, "material" that the entire Israeli social entity must reckon with, since the subject lives within it, constantly burrowing deeper.

To a certain extent the society justifies its own existence through its struggle with that subject. Literary works in this country are different from those of Holocaust survivors in other languages, which stand by themselves and are bound to a social milieu that is much less self-enclosed. There are perhaps only two nations that must grapple with this "material" as social entities, that cannot ignore it, for it is part of their national identity—the Israelis and the Germans. It seems to me that we would do well to undertake comparative research in the way that our literature and that of the Germans have dealt with the experience that was a collective trauma for both peoples—the murderers and the victims.

People in Israel do not confront the gaping maw of the recent past in the same way, as different groups within the population come to it with different memories. Few among those who live with us today have gone through the fire. Many more were burned by it in one way or another—a person who was saved from the very horrors of the Holocaust is not the same as someone who was saved at the threshold of the period; nor is, someone who was imprisoned in a camp the same as a person who remained outside it. *A fortiori,* someone born in Israel, for whom that experience was merely a collective "national" experience, is not similar to a refugee from the Holocaust, for whom it was part of his existential being.

2

In order to distinguish among various literary reactions typical of various population groups, perhaps one must first ask several preliminary questions, such as: Which social groups produced the writers who grapple with this subject? To whom are their works addressed? What materials did they choose for themselves to construct the fictional world that relates to the subject of the Holocaust? Finally, and most important: Does this subject belong to the sort that a man cannot see and live with, that is, a subject that is actually beyond the power of the writer's pen (such as a son who kills his mother, which Eliot in his *Hamlet and his Problems* [*Collected Essays 1917–1932*] claims to be beyond the power of writers)? What is, therefore, the way writers choose to express the fundamentally indescribable?

Another topic leads us to the area of literary form: the question that writers confronted was how to raise the issue. By depicting the fate of individuals who represent the masses, by means of synecdoche? Or by casting a general and epic light, rich in synecdoche and general descriptions?

Each of these approaches entails its own problems, and various writers "solved" the artistic problems bound up with their approaches in various ways.

3

The subject of the Holocaust, therefore, is multi-faceted and not treated in the same way by every writer. Various writers from various population groups have written on the subject in various ways. It is possible to distinguish among several approaches to the subject according to the social "origin" of the writer.

Among those born in Israel, there is an effort to understand the experience of the Holocaust through characters from "over there" who appear and pose a problem to the native Israeli. He, in turn, must deal, by means of the figure before him, with the world which that figure represents.

Another way also characteristic of native Israelis is to intensify those figures and raise them to the level of the symbol. The writers interpret that symbol and give it historiosophical significance.

Other writers have spread out their canvas and have attempted to deal with historical situations: pictures of the masses, the movements of groups in geographical space, constantly alternating between the observation of individuals and the illumination of large groups.

The survivors themselves reacted to the subject in a different way. What was for most of the native Israelis a historical event with collective significance was for most of the survivors a traumatic childhood memory. What the first group saw from the outside was seen by the second group from within. Each brings things from his own life when he describes the way in which the lives of his heroes were shaped in the recent and more recent past (following the Holocaust)—in the shadow of that traumatic childhood experience —and the way they continue to live despite the mark of that past.

4

Judith Hendel was one of the first Israeli-born writers who felt that the characters who came from over there "were another kind of people." Just as Aharon Megged in *Yad Vashem* presented the native Israeli in contrast with someone who was bound up with the Diaspora and with the Holocaust and emphasized the opposition between the two attitudes, Yosef Bar-Yosef also juxtaposed the native Israeli, Yonatan Argaman, and the Holocaust survivor in his book *The Life and Death of Yonatan Argaman.* The survivor is sent to his death by the native Israeli, who feels guilty toward him.

A juxtaposition of that sort is also found between Uri and Mika in *He Walked in the Fields* by Moshe Shamir, and the lack of understanding and the mutual attraction between the lovers is also explained by the opposing forces within their historical "origins," which provide the background.

And, to be more specific: Judith Hendel feels the right of "the other people" to be different, even though the country's poor people are unwilling to grant them that right and accept them as they are.

Shlomo Nitzan also subjects native Israelis to criticism, and most of the heroes of his novel, *Among Themselves,* are native Israelis or their parents, pioneering immigrants. But the children pilot ships full of immigrants to Israel, and one of the heroes finds his grandfather among the immigrants. At first he pins high hopes on his grandfather, but in the end he is disappointed. All his expectations are proved false. The grandfather does not fit the image that he had fashioned for himself, and the author criticizes the grandson's very expectations for a "hero" and his disappointment when he discovers that the hero was actually an anti-heroic refugee from the Holocaust.

Hanoch Bartov's hero in *The Brigade* discovers Holocaust survivors who are strong and proud. An emissary of the partisan movement, with whom the soldiers of the Brigade meet, is a proud figure who arouses enthusiasm and pride. The heroes of the novel meet with refugees and with the persecutors. They, the soldiers of the Jewish Brigade, cannot behave like ordinary mortals and are not prepared to take revenge for the blood that had been shed. That is their weakness as Jews, and that is also their moral strength. Apparently native-born Israelis seek and find something of their identity in their identification with the fate of the Jewish people and the experience of the Holocaust. That is, of course, an externalized view, but it implies a sincere effort to make a connection between historical experience and historical identity.

A similar problem appears in the novel *People of Sodom* by Ehud Ben-Ezer, which was meant, perhaps, to be essentially a suspense novel. At the Dead Sea he brings together Germans, the children of former Templars, an American Jew who saw the Holocaust of the European Jews with his own eyes, and very *macho* Israeli soldiers.

Ben-Ezer's characterization is not sufficiently faithful and serious, but he reveals a certain aspect of the matter:

Look, Zvi came back and sat down next to them. Let's be logical. I was born here in this country. That's a fact. What happened to the Jews, in my opinion, in a general, human way, how can I put it? . . . It's very sad. That's a fact. I would be sorry for any people that had something like that happen to them. But what can I do? I don't feel close to them at all, personally. Believe me, my family came here years ago. Not one of us was killed there. Why does he want me to kill him? For someone who was in Europe—fine, I really understand him. But me? My father, and my father's father, we were all born here in the East. I feel part of this region. No sense of belonging to the Jewish people. Tell me, what does he want from me? How does that concern me? (Hebrew edition, pp. 204–5.)

This passage demonstrates the viewpoint of the hero (Zvi), not of the author. The author's relation to the subject is more complex than that of his hero. The hero's way of looking at the subject of the Holocaust in *People of Sodom* is entirely externalized. He is not willing to lie and relate to the collective exterior experience as though it were his personal inner experience. Although the author does attribute a certain amount of criticism to his hero, there is no great gap between his world view and that which is current among those "heroes." What is doubtlessly true is that although both fictional and actual Israeli youths attempted to come into contact with the pain and to understand it, they never succeeded in understanding the essence of the matter. The author is aware of the spiritual limitations of the uninvolved hero, who is unable to take a spiritual position on the subject, which is distant from him.

A similar approach appears in the contrary fashion in the work of Yosef Bar-Yosef, *The Life and Death of Yonatan Argaman*. Bar-Yosef has written a melodrama based on a modern incarnation of the myth of "the poor man's ewe." The hero of the book, Yonatan Argaman, killed an Arab and brought about the death of a Holocaust survivor. First he made love to the survivor's girlfriend and then sent him, as King David sent Uriah the Hittite, to die at the front. Argaman attributes broader significance to his guilt:

Yes, it's only now that I think that I felt guilty because I was healthy and my body was sound and upright in a world of death camps, and that's why, because I was of sound body, he called out defiantly, but with his head down, I could take you away from him and take pleasure in you.
(Hebrew edition, p. 182.)

That attitude (in a book that preceded Ben-Ezer's work by ten years) is contrary to the attitude of Ben-Ezer's hero. Neither of the two writers accepts the position of their heroes. Ben-Ezer has no illusions and does not believe that his hero will repent and accept the burden of his guilt. Bar-Yosef's hero is depicted as a stereotypical *sabra;* he is capable, as it were, of conquering all the women, and he has no moral inhibitions, but when he sends the survivor to death for the second time, he does feel guilty. In his eyes the "killing" of the survivor is a kind of repetition of the murder of the Jews in the camps. His relation to the Holocaust therefore causes an extreme change in the image of the *sabra* as a stereotype of a "superman."

These two writers relate to the arrogant *sabra* in one way or another in a rather critical fashion. Ben-Ezer accepts him as he is and observes him from the outside; Bar-Yosef attempts to change him into a kind of victim of the guilt feeling that history and his own actions have planted within him.

Megged, too, in *Yad Vashem,* deals with the subject of guilt feelings. Here the person who is in the right is Grandfather Zisskind, and the guilty ones are the grandchildren, the *sabras,* Raya and Yehuda. The grandfather claims that those who were murdered, his grandson Mendele and his son Ossip, were the cream of Jewish society, and the survivors here are shoddy goods in comparison with those jewels!

"Everything here . . . is no more than a puddle of tap water against the big sea that was there! What have you here? A mixed multitude! Seventy languages! Seventy distinct groups! Customs? A way of life? (p. 32 in this volume.)

Once again the author identifies to a great extent with the grandfather and does not accept the arguments of his grandchildren. He directs the reader to adopt a negative attitude toward those young people who refuse to name their son after the grandchild who was lost in the Holocaust. The writer, who is almost a *sabra* (he was born in Poland in 1920 and immigrated to Israel in 1926), takes an anti-*sabra* attitude. He accepts the opinion of the survivors that the grandchild who died (Mendele) was and still is a more complex and interesting person than the young *sabras,* who were born, as it were, of the sea. From that point of view Bar-Yosef and Megged are quite close to the way in which Ben-Zion Tomer presented the problem in his play *The Children of the Shadow.* The *sabras* (or the survivors who pretend to be *sabras*) must admit to the existence of the children of the shadow in order to accept the guilt of their own survival, their true identity and belief in themselves.

The writers plumb the depths of the significance of the Holocaust or of the minds of the survivors, but most of them take a social and historical position that opposes, as it were, the position of the native Israeli "heroes." They "reveal" the weakness of the "native Israelis," who cannot cope with the Holocaust and its survivors. They attempt to correct, as it were, in their writing and fiction the distortions and the harm wrought by the members of their generation orally and in reality. Their fiction must be seen as a kind of testimony by guilty *sabras* who, as the children of a historical group whose best sons were murdered or destroyed spiritually, are attempting to repent.

5

Many writers have attempted to deal with the Holocaust from a general point of view, to see in its heroes and their deeds general symbols of the situation of the Jew in the world—no longer a "modest corner" concerned with a single person or situation, but a general illustration of Jewish existence during the last generations.

I refer to the works of Haim Gouri, *The Chocolate Deal;* to *Adam Resurrected* by Yoram Kaniuk; to *Touch the Water Touch the Wind* by Amos Oz; and to *The Dissembler* by Hanoch Bartov. These writers try to understand the whole structure, the essence of the roots of the Holocaust experience. A central work in that area is Kaniuk's novel, *Adam Resurrected.* Kaniuk tried to understand the character of the Holocaust from the point of view of a man who survived physically but not mentally. His hero is a survivor of the Holocaust who has found a kind of small-scale peace, as it were, in a mental hospital in Arad. Like other Holocaust survivors, he is pursued by guilt feelings because he remained alive, while his wife and daughter were murdered. His name is Adam Stein, and in the past he was a comedian and circus clown. After he saved the Commandant's life, he received his own as a gift. But he was humiliated and degraded, made to live together with the Commandant's dog Rex and forced to behave like the dog. He "plays" the dog at the very time that the Commandant and his colleagues are systematically wiping out his Jewish brethren.

In this work Kaniuk tried to do what his German contemporary, Günther Grass, attempted, in his own fashion, in *The Tin Drum.* Like Grass he feels that the only way to grapple with that enormous and dreadful subject is to turn to the grotesque. Only the grotesque can grapple with an emotional experience that is far beyond the power of human intelligence. The only way to deal with absolute dehumanization of the human being is (in Kaniuk's view) through the grotesque. The writer no longer uses a modest synecdoche (little corners and small characters who function as details representing the whole), but bizarre and tortured metaphors that symbolize the entire phenomenon. Those are extreme metaphorical images, by means of which he describes, in an almost insane manner, an experience that makes one insane. Kaniuk's main metaphors are "man" and "dog." In a certain social context man becomes a dog, and the dog lives better than human beings. (The question is: Is it really better to be a living dog than a dead lion?)

In one chapter of the book, a Purim party takes place at the mental hospital, during which everyone plays the role he played during the Holocaust. The link between the Holocaust and the mental hospital, *Purimshpeil* and kindergarten, is a mad, metaphorical connection, allowing the author to grapple with the experience. Other metaphorical bonds of that kind describe Commandant Klein, who becomes Mr. Weiss, a scholar of Semitic languages; a child who becomes the "last" creature; a man who is a dog; and King David in the mental hospital, which is a refuge for survivors and at the same time a culinary paradise.

Although the novel contains strange and diverse characters, they do not stand by themselves, but are rather projections of a "collective ego," scraps and tatters of a general metaphor. The author is not, in fact, interested in one detail or another that can be defined clearly in terms of time and place. The identity of each individual bursts apart in this work, and the characters live in both the mental hospital and the death camp at the same time. The struggle against madness is a kind of cathartic effort to overcome it, to paint a grotesque painting on the wall in order to attract evil spirits and wild beasts and, at the same time, to drive them off, to learn to live with the living horror that is within us in an attempt to give it an image and a figure.

Just as Günther Grass conjured up the warped figure of Oskar to grapple with his past—the past of murderous fathers and decaying sons—similarly Kaniuk conjures up the figure of the dog-man in order to live with his own past, the past of one who has survived unscathed and must account for his own survival to those who were not saved.

Amos Oz, in *Touch the Water Touch the Wind*, also attempts to deal with the great historiosophical questions of Judaism after the Holocaust. His principal heroes, Elisha and Stepha Pomeranz, do not exist in themselves, but are representatives of two major groups in the Jewish world. They are a Polish couple who were separated by the Holocaust: the man is an unknown genius who turns up in Israel, and the woman, who is also a kind of unknown genius, first worked as a Russian in the service of the KGB until she, too, returns and encounters her former lover and husband in Israel. The descriptions of the pair's actions are on a "symbolic" level, and each of their actions symbolizes a certain stage in post-Holocaust Jewish history. In the end the two are swallowed up by the earth like the biblical Korach and his followers.

The author wishes to describe post-Holocaust Jewish existence by means of great symbols, to distance himself by means of the symbols in order not to have to confront the dreadful ordinary pettiness face to face. Neither Oz nor Kaniuk actually went through the experience from within. They came to it from the outside and tried to grapple with the dreadful vision by pseudo-visionary means.

Hanoch Bartov, too, in his novel, *The Dissembler*, tries to ask major questions by means of a character, whose combination of traits, as it were, represents the meaning of Jewish existence. The novel was written as a suspense story, on the one hand, and as a modern picaresque novel in the style of *Felix Krull*, on the other hand.

A man was murdered in London, and the security services of various countries all claim a sort of priority on his identity. It turns out that the character had roamed the world using several identities at the same time. He was Heinz, Henri, and Avshalom all at once. Through the dissembling swindler the author tries to present the polysemous quality of Jewish existence. A single character was persecuted in the camps, lived in the underground, returned to Germany, and identified himself as a Canaanite-Israeli born in Hebron and as a survivor of the Holocaust all at the same time. The question of who the man was in the last analysis is never answered, because Bartov chose to leave the enigma unresolved and the possibilities open. What is clear is that the man could have been any of the people, all of those identities together, or each one of them separately.

Something about the problem of Jewish identity is revealed in another way by Saul Friedländer in his memoirs, *When Memory Comes*. Friedländer also sought, perhaps, to make his personal memories a representative sample of all of Jewish existence. Friedländer is naturally much more detailed, trustworthy, and precise than Bartov. He presents a synecdoche based on his life story, unlike Bartov, who aspires to a metaphor that amalgamates all the elements (although, from the artistic point of view, it did not break out of the limitations of the suspense novel, which he attempted to "use" in order to reach a broader and deeper meaning).

All the books to which we have referred here seek to grapple with the major symbols of the Holocaust, Jewish rebirth, and Jewish identity. One took the path of the grotesque; the other the path of the symbolic novel; the third used metaphorical and disfigured characters; and the fourth depicts a picaresque figure who apparently seeks to swindle people and create identities for himself, but who is found to speak (in his own way) the whole truth—that survivors and native Israelis are different aspects of the same existence.

6

A third way of dealing with that experience is that taken by those who seek to examine the topic through the historical novel; neither an encounter with survivors, nor vast symbols of death and rebirth, but the description of the historical development that led to the destruction of European Jewry by means of a great many synecdoches, each illustrating one of the details that are meant to present the epic story of that development.

That is what was done, for example, by Naomi Frankel in *Saul and Johanna* (1956–1967). What interested her was the formation of a Jewish consciousness by a family assimilating into the ever-more-hostile German society. She tried to describe the effect of various social forces in Germany at the time of the ascent of the Nazis. Thus in her book certain characters represent communism, as opposed to figures representing German industry. Junkers versus liberals, and humane Germany versus the emerging Nazi Germany. The Jews are also conceived from an ideological point of view. A varied spectrum of Jews is presented: from the most assimilated, such as the Blum and Levi families, to those who observe the commandments and were quicker than their fellows to sense the coming disaster, such as the Stern family. Even when Naomi Frankel tries to depict material which is not purely historical, such as the love of Edith for Emil, the Nazi, and afterward for Erwin, the communist, her writing has social and historical meaning. It is not the story of the love of a woman for men, but the love of a Jewess for men who represent various strata of the non-Jewish German society.

Saul and Johanna are two young people who found their solution to social pressures by taking the path of Zionism. The author seeks to portray Zionism as the true escape from the swamp of assimilation, which did not bring salvation from the threats of disaster that began to gather like black clouds on the horizon.

An illustration of history can also be found in the novel by Jonat and Alexander Sened, *Between the Dead and the Living*. The authors try to understand what happened to a group of young people who were left in Poland during the Holocaust, and what happened, in contrast, to one of their number who managed to reach Palestine. One juxtaposed with the other, one beside the other. The authors are aware of the historical significance of their novel, and even though many of the protagonists and the "existential" plot are essentially fictional, many parts of it are "documentary" and refer to events that actually happened. The novel reaches its climax in the documentary passages that describe the Warsaw ghetto uprising. What the authors attempt to do is confront the heroes with death and show how they preserve their humanity in struggling against horror. The authors frequently emphasize the human and quotidian, the nightlife that "flourished" in the ghetto, a man's love for his wife, and a girl's love for her boyfriend. The book is written as a kind of human frieze on the great wall of history. It is a heroic novel that attempts to "declare" that horror, death, and cruelty cannot defeat the young people who wished to preserve the image of God in the face of the unbelievable. This novel is, perhaps, the book of the heroism and revolt of its generation. It tries to approach the subject both from the angle of the human situation in the face of horror and from the individual's situation as part of an impersonal historical process that took place both in the Diaspora and in Israel —one that determined the fate of the nation.

I must also mention Yehuda Amichai's book, *Not of This Time, Not of This Place* (1963). Amichai tried to settle historical and existential accounts with the Holocaust. The hero of his novel, Yoel, returns to the land of madness in order to find his lost youth and complete his deficient identity. He manages to find himself only after he chooses love (the love of his hated childhood) and gives up revenge. Someone for whom the Holocaust was both a personal and a historical memory (for that was his own country of origin) can, as it were, raise up the tabernacle of his personality only after he has succeeded in relating to his past as to a lost childhood. He feels that he must restore the existential cycle, which had been snapped, although his days were swept by the winds of impersonal history. Amichai's novel is not a historical novel, but an existential one that seeks to grapple with and overcome historical experience.

7

Different from the preceding are the writers who are survivors: Itamar Yaoz-Kest, Aharon Appelfeld, Uri Orlev, and David Schütz. It is not surprising that they tend in general (Yaoz-Kest is exceptional here to a certain degree) to write shorter works—stories and novellas. They attempt to view the experience from a narrow angle of vision, to present testimony about what happened to them and to their protagonists, not to resolve historical issues and not to embody history in a symbol that comprehends the entire experience. They write short impressions of a great and terrible event, and in their compressed vision there is artistic greatness.

I am of the opinion that Appelfeld has produced major achievements in his short stories, such as "On the Saint George Islands," "Bertha," or "Another Attempt," stories of survivors who bear the past with them like a hump on their backs and cannot escape it. Better than most other writers known to me, Appelfeld has presented the survivor who has not survived, and will never survive, because he bears his memories with him like a can of worms. When the driver, the "hero" of "Another Attempt," dies, it is a posthumous death. What ought to have happened years ago, in a camp or in the forest, happened to the hero in the place that he reached, as it were, as an inheritance. We learn from Appelfeld's works, from "Smoke" to "The Burning Light," that in his world there are no survivors. Anyone who has passed through the seven circles of hell brings hell with him. Even the land of our fathers in "The Burning Light" seems to the "survivors" as if it were another version of death and detention camps. The horrors have been internalized, and one cannot free oneself from them, and those who survived physical death create situations of horror and suffocation for themselves wherever they go. Time does not heal the wounds, nor does it soothe them.

From that point of view, David Schütz is similar to Appelfeld. The heroes of *The Grass and the Sand,* Michael and Emanuel, who only appear to be survivors, bear their past with them to Israel, which was to redeem them, as it were, from all their sufferings. That is also the case with *Until Tomorrow* by Uri Orlev, who also brings his main protagonist to Israel. Like Appelfeld's heroes (and later those of Schütz), he, too, is pursued by memories of the Holocaust: children and adults in an attic in the ghetto, a girl who is carried in a knapsack after her mother's death, two children who rush to fight for their murdered mother's bed—in general, little children who wish to survive and who succeed in reaching a safe harbor, but, as we said, their repose is only apparent, for they have no portion in spiritual tranquility. They have faced the adversities of history and have remained alive, but the damage cannot be eradicated from the tablets of their hearts, just as one cannot erase the entire experience from the tablet of human historical memory.

The survivors remain vulnerable and tormented. The Zionist home did save their bodies, but it could not restore their spiritual repose.

8

In Israel, viewed as "the largest insane asylum on earth," survivors and remnants live among each other, witnesses and "observers" of the most insane episode in human history. Each group tried to deal with that experience in its own way, producing various models of literary reactions to that historical experience. All of their creations are a human effort to depict in order to remember and to remember in order to learn to live with the trauma. Literature plays a role in the life of the nation similar to that played by psychoanalysis in the life of an individual. The latter evokes traumatic memories from the depths of the past in order to cure disease and unify the scraps of a personality, and the former commits traumatic memories to writing in order to cure a national malady and to reconstitute the identity of a persecuted and beaten nation.

BIOGRAPHICAL NOTES

YEHUDA AMICHAI was born in Würzbürg, Germany in 1924, and came to Palestine in 1936. He served in the British Army from 1942 to 1946. He is known primarily as a poet, although he has also published short stories, novels, and plays, which have been translated into numerous languages. In English, his most recent collections of poetry are *Songs of Jerusalem and Myself* (1973), *Amen* (1977), *Time* (1979), *Love Poems* (1981), and *Great Tranquility* (1983). His novel, *Not of This Time, Not of This Place,* appeared in English translation in 1968, and a collection of his short stories, *The World Is a Room,* was published in English in 1984. He has been awarded the Israel Prize for Literature.

AHARON APPELFELD was born in Czernowitz, the Ukraine, in 1932. During the years of Nazi occupation, he was interned in the Transnistria concentration camp, from which he eventually escaped at the age of eight, roaming the forests for the next three years. He arrived in Palestine in 1946.

He teaches Hebrew literature at Ben-Gurion University in Be'er Sheva, Israel. He has written a number of novels and short stories. The English translations of his novels include *Badenheim 1939* (1980), *The Age of Wonders* (1981), and *Tzili* (1983). He has been awarded the Israel Prize for Literature.

HANOCH BARTOV was born in Petach-Tikva, Palestine in 1926. He served in the Hebrew Brigade of the British Army from 1942 to 1946, and then in the Israel Army during the War of Independence in 1948. From 1966 to 1968 he served as cultural attaché to the Israeli Embassy in London. He is a novelist, journalist and playwright. "Enemy Territory" is the concluding section of his novel, *The Brigade,* which was published in English translation in 1968. This was followed by another English translation, *Whose Little Boy Are You?* (1978).

YITZHAK BEN-MORDECHAI was born in Tel Aviv, Palestine in 1946. He has published three collections of short stories in Hebrew.

YOSSEL BIRSTEIN was born in Biała Podlaska, Poland in 1920, and emigrated to Australia in 1937. Arriving in Israel in 1950, he lived in a kibbutz for a number of years. He has published novels and collections of short stories in Hebrew. He also writes in Yiddish, and has published a book of Yiddish poems in Australia.

MICHAL GOVRIN was born in Tel Aviv, Israel in 1950. She received a doctorate in the history of theater from the Sorbonne and teaches drama at the Hebrew University in Jerusalem. She has directed plays for Habima in Tel Aviv and in Jerusalem. She has published poetry and short stories in Hebrew. "La Promenade" is one part of a triptych.

SHULAMITH HAREVEN is a poet, essayist, translator, and writer of fiction. Numerous collections of her poetry and fiction have appeared in Israel. Her novel *City of Many Days* was published in English translation in 1977.

AHARON MEGGED was born in Włocławek, Poland in 1920, and came to Palestine in 1926. He established the literary weekly *Masa,* and served as its editor for fifteen years. From 1968 to 1971 he served as cultural attaché to the Israeli Embassy in London. He writes fiction and drama. Translations of his novels include *Fortunes of a Fool* (1962), *Living on the Dead* (1970), *The Short Life* (1980), and *Asahel* (1982).

URI ORLEV was born in Warsaw, Poland in 1931. He was in the Warsaw ghetto from 1939 to 1943; he was imprisoned in the Bergen-Belsen concentration camp from 1943 to 1945 and came to Israel after the war. He writes novels, short stories, and children's books. *The Lead Soldiers* (excerpted in this anthology) appeared in English translation in 1979.

DAVID SCHÜTZ was born in Berlin, Germany in 1941 and came to Israel in 1948. "Mrs. Eckhardt's Story" is an excerpt from his novel, *The Grass and the Sand* (1979), which has not as yet appeared in English translation.

BEN-ZION TOMER was born in Yolgorei, Poland in 1928. At the onset of war he fled to Russia and was deported to Siberia. He arrived in Palestine in 1943. During the War of Independence he fought in the Palmach and was captured by the Jordanians. From 1966 to 1968 he served as cultural attaché to the Israeli Embassy in Brazil. He has written poetry, fiction, and drama. His play *Children of the Shadows* has been translated into English.

ITAMAR YAOZ-KEST was born in Hungary in 1934 and was interned in the Bergen-Belsen concentration camp in 1944. He came to Israel in 1951. He has written poetry and fiction and is the editor at the Ekked publishing house in Tel Aviv.

GILA RAMRAS-RAUCH (editor) was born in Tel Aviv and received her higher education in the U.S. and Israel (M.A., City University of New York; Ph.D., Bar-Ilan University). She has published numerous articles, in English and in Hebrew, on world literature, including Hebrew literature. Her books in English include *The Protagonist in Transition* (1982). A biography of the early twentieth-century writer L.A. Arieli is currently in preparation. She has taught at the University of Indiana, the University of Texas, and the Ohio State University. Currently, she holds the post of Professor of Judaic Studies at Hebrew College in Boston, Massachusetts.

JOSEPH MICHMAN-MELKMAN (co-editor) was born in Amsterdam in 1914. During World War II he was interned in Bergen-Belsen. After the war he served as the head of the cultural and immigration department of the Jewish Agency in Holland. He settled in Israel in 1957 and became the director of Yad Vashem, the archive and exhibit memorializing the martyrs of the Holocaust. In 1960 he became the cultural director of Israel's Ministry of Education. He has published numerous anthologies of Hebrew poetry and prose.

GERSHON SHAKED is Professor of Hebrew Literature at the Hebrew University, in Jersusalem. He is the author of the three-volume *History of Hebrew Narrative Fiction 1880–1980* and sixteen other books. He has been Visiting Professor at Hebrew Union College, Jewish Theological Seminary, University of California at Berkeley, and Harvard University.